ADVANCES IN LIFELONG EDUCATION

ORGANIZING SCHOOLS TO ENCOURAGE SELF-DIRECTION IN LEARNERS

Other titles in the Series

ORGANIZING SCHOOLS TO ENCOURAGE SELF-DIRECTION IN LEARNERS

by

RODNEY SKAGER

UNESCO INSTITUTE FOR EDUCATION, HAMBURG

and

PERGAMON PRESS

OXFORD · NEW YORK · TORONTO · SYDNEY · PARIS · FRANKFURT

U.K.	Pergamon Press Ltd., Headington Hill Hall, Oxford OX3 0BW, England
U.S.A.	Pergamon Press Inc., Maxwell House, Fairview Park, Elmsford, New York 10523, U.S.A.
CANADA	Pergamon Press Canada Ltd., Suite 104, 150 Consumers Road, Willowdale, Ontario M2J 1P9, Canada
AUSTRALIA	Pergamon Press (Aust.) Pty. Ltd., P.O. Box 544, Potts Point, N.S.W. 2011, Australia
FRANCE	Pergamon Press SARL, 24 rue des Ecoles, 75240 Paris, Cedex 05, France
FEDERAL REPUBLIC OF GERMANY	Pergamon Press GmbH, Hammerweg 6, D-6242 Kronberg-Taunus, Federal Republic of Germany

First edition 1984

Library of Congress Cataloging in Publication Data
Skager, Rodney W., 1932-
Organizing schools to encourage self-direction in learners. (Advances in lifelong education ; v. 9) Includes bibliographical references and index.
1. Continuing education—Germany (West)—Case studies. 2. Continuing education—Hungary—Case studies. 3. Continuing education—Philippines—Case studies.
4. Continuing education—United States—Case studies.
I. Title. II. Series.
LC5256.G4S56   1984   374   83-19514
ISBN 0-08-026784-X Hardcover (Pergamon)
ISBN 0-08-026785-8 Flexicover (Pergamon)
ISBN 92 820 1031 7 Hardcover (UIE)
ISBN 92 820 1032 5 Flexicover (UIE)

In order to make this volume available as economically and as rapidly as possible the author's typescript has been reproduced in its original form. This method unfortunately has its typographical limitations but it is hoped that they in no way distract the reader.

The Unesco Institute for Education, Hamburg, is a legally independent entity. While the programmes of the Institute are established along the lines laid down by the General Conference of Unesco, the publications of the Institute are issued under its sole responsibility; Unesco is not responsible for their content.

The points of view, selection of facts and opinions expressed are those of the author and do not necessarily coincide with official positions of the Unesco Institute for Education, Hamburg.

The designations employed and the presentation of the materials in this publication do not imply the expression of any opinion whatsoever on the part of the Unesco Secretariat concerning the legal status of any country or territory, or of its authorities, or concerning the delimitations of the frontiers of any country or territory.

Printed in Great Britain by A. Wheaton & Co. Ltd., Exeter

About the Author

RODNEY SKAGER (United States) is a Professor in the Graduate
School of Education at the University of California, Los Angeles.
He has broad experience in the field of educational evaluation
and in the disciplines of measurement and educational research
methods. Professor Skager is also associated with the Center
for the Study of Evaluation at UCLA. Before joining the faculty
of the School, he was a research psychologist with the Educational Testing Service in Princeton, New Jersey, and later with
the America College Testing Program in Iowa City, Iowa. While
on academic leave during 1975-1976, he served as Senior Educational Research Specialist at the Unesco Institute for Education in Hamburg.

Contents

Contents

Contents

Contents

Contents

Foreword

The concept of lifelong education has been viewed as a major positive response to the new educational needs that have arisen as a result of various factors and forces such as (a) unprecedented developments in different fields of knowledge, particularly in science and technology, (b) contemporary problems emerging from the consequences of these developments in the personal and social life of people of all age groups, and (c) an increasing, worldwide awareness of achieving a better quality of life for individuals and their collectives. Granting the value and significance of lifelong education as a potent means of meeting the new learning needs of all in the personal, social and vocational domains of their lives, one major question remains to be answered: How can this broad and abstract concept of lifelong education be translated into practice?

Answering this question satisfactorily is not at all easy. Clearly, many and varied steps have to be taken in order to realize the aspirations of lifelong education on a global scale. But one such important step proposed by many educational thinkers, researchers and practitioners is to encourage self-directed learning among children and adults.

It is desirable to develop skills and competencies of self-direction in learning among people from an early age in their lives through different learning environments and educational structures of formal, nonformal and informal character. For example, the home as an educational structure provides an informal learning environment that produces the first and persistent, though subtle, impact on the learning skills and attitudes of

an individual, and is likely to influence the process of fostering self-directed learning. Another important educational structure, more formal in nature, which can contribute significantly
towards encouraging self-direction in learners, is obviously the
school.

This book presents some useful experiences and observations on organising schools to encourage self-direction in
learners and helps us in moving towards the practical application of the concept of lifelong education. It embodies the report of a research project and provides a comparative and per-
ceptive analysis of four concrete experiences for understanding
and indicating how curricula, learning strategies and other
similar aspects of the overall educational practice in a school
can be organised to encourage self-directed learning. The
analysis is based on intensive case studies of four schools selected from the Federal Republic of Germany, Hungary, the
Philippines and the USA.

But before presenting this analysis, the book examines
some of the more fundamental issues concerning theories of human
learning in the context of developing self-direction, operational principles of learning environments hypothesized to contribute to the development of self-direction in learning, and so
forth. It is in relation to these basic elements that the analysis of case study materials has been carried out. Thus, the research project, and hence its report as embodied in this book,
tackles both conceptual and operational aspects of self-directed
learning in an interactive manner.

This project constitutes one of the several studies that
the Unesco Institute for Education (UIE) has carried out since
1972 on various facets of lifelong education in co-operation
with researchers and other educators from different parts of
the world. The findings of this study are relevant to policy-
makers, curriculum workers and school practitioners. It is
hoped that the report will contribute towards reforming certain
aspects of school practice in order to enable the learner not
only to meet the new challenges of change but also to become an
active and judicious participant in the process of bringing
about change itself.

We are grateful to Professor Rodney Skager for very effectively conducting and co-ordinating this important research
project on behalf of UIE. Our thanks are also due to those
cited in Appendix A who co-operated with us in designing and

xvii

conducting the case studies and all who carried out other activities connected with this project. We wish to express our deep sense of appreciation and thankfulness to the authorities of the four institutions studied for giving our collaborators all the facilities needed for conducting the studies.

Ravindra H. Dave

Director
Unesco Institute for Education

Introduction

The research program of the Unesco Institute for Education has addressed the concept of lifelong education along two parallel avenues of inquiry. On the one hand, the meaning of lifelong education has been elaborated through exploration of its conceptual roots in the social science disciplines as well as through detailed examination of implications for various facets of education such as curriculum design, teacher training and evaluation. While this primarily theoretical and conceptual work has proceeded, empirical projects have also been undertaken. The latter have often taken the form of case studies of institutions or programs which incorporate significant elements of the concept of lifelong education. These studies have been conceived partly as a means of testing and elaborating the conceptual work and partly for the purpose of identifying for a worldwide audience practical ways of applying the principles of lifelong education.

This project is aimed both at further conceptual development and practical application. While also using the case study approach, its particular focus is on the role of schools in the formation of important attitudes, competencies, and motives in the learner. The project identifies self-direction in learning as a key human factor in the implementation of the principles of lifelong education and the school as the critical social institution in the development of self-direction.

The project examines earlier notions about the psychological characteristics of the self-directed learner in the school context. Revisions in this earlier thinking appear to be in order, especially in the light of comparisons between high and low self-directed learners made in two of the studies reported here. Most importantly, however, this report will describe four different schools, each an unusual institution within its own national context. In spite of differences in other respects, each school is also distinguished by its stress on the encouragement of learner self-direction.

The project was coordinated by the Unesco Institute and required international cooperation as is usually the case with the Institute's research activities. When a common framework of inquiry exists, work in different countries has the significant advantage of providing both diversity and generality. Parallel investigations in different economic, social, and political contexts have the potential for turning up alternative concepts of teaching and learning in addition to a rich variety of practical means for organizing the learning process. At the same time, the generality of concepts can be tested in ways that are not possible within a homogeneous culture. The latter is a special concern in this research. A conception of the "self-directed learner", developed within a society that values individual achievement and success in interpersonal competition, may differ in significant respects from one developed in a society stressing collectivism and cooperation.

Another type of diversity was also incorporated in the project, though not by design. The four institutions studied represent three different levels of schooling. The U.S. study deals with a six-year elementary school. The Philippine and Hungarian studies are of four-year high schools, and the study from the Federal Republic of Germany is of a transitional school incorporating the last two years of secondary school and approximately the first two years of university education. This diversity of levels was a by-product of the decision that self-direction in learning would serve the overriding criterion for the selection of schools, rather than comparability of age or grade level.

No matter how timely and well thought-out the type of research reported in this book may have been, it could not have been successful without the full cooperation of appropriate institutions and researchers in the countries involved. Schools rarely have trained educational researchers as part of their regular staffs, so it was necessary to identify both schools as well as outside research personnel who would be able and willing to undertake the kind of work proposed. In Hungary the research personnel were in part associated with national research institutes. In this country the research was sponsored by the Institute for Educational Research of the Hungarian Academy of Sciences, and principal responsibility for carrying out the study and authoring the final report was in the hands of a researcher based at Pécs. The U.S. study was conducted by research staff from the Center for the Study of Evaluation, a federally supported research and development center, located in the Graduate School of Education of the University of California at Los Angeles (1). The Federal Republic of Germany and Philippine studies were also conducted by personnel associated with universities, acting in an independent capacity rather than as representatives of their respective governments. In the case of the former, researchers were located at the Pedagogical Seminar of the University of Göttingen, and the Oberstufen-Kolleg at the University of Bielefeld. The Philippine study was carried out by research staff at the Science Education Center, Educational Development Center, of the University of the Philippines. In the case of all four of the studies, support for local research activities was provided by agencies within the countries involved.

The most important aspect of coordination by the Institute involved the development of a common framework for studying schools and learners. While there was no reason to insist on rigid conformity among the separate national studies, it was important that a communality of intention should exist as to the goals of the research, as well as a common set of dimensions by which the schools and learners would be described. This was mainly achieved, and will be reported in Chapter 3.

The development or selection of assessment instruments such as observation schedules and measures of attitudes and opinions was done independently by the national research teams. This was desirable, given the questionable appropriateness of such instruments when used in cultures other than the one in which they were developed. Moreover, modes of assessment that are acceptable in one place may not be acceptable in another. For example, public distrust of the intentions of social science researchers made it impossible in the U.S. study to use any test or questionnaire that might be interpreted as a type of personality assessment. The same was true for very different reasons in the Federal Republic of Germany study. There the skepticism of students and staff in the school as to the validity of such instruments would have blocked their use even if proposed. Fortunately, there are many approaches to assessment, and adaptations were made by each of the national research teams.

A second essential aspect of the Institute's coordinating role involved hosting project meetings before the national teams began their work and again after the case studies had been completed. These intensive work sessions, involving Institute staff, the study directors, other local personnel,

and myself as coordinator, performed the vital function of initially clarifying goals and concepts and helping to synthesize
findings at the end of the project. Communication, with the
objective of achieving mutual understanding of terms, concepts,
and intentions, must be the central concern of cooperative,
multinational research. The Institute has been, and continues
to be, a successful facilitator of this kind of communication.

This report will examine the concept of the self-directed
learner as it has been elaborated in previous work, especially
work deriving from the study of lifelong education. Possible
negative relationships between the common practices of schools
and the development of learner self-direction will be cited.
The schools participating in this research will be described
holistically in the light of their national and local contexts.
The approach to research taken by each of the national studies
will also be described. Next, the special studies comparing
high and low self-directed learners in two of the schools will
be summarized and compared, leading to proposed revisions in
the concept of self-direction. Finally, various aspects of the
schools will be compared along common analytical, descriptive
dimensions. An effort will be made to synthesize these findings
and to arrive at generalizations about the practice of schooling
and the enhancement of self-direction. Many individuals made
significant contributions to the research described here. Most
worthy of note are the researchers and their co-workers who conducted the case studies. Their names and institutional affili-
ates are listed in Appendix A. Other individuals in the countries involved and in regional Unesco offices, some of them unknown to me, are also deserving of gratitude for helping to
identify participating institutions and research personnel and
for finding ways to support the case studies themselves. I am
especially grateful to Karl-Heinz Flechsig of the University
of Göttingen and Otto Mihaly of the Hungarian Academy of
Sciences. Professor Flechsig was also able to contribute most
generously of his time and ideas in the planning and synthesizing phases of this project, while Dr. Mihaly provided valuable
suggestions for realising the manuscript for this book. In the
latter regard, Professor Hartmut von Hentig, Director of the
Oberstufen-Kolleg at Bielefeld, also generously provided important insights and corrections of fact and interpretation.

Members of the staff of the Institute were equally supportive. Dr. M. Dino Carelli, Director of the Institute until
his recall to Unesco, Paris, in the Fall of 1979, placed the

resources of the organization firmly behind this project as
well as the earlier work that served as a conceptual basis. He
has always been generous in his support and willingness to offer
sound advice. This same support has been extended by the new
Director, Dr. R. H. Dave. Institute staff members who contributed significantly in the exchange of ideas at one or both of
the project meetings included Arthur Cropley (now of the University of Hamburg) and Leonard Goad of the UIE research staff
(whose comments on the draft manuscript were invaluable), and
Kenneth Robinson, Dennis Buckley, Jeremy Greenland and Paul Fisk
of the editorial staff. As has been the case in the past, Louise
Silz provided invaluable assistance by taking care of administrative arrangements and secretarial support for the project, and
Elke Schlinck-Lazarraga painstakingly typed the camera-ready copy
of the book.

NOTE

1. Funding for the U.S. study was provided by a grant from the
   Spencer Foundation. The case study was not conducted under
   the regular research program of the Center for the Study
   of Evaluation and is not to be construed as an "officially"
   sponsored enterprise.

Chapter 1

Lifelong Education, the School and Self-direction in Learning

LIFELONG EDUCATION

Lifelong education has been proposed and elaborated as an organizing or master principle for education in the modern world (see, for example, Faure (1972)). It is a vision of the learning society in which opportunities to learn new skills and competencies as old ones become obsolescent are available to individuals of all age-levels and social backgrounds.

Cropley and Dave (1978) have helped significantly to clarify the concept of lifelong education. The latest book by these two authors is one of a series of works (see, e.g., Lengrand (1970), Dave (1973), and Skager and Dave (1977)) which have analyzed the concept of lifelong education and derived principles summarizing how the educational offerings of a society might be organized in the perspective of lifelong education. These authors have also attempted to specify the kinds of skills and attitudes that learners would need in order to take advantage of the opportunities that are available.

In Cropley and Dave's (1978) recent formulation, lifelong education is appropriately viewed as a system. The term "system" carries with it connotations of comprehensiveness and integration. This is readily apparent in the five system characteristics proposed in the work just cited, and summarized below.

Totality
Under a system of lifelong education, opportunities for learning would be available throughout the lifetime of the individual. The school, now the primary vehicle of formal

education, would become but one of a variety of subsystems for
the delivery of education. Earlier, Spaulding (1974) elaborated on the types of opportunities which would become univer-
sally available by expanding the familiar categories of formal,
non-formal, and informal education into a more differentiated
continuum, beginning with formal institutions such as schools
and universities and ending with highly informal delivery systems such as the communication media.

Integration
        The fragmentation and dissociation of educational sub-
systems in most societies has been frequently noted by writers
on lifelong education. The home, the school, the work place,
and the communication media all incorporate essential educational functions, yet often operate independently and even at
cross purposes. Worse, the traditional school as an institution is almost invariably monopolistic in its control of certification and credentialing through formal credits and di-
plomas. Non-formal education, often the only means of self-
development for the poor and those who are beyond the normal
school age, is typically pitted in an unequal struggle for
recognition against national educational establishments and
traditional attitudes among employers. La Belle and Verhine
(1974) have documented this problem in the case of the South
American sub-continent, for example. Under lifelong education,
the school would become only one among a variety of coordinated
educational subsystems.

Flexibility
        The curricula, learning processes, and goals of education
must be continually adapted to meet new knowledge and competency
requirements in modern societies. Education must also incorporate developments in technology, especially those associated with
interactive machines and media. Lifelong educational principles
incorporate the belief that there is more than one way to teach
and learn, just as there is more than one place for learning.

Democratization
        The principles of lifelong education hold that education
should be available to all and in forms that are adapted to
meet the needs of people of different capacities and backgrounds. As Cropley and Dave imply, lifelong education is anti-
elitist. When fully implemented, its principles would avoid
the allocation of opportunity to a chosen few while the majority
lack the means for achieving further development. This is
certainly one essential aspect of the democratization theme.

Skager and Dave (1977) also suggested somewhat earlier that the democratization principle of lifelong education also applies to relationships between people in the educational process. There has been a strong sense of recognition in writing on lifelong education that authority can be exercised in ways which develop habits of passivity and dependence among learners. People who grow up perceiving the role of the learner as one of total reliance on a teacher for guidance and feed-back are not likely to develop into individuals capable of self-directed learning later in life. They will not take advantage, it is widely believed, of the opportunity to learn when there is no teacher to provide direction. Lebouteaux (1973) summarizes this point made by many writers on lifelong education by suggesting that learners should emerge from school no longer needing school for their future learning.

Self-Fulfillment

Cropley and Dave (1978) conclude, "The ultimate goal of lifelong education would be to improve each individual's quality of life" (p.14). Maslow's (1954) concept of *self-actualization* is very close to this goal, implying, as it does, becoming whatever one is capable of being. But society can merely provide opportunities and tools. Personal characteristics and attitudes weigh heavily wherever learners are given the opportunity to make choices. While these characteristics have been discussed in a variety of works, it is clear that the desire to engage in self-directed growth, and that the requisite skills and competencies to engage in such growth successfully, are prerequisites to any hope for self-fulfillment.

This last system characteristic of lifelong education, especially, raises the issue of what kinds of competencies, attitudes, and motivation are required in learners. Realization of the principles of lifelong education depends as much on the willingness of citizens to take advantage of opportunity as it does on the availability of such opportunity. To build a society that is fully responsible to the educational needs of virtually all of its members is pointless if those individuals are unable to recognize their need for self-development and resist any situation that makes it possible for them to do anything about meeting that need.

Cropley and Dave (1978) contrast "lifelong education" with "lifelong learning" in this regard. While often used interchangeably, the terms have different referents. Learning is a process resulting in changes in the individual that are

ultimately recognizable in that individual's behavior. It needs
to be added, perhaps, that as used here the term "learning" also
implies intentional, systematic activity, rather than the accidental or incidental acquisition of information. "Education",
on the other hand, refers to the organization of events that
makes learning possible. Learning refers to the behavior of
individuals who are interacting productively with those systems.

THE CONCEPT OF EDUCABILITY

The immensely complex problem of developing and coordinating the elements of an educational society is an inevitable
preoccupation for those who sense the potential of lifelong
education. But the parallel problem of whether or not large
numbers of learners would be willing to take advantage of the
opportunities provided deserves at least equal consideration.
For example, Cropley (1976) cites a report on a group of tech-
nologically displaced workers who did not take advantage of
training in new skills because they saw formal learning situations as appropriate only for children. This phenomenon is
not likely to be an isolated one.

Dave's (1973, 1975) elaboration of the concept of educability reflects this alternative concern with people as contrasted to institutions. While encompassing a much broader
array of human characteristics than can be the focus here,
Dave's definition of educability conveys the idea that a complex set of competencies, attitudes, and motives are characteristic of people who are "educable". The concept includes
basic learning skills, the ability to make use of different
modes of learning and, most important from the perspective of
this book, the "ability to organize one's own learning experiences through identification of needs, planning and carrying
out learning activities, and evaluating one's own accomplishments" (Dave, 1973, p.23).

Educability is a meta-concept. It encompasses all human
characteristics that influence learning, including the most
basic learning skills. Yet, at the core of this concept is
the more circumscribed, though still complex, concept of self-
direction in learning (Skager, 1978). *Self-directed learners
recognize their own needs for personal growth, plan and carry
out appropriate learning activities, and evaluate their own
progress.* They may work independently and autonomously, or

co-operatively with others. But it seems axiomatic that only intrinsically motivated, self-directing individuals would be able and willing to take advantage of a system of education which extends beyond the school and throughout the lifespan, and in which voluntarism rather than coercion is the basis of participation.

THE SCHOOL AND LEARNER SELF-DIRECTION

The role of schooling in the origins of educability and self-direction is both central and controversial. Hargreaves' (1974) chapter (in the book *Educability, Schools, and Society*) summarizes a controversy about what is to be done about schools that really began with Goodman's (1962) classic *Compulsory Mis-Education* and continues to the present day. Hargreaves divides radical criticism and proposals into two camps, the "de-schoolers" and the "new romantics".

Deschooling

The *deschoolers*, of whom Illich and more recently Holt are perhaps the best known representatives, would eliminate schools as we know them. These writers base their opposition partly on a general distaste for the increasing power of bureaucratic institutions in most modern societies, partly on grounds of economic practicality, partly on the belief that schools are inherently geared to the needs of elitist groups, and especially relevant to this discussion, partly because they perceive a hidden curriculum which indoctrinates crippling dependencies in the learner, e.g. that all learning requires a teacher or that learning can only occur in a school. The school, in their view, is by its very nature antithetical to the development of self-direction in learners.

The alternative proposals of the deschoolers are not pertinent here, other than to note that they incorporate non-formal, community based educational subsystems of a type that would presumably also be a part of a fully articulated system of lifelong education. In fact, the similarities of concrete proposals tempt one, at times, to define lifelong education as a movement toward deschooling that manages to rationalize the retention of the school, contradictory as this assertion might appear.

The New Romanticism
    In their evaluation of the school and its potential,
writers on lifelong education are much more in harmony with the
second camp of radical critics than they are with the deschoolers. Hargreaves labels this relatively large group of
critics as the *new romantics* because its members have advanced
proposals that echo the educational principles of romantic
philosophy. A number of familiar names are associated with
this perspective, initially Friedlander and Kozol, and later
Holt (until his switch to the deschooling camp), Kohl, Neil
Postman, and Rogers. There is also a connection with some of
the ideas of A. S. Neil.

    The new romantics, radical as they may be in the eyes of
supporters of the traditional schooling, are reformers rather
than revolutionaries. They do not offer mere splints and ban-
dages, but neither do they hurl plastic explosives. Most important is the great emphasis they place on the process of
"learning how to learn". Ideally, the most important thing
that schools can teach is not subject-matter content, however
advanced, but rather how to go about the learning process successfully. Learning skills, above all reading, are obviously
ancillary to this kind of development, and school often impart
these skills effectively. But other aspects of the hidden
curriculum are likely to inhibit the process of development.
The reformers see as highly counterproductive to the development of "learning how to learn"

1. emphasis on memorization as a mode of learning,

2. concentration on the answer rather than on the
   process by which the answer is attained,

3. imposition rather than voluntarism, and

4. the development of defensive or manipulative
   strategies for meeting past requirements that
   have no apparent meaning or utility.

Likewise, relationships with authorities, especially teachers,
are negative influences when initially motivated students are
not trusted to work independently and when evaluation is
threatening or exclusively the prerogative of the teachers.
The second aspect of the democratization theme of lifelong education noted earlier is entirely consistent with this position.
Democratization implies the development of relationships based
on mutual trust and cooperation rather than on power and arbitrary authority.

These reformist views have been fully incorporated into the generally held assumptions and proposals of writings on lifelong education. For example, lifelong learners, Marbeau (1976) suggests, have been "exposed to situations of responsibility and autonomy in (the) school years, for they offer the best means of acquiring a taste for personal effort and a desire to progress". This idea that self-directed learning develops out of a history of democratic relationships with authority, the opportunity to choose, and the responsibility to evaluate one's own efforts is not only supported by contemporary liberal and radical thought, it is compellingly logical. How could self-direction develop among learners who are never allowed to exercise the slightest degree of responsibility for their own learning? But it is still an assumption for all the apparent logic, although at least some empirical work, especially that of De Charms (1972), supports the view that important aspects of self-direction can be deliberately enhanced in the school setting. Whether or not such learning extends into later life, however, is still an open question.

The research reported in this book assumes that schools are of great importance in the development (or inhibition) of self-direction in learning. This assumption is widely held. Even the deschoolers, while decrying the negative effects of institutionalized learning, take for granted the capacity of schools to bring about passivity and dependency in learners. The reformers agree, but by implication argue that a social institution that is powerful enough to shape the individual's approach to learning so negatively could, with suitable restructuring, have equally strong and permanent positive effects. Neither may be right, but the school is nevertheless with us and is likely to remain with us for an indefinite period as the primary vehicle for the education of youth.

THE CASE STUDY AS A MODE OF INQUIRY

The case study is an approach to educational and other social science research derived from clinical practice, originating in fact with Hippocrates. It is a strictly non-interventionist approach to research. It avoids attempting to influence or control the situation under study in order to test *a priori* hypotheses experimentally. Rather, an educational case study seeks to describe and to understand or explain by means of direct and detailed knowledge gained through observation and even participation. It usually depends heavily on the

interview and on formal and informal observation. As applied
to an entity as complex as a school, the case study aims at a
holistic description of the institution in the context in which
it operates. This descriptive portrait obviously must be constructed from more focused examinations of interrelated facets
(the curriculum, the teaching/learning process, the organizational structure, etc.), but it does not concentrate on any
particular element at the expense of the whole.

The first objective of a case study is to present an accurate description of the situation observed: it is not conducted to present or defend an *a priori* viewpoint. The case
study usually follows description with diagnosis or explanation,
although the two endeavors should be kept separate. Diagnostic
or explanatory statements are limited to the particular case
studies rather than applied to schools in general. However,
conclusions from individual case studies may serve as hypotheses
to be tested in other types of research, and the development of
such hypotheses is the second goal of the case study. The
successful case study thus provides descriptive information
about praxis that may be useful in other places, as well as
speculations and hypotheses that may serve as the basis for
later research of a different type.

GOALS OF THE RESEARCH

Having selected the case study approach, this research
did not attempt to establish that one or more of the schools
studied was successful in turning ordinary students into self-
directed learners. This question (in so far as it is realistic)
would presumably be addressed by a large-scale program of longitudinal, comparative research. Such research would be conducted to determine whether certain types of schools (as defined
by organization, curriculum, teaching/learning processes, etc.)
were more effective in encouraging learner self-direction in
and out of school than were other types of schools. Such research would also be longitudinal in order to establish whether
self-direction in learning associated with the school environment would extend into adult life for a significant number of
years after the end of formal schooling. The scope of this
type of research would be large, even if we were conceptually
ready to conduct it.

The research which forms the basis of this publication is
concerned first with advancing conceptual clarity, especially

relating to the characteristics of the self-directed learner. It will be shown that significant progress has been made in describing how self-directed learners *behave*, but also that there is another, much less tractable, level of description. What kinds of personal traits or characteristics do self-directed learners possess? How do we account for the observed behavior of self-directed learners in terms of theories about motivation and personality? Two of the four studies which formed part of this research dealt directly with this issue, and they, in part, produced findings that disconfirmed some prior expectations.

As important as conceptual clarity may be, this research is not directly concerned with identifying aspects of schooling that are of importance in the encouragement (or inhibition) of self-directed learning. There are many conventional ways to describe schools. We can count the number of books in the library, determine the ratio of teachers to students, calculate the number of hours per day spent in academic learning as compared to organizational or recreational activity, or assess the achievement of the students. Even without having reflected much on the nature of self-directed learning, it should be obvious that none of the above indices are likely to be in any way directly relevant to its study. Neither, *per se*, is something as modern as assessing the degree to which an instructional program is individualized to take into account the level of development, abilities, and optimal learning modes of individual students. This is because individualization *per se* may imply nothing more than efficiency, with learners entirely dependent on authorities for instruction on what to do, explanations of how to do it, and evaluations of whether or not they have been successful. This project has thus developed and applied a set of dimensions for describing schools that reflects what is pertinent to the study of self-direction and schooling.

Thirdly, there are the schools themselves. All four were identified as institutions which emphasized the development of self-direction. This report will develop portraits of these schools, both generally as well as in terms of dimensions especially relevant to self-direction. Each institution will be described in terms of organization and governance, of curriculum and of teaching and learning processes. It will become apparent that each institution, in its own way and within its own content, offers alternatives that are not available in typical schools in the country in which it is located. In no case is this because each offers something different in the way of program and process that relates in apparently important ways to the development of self-direction.

To summarize, the research reported in this book has three major goals:

1. the application and revision of an earlier conception of the personal characteristics of the
   self-directed learner;

2. the development and application of dimensions
   for describing schools that will give as much
   relevant information as possible about the
   manner in which those schools are attempting
   to encourage and maintain self-direction in
   learners; and

3. the description of the four participating
   schools in terms of organization and government,
   curriculum, and teaching and learning processes.

In other words, this study combines research on the characteristics of self-directed learners in the school environment with analytical and holistic descriptions of the schools in which they are enrolled.

ORGANIZATION OF THE REPORT

The first chapters of this report provide the conceptual groundwork for the research. This initial chapter, in addition to describing the goals and approach of the research, has introduced the concept of lifelong education and related it to the concept of educability and more specifically to self-direction in learning. Chapter 2 will sharpen the concept of self-direction by differentiating it from related concepts and by describing the behavioral and personality traits of the self-directed learner. Chapter 3 will complete the conceptual introduction by describing dimensions of learning environments which have been hypothesized to encourage self-direction and by relating these to several theories about human learning. Together, this material leads to the specific questions to be answered in the case studies, which are listed and briefly elaborated at the end of the third chapter.

Chapter 4 describes the participating schools in the four countries and the criteria which led to the selection of each for this research. This chapter is supplemented in the Appendices by additional descriptive material about the research itself. Appendix B summarizes the organizational and planning phases of the research, and Appendix C provides details about the particular research strategies adopted by each research team.

Chapters 5, 6 and 7 present the main body of findings of the research. Each of these chapters focuses on a relatively broad, though also readily differentiated, aspect of the institutions studied. Thus, Chapter 5 describes the organization and governance of the schools in relation to decisions about teaching and learning. Chapter 6 addresses the curriculum at each school, partly as reflected in what students learn. Chapter 7 completes this particular group by analyzing the process of teaching and learning at each institution.

Chapter 8 presents the findings of two roughly parallel empirical studies which had not been planned initially, but which contributed significantly to the research. These studies compared high versus low self-directed learners in two of the schools (Philippines and U.S.A.). The findings of these two special studies of learners confirm most of the prior expectations about the characteristics of the self-directed learner, but also raise some provocative new questions.

Finally, Chapter 9 brings theory and findings together in the light of a pair of alternative assumptions about the nature of environments which encourage self-direction in learners. To differing degrees, the four schools are shown to reflect practices which can be traced to both of these assumptions, although the latter would appear to be at least moderately contradictory in terms of the practices each prescribes.

SUMMARY

Viewed as a social system, lifelong education proposes to make educational opportunities available to learners in places that are fully accessible, in a mode that is suitable to the learner's skills and capacities, and at whatever point in life that it is needed. However, even granting that something approaching this kind of total availability and flexibility were to be achieved in a given society, it does not necessarily follow that the typical potential learner at an age level beyond compulsory schooling would be motivated and prepared by prior

experience to take advantage of the opportunities offered. If
the typical learner sees formal learning, even when offered in
non-formal delivery systems, as something that only occurs in
the first stages of life and only in institutions called schools,
then achieving a system of lifelong education at the institutional level will have been for naught. In short, the learner
cannot be left out of the equation.

The meta-concept of educability, often associated with
writings on lifelong education, incorporates all the characteristics of learners that would make them fully able to take
advantage of any educational opportunity that might be available.
At the heart of the concept of educability lies the somewhat
more delimited concept of self-direction in learning. The
self-directed learner, by being able to plan and carry out
learning independently or in co-operation with others, is able
and motivated to take advantage of opportunity in whatever form
it occurs. Any non-coercive system of lifelong education would
be heavily dependent on the presence of self-directed learners
in large numbers in the general population.

For virtually all citizens of developed societies and for
many citizens of developing societies, the school provides
life's single educational experience. Yet the ordinary school
has been castigated by contemporary educational reformers for
fostering dependency and passivity in learners rather than independence and motivation to learn. Even if schools manage to
impart the basic learning skills that comprise the foundation
of educability, they may, in the opinion of these commentators,
inhibit or even suppress learner characteristics which lead to
self-direction.

The research to be reported in the pages which follow,
fits in this context. It seeks to define more precisely what
self-directed learners are like in the context of the school,
as well as to describe, along common dimensions, the characteristics of four schools that have as major curricular goals the
encouragement of self-direction in learners. The research reported in this book is consistent with a contemporary reformist
view which holds that it is not inevitable that schools *per se*
inhibit the development of self-direction in learners, but
rather it is the way in which many schools are organized and
the learning process carried out that needs to be revamped.

Chapter 2

The Concept of Self-direction in Learning

DISTINGUISHING BETWEEN SELF-DIRECTION AND INDEPENDENCE

The term "self-direction" implies for many the notion of an independent, even individualistic, learner who prefers to work alone in the pursuit of highly personalized goals. This perception is inaccurate on two counts. First, self-direction in learning must be viewed developmentally. The image of full independence or autonomy refers surely to a mature adult. But even relatively young children manifest significant aspects of self-direction under appropriate conditions, as research to be cited in the next chapter has revealed. If self-direction as a recognizable pattern of learning behavior emerged only in adulthood, then one might wonder whether schooling or any other early experience had anything to do with the matter.

Secondly, learning need not be independent or individualistic in order to be self-directed. It is the motivation to *choose* to learn, and to act on that choice, that most distinguishes the self-directed learner. Whether or not the learning itself is carried out independently, co-operatively in a learning group, or even dependently at a computer terminal or under the authority of a master teacher (as in the classical apprenticeship role) is immaterial. All three modes can be manifestations of self-direction in learning.

Dave (1975) has made an explicit connection among the concepts of self-directed learning, educability and lifelong learning. He has emphasized that self-direction in learning incorporates independent learning in addition to other types of learning.

Self-directed learning refers to the planning and .

18

management of learning by individuals (either singly
or collectively) to accomplish their personal, social,
and vocational development by recognizing specific
learning needs from time to time and fulfilling them
through suitable techniques, resources, and learning
opportunities.

Dave particularly stressed the importance of *inter-learning* as a mode of self-directed learning. Inter-learning is a
group process in which two or more individuals freely exchange
the role of teacher and learner "... without feeling the heavy
weight of the teacher-learner hierarchy". The interpersonal
aspect of the democratization theme of lifelong education is
readily apparent in Dave's conception of inter-learning. The
self-directed learner may work entirely alone, but this is
neither a necessary condition of self-directed learning nor in
many circumstances is it a desirable one. As an exclusive
strategy, independent learning ('self-learning' in Dave's terms)
severely restricts both the opportunities available to an individual as well as his or her potential for contributing to
the learning of others.

RECOGNIZING SELF-DIRECTED LEARNING BEHAVIOR

Systematic learning is usually identified with some sort
of activity extending over time. It involves intercourse with
the environment, the use of tools such as books or other learning aids, or interaction with other people in co-operative
ventures. It is ordinarily possible to determine through observation that an individual is engaging in a learning activity,
irrespective of whether or not that activity is successful.

While it is relatively easy to establish that an individual is engaging in systematic learning, it is much more difficult to determine whether or not the learning activity is self-
directed. This problem is not intractable as it might seem,
however. What are needed are suitable criteria for defining
the learning as self-directed in nature.

Tough's (1971) research on independent learning activities
of adults generated such criteria. While this writer did not
use the term "self-directed", his view of the behavioral and
motivational nature of independent learning coincides with the
perspective of this book and the project which it summarizes.
It should be noted that the term "independent" reflects Tough's

primary interest in learning that occurs in non-institutional situations. It is by no means restricted to instances of Dave's concept of self-learning, e.g., learning solely by oneself. Tough restricted the application of the concept of independent learning to activities that are

a) intentional,

b) involve a series of learning episodes, and

c) part of a project with coherent goals.

The nature of learning episodes in Tough's conception was summarized in an earlier book (Skager, 1978), but needs to be examined more carefully here. An activity can be classified as a learning episode if characterized by the following:

1. The learning that occurs is *intentional* as contrasted to accidental or incidental. This intent remains dominant throughout the episode.

2. The learner engages in the activity in order to develop some reasonably *definite knowledge or skill* rather than for general self-improvement without a prior decision as to what the nature of that self-improvement might be. Tough defines "knowledge and skill" very broadly, including any kind of intentional change in the learner from the relatively trivial to the fundamental, and including harmful as well as trivial changes.

3. The learner wishes to *retain* the knowledge or skills for some definite period of time. In Tough's studies, the period of intended retention required for classifying a given activity as a learning episode varied from a few days to a lifetime.

Examination of the first three criteria suggests that the mere observation of behavior, while normally sufficient to determine whether an activity is a learning activity, is often an insufficient basis for establishing that the learning is independent or self-directed. While it often may be possible through careful and systematic observation to determine that learning is intentional, directed at the attainment of a specific knowledge or skill, and to be retained for a significant period of time, it would be far easier and usually more valid to solicit the learner's own assessment of the origins of his or her behavior.

It is also important to recognize that the first three criteria exclude some types of learning. Specifically, learning that is incidental to another type of activity is hardly a sign of self-direction as far as learning is concerned. Likewise, learning that has no reasonably specific goal or purpose, that is not directed towards the achievement of a definite change in the learner, does not count.

Finally, the intention to retain the knowledge or skill for some definite period indicates that the learner intends to make some use of what has been learned, and is fully consistent with the perspective taken here.

The last criterion has been separated from the others because it is the most subjective.

4. The intention to learn some definite knowledge or skill must be the *predominant motive* for engaging in the activity.

In Tough's conception, "predominant" means "more than half of the person's motivations". There is often more than one reason for engaging in an activity, and this criterion recognizes that motivation is potentially complex, including the motivation to learn something. (1)

Tough's criteria reflect the fact that they were derived from the study of adults pursuing specific, self-initiated projects outside of formal schools. The projects had definite beginnings and equally definite termination points and always involved a series of "episodes" rather than a single activity at one point in time. The projects were also undertaken to accomplish predetermined goals.

It is clear that adults who engage in intentional learning, as defined by Tough, are all self-directed learners as the concept is used here. However, there is no intention of suggesting that all self-directed learning occurs in circumscribed projects with definite goals and clearly defined points of termination. Self-directed learners may engage in systematic learning because they are interested and stimulated by some educational content, while at the same time having no definite goals nor any idea as to the point at which the learning would be "finished". Also, children in the school context may show significant aspects of self-direction in learning without necessarily engaging in projects with definite terminal points.

None of this detracts from the relevance of Tough's criteria, merely from their comprehensiveness.

SELF-DIRECTED LEARNING AS A MANIFESTATION OF THE IDEAL OF RATIONALITY

The work just described is out of the tradition of empirical education research. However, the concept of self-direction can also be anchored philosophically. The concept, "rationality in action", as articulated by Peters (1974), applies to the self-directed learner, although the concept is itself very broad in scope. In Peters' (1974) formulation, "Rationality in action is manifested in choosing means to ends, in the scheduling or planning of a series of choices over time in order to satisfy a number of conflicting wants, which give no special priority to the present". Peters (1976) later observes that rational people operate on the basis of three kinds of internalized norms:

1. They are concerned with consistency and the avoidance of contradictions, including the consistency of means with ends. They seek to resolve conflicts between existing beliefs and discrepant experience or information.

2. They have a clear sense of what considerations are relevant in formulating beliefs and in making choices.

3. They inquire actively for new evidence in the attempt to verify assumptions against new experience.

The Peters' concept of rationality in action is a highly generalized, exclusively cognitive view of the fully developed human mentality. The definition and three principles describe the orientation of the philosopher, research scientist, or even theologian, in short the scholar in the process of exploration. But, translated into everyday terms consistent with ordinary human learning, the statements readily characterize the self-directed learner who recognizes that something must be learned and selects an appropriate way to engage in learning, who integrates new learning with prior learning by resolving discrepancies, and who is able to use pertinent information to evaluate his or her own progress. As a rational individual, the self-directed learner is also able to downgrade the priorities of the present in the interest of the future.

Peters describes the concept of rational action as a re-
formulation of Piaget's developmental principles of assimila-
tion and accomodation. These presumably universal human dispo-
sitions may be enhanced or suppressed by a given culture, but
define man as a purposive, rule-following organism. Anthropological evidence reported by Greenfield and Bruner (1969) and
cited by Peters suggests that cultures which encourage children
to learn through experience provide more developmentally stimulating conditions than do cultures which force children to depend on authority for answers. The implication is that rationality develops through certain kinds of conditions, all of which
are controlled by the cultural context, even though experience
within that context may differ among individuals.

Peters' is a useful conception for this research, as long
as it is perceived realistically as an ideal. Rational individuals are likely to be self-directed learners, that seems clear.
However, it is not so apparent that all instances of self-direction in learning, such as those exhibited by children in the
classroom or by some of the adults involved in the projects
described by Tough, imply fully-developed rationality. Self-
direction in learning seems to be a necessary pre-condition for
rationality, but self-direction in learning can also characterize the activities of children or adults whose developmental
level is still considerably short of the very high level described by Peters.

CHARACTERISTICS OF THE SELF-DIRECTED LEARNER

Tough's (1971) work has shown that it is possible, within
a reasonable degree of certainty, to determine whether or not
an individual's motivation for engaging in a learning activity
is self-directed. Generally speaking, it is possible to recognize the self-directed learner in action, especially if it is
also possible to question that learner about his or her intentions and goals.

Unfortunately, we are in a region of hypothesis and speculation in the attempt to isolate and describe the personal characteristics of self-directed learners. In other words, while
it is possible to be reasonably certain that people are self-
directing in their learning activities, that knowledge tells us
nothing about how they developed into self-directed learners or
whether or not self-directed learners in general have any personal characteristics in common. This kind of knowledge is

potentially important since it would presumably be of great
help in the design and evaluation of learning environments that
facilitate the development of self-direction.

Speculation or not, we have to start somewhere. In the
book that led to this report, Skager (1978) identified seven
personal characteristics of the self-directed learner based on
a survey of earlier work by a number of theorists and researchers, including Berlyne (1965), Biggs (1973), Dave (1975), March
(1972), Maslow (1954), Joyce and Weil (1972), Rogers (1969),
Wroczynski (1974), Skager and Dave (1977). These characteristics are reproduced here with slight revisions.

1. *Self-acceptance*. As used here, self-acceptance
   refers to positive views about the self as a
   learner. It is grounded in extensive and successful prior experience. Not only does self-acceptance mean, "I can do it", it also refers to a
   positive valuing of the self as an entity worthy
   of improvement.

2. *Planfulness*. Planful learners are able to
   a) diagnose their own learning needs,
   b) set appropriate personal goals in
      the light of those needs, and
   c) devise effective strategies for
      accomplishing the learning goals.
   Such individuals make use of the help and advice
   of others at any stage in the above process, but
   it is because they choose to do so. The planful
   learner may also arrive at such personal goals
   during the learning process, e.g., may engage in
   learning for the purpose of goal setting.

3. *Intrinsic motivation*. Learners who are intrinsically motivated persist in learning activity
   in the absence of external controls in the form
   of rewards or sanctions. They are likely to
   continue learning outside of formal learning
   situations and to delay or even forego various
   kinds of competing gratifications in order to
   proceed with learning.

4. *Internalized evaluation*. Self-directed learners
   are able to act as their own evaluation agents.
   They can give accurate estimates of the quality
   of their own performance based on evidence they
   collect themselves. Learners who have internal-

ized the evaluation process may solicit feedback
on their own performance from knowledgeable
others, but they will accept external evaluation
as valid only when the qualifications of the
judge are established independently of social
role and when the evaluation agrees with their
own evidence.

5. *Openness to experience*. Learners who are open
to experience engage in new kinds of activities
that may result in learning or goal setting.
However, consciousness that either of the latter
may occur is not necessarily the reason for
entering into new kinds of activity. Curiosity,
tolerance of ambiguity, preference for complexity,
and even playfulness (all cited by other authors)
represent motives for entering into new activities and imply openness to experience. Further
delineation of this construct may reveal that it
comprises several component constructs.

6. *Flexibility*. Flexibility in learning implies a
willingness to change goals or learning mode and
to use exploratory, trial-and-error approaches
to problems. It does not imply a lack of persistence in learning itself. Failure is countered
with adaptive behavior rather than by withdrawal.

7. *Autonomy*. Autonomous learners choose to engage in
types of learning that may not be seen as important
(or that may even be perceived as dangerous) within
a particular cultural context. Such individuals
are able to question the normative standards of a
given time and place as to what kinds of learning
are valuable and permissible. However, autonomy
is exercised by the learner in the service of a
wider perception of personal and social utility.

Two of the seven characteristics, Planfulness and Internalized Evaluation, describe an individual who is able to engage in *self-evaluation*. This is such an important element of
the concept of self-direction in learning that it is worth con-
sidering in more detail. Sawin (1969) has done so, and his
analysis of this characteristic reads almost as if it were a
highly concrete version of Peters' (1976) concept of the rational man in action.

1. The learner should comprehend the fallacy of generalizing from a single instance. There should be a willingness to suspend judgment until sufficient evidence has been collected.

2. The learner should be able to determine whether evidence is, or is not, relevant to what is being evaluated.

3. The learner should understand that his or her own beliefs about what he or she can and cannot do may not be accurate, and that it is often necessary to seek information about personality capabilities from knowledgeable others.

4. The learner is aware that varied or comprehensive evidence should be obtained on the performance being evaluated.

5. The learner should be able to focus on a few specifics rather than trying to evaluate everything at once. This is analogous to testing a hypothesis through the use of sampling procedures.

6. The learner should be able to conduct a content analysis of his or her own work. Learners should be able to detect patterns in their own errors, for example.

Sawin's self-evaluative skills represent competencies and attitudes that can be learned by ordinary people. There seems to be no reason why these kinds of skills could not be taught and practiced in schools, as they undoubtedly are at times. Yet the broader concept of self-direction implies more than a collection of competencies and skills, no matter how important. It incorporates the development of certain deeper, more pervasive aspects of the personality, especially in relation to motivation, openness and flexibility, and the concept of the self.

In the development of these deeper aspects of the self, the school is only one among many influences, probably a less important one than the family, the community, and the genetic inheritance. As social institutions, schools are not likely to be in a state of dissonance with the surrounding community and dominant patterns in their learners' families, at least not for long. But schools are the environment in which the earliest and most extensive formal learning takes place in

most societies. Nowhere is the influence of the school, for
good or bad, thought to be insignificant, especially in the
lifelong orientation it provides to the learning process.

SUMMARY

The concept of self-direction of learning incorporates
what is often referred to as independent or self-learning.
However, individuals who choose to learn solely in an independent, isolated manner both cut themselves off from co-operative
modes of learning and fail to make positive contributions to
the learning of others. Self-directed learners may also learn
co-operatively (inter-learning) or even in a partially dependent relationship with an authority. The essential element in
self-direction is thus choosing to learn and selecting the most
appropriate mode of learning, rather than working alone *per se*.

It is relatively easy to recognize the self-directed
learner at the behavioral level. Such learners engage in self-
selected learning projects over a significant period of time
in order to attain certain predetermined goals. However, they
may also persist in systematic learning because of personal
interest without being aware of definite goals or terminal
points in the learning process. Self-directed learning is
never casual or incidental, but invariably intentional and
conscious. Self-directed learners make rational choices based
on perceived needs and are able to establish future priorities
in the face of conflicting current preoccupations. They are
also able to choose modes of learning which are appropriate to
the ends they may wish to achieve.

While it is relatively easy to recognize self-direction
in learning at the behavioral level, the personal characteristics of self-directed learners can only be hypothesized at this
point. Self-directed learning depends in part on generalized
learning skills and competencies. But there must also be an
internalized motivational basis for learning, an appropriate
concept of the self, as well as other personality components.
These characteristics of the learner may be influenced by many
factors, schooling being only one. Nevertheless, schooling is
widely accepted as an especially critical institutional influence because of its universality in developed societies and
its potential for either enhancing or inhibiting other influences on the learner's development.

NOTE

1. Operationally, Tough and his co-workers dealt with the
   assessment of the fourth criterion by having their subjects
   distribute 100 points among each of the reasons for engaging
   in the activity. If more than 50 points were assigned to
   the desire to develop and retain a particular set of skills
   or competencies, the activity was ruled as intentional.
   This is an adaptation of a long-known psychophysical method
   (method of constant sums).

Chapter 3

From Theoretical Perspectives to Research Questions

This chapter begins with a review of several hypotheses about the relationship between self-direction and the environment in which learning takes place. The major theories of human learning are next examined from the same perspective. Relationships between what the theories have to say about the learning process and the hypotheses about self-direction are noted. Finally, the specific research questions, formulated to guide the case studies, are derived in the light of the previous material and related research.

SELF-DIRECTION AND THE LEARNING ENVIRONMENT

Skager (1978) proposed eight principles of learning environments which seem likely to contribute to the development of self-direction. The principles have the status of hypotheses synthesized partly from conceptual writings on educability as an aspect of the concept of lifelong education, partly from the literature on models of teaching, and partly from empirical work on independent or self-learning. These principles served as a basis for examining relevant learning theories (Skager, 1979) and also aided in planning research strategies for the case studies. The principles are stated and briefly discussed below.

Flexibility in the Learning Situation
The learning situation should incorporate flexibility in (a) the amount of time to be devoted to a given learning activity, (b) the place where learning occurs, (c) the mode or method of study, and (d) the content to be learned.

Unless there is flexibility in the learning situation, learners presumably will not develop the ability to make intelligent choices or learn to exercise other aspects of self-direction. However, 'flexibility', as conceived here, does *not* mean that learners should have the freedom to do nothing. This and the principles which follow, refer to environments, primarily institutional, deliberately designed to promote learning. Situations in which it is assumed that children will decide to learn on their own if adults are sufficiently patient, are not the subject of this or other principles. In addition, the principle of flexibility is meant to be relative in its application, taking into account the level of maturity of the learner.

Encouragement of Choice
> Learners should be actively encouraged to make their own choices as they develop the competency to do so.

Even relatively young learners can often make intelligent choices about the mode of learning that is most suitable for them. In an individualized program, for example, they can also learn to allocate time to different activities through the application of systematic planning techniques. However, choice of content is the most sensitive and difficult choice, since the needs of the society as well as the predilections of the learner inevitably enter into the equation.

Teaching as a Facilitating Activity
> Teaching should be defined as an activity that facilitates learning through stimulation, helping, and the arrangement of opportunities.

While it is clearly part of the teacher's role to give feedback on the quality of the learner's performance, this should be done in a way that fosters the development of self-evaluative skills and avoids undue dependence on authority for evaluative feedback. Underlying this principle is the assumption that highly directive, authoritarian teaching expresses a hidden curriculum under which children do not have the opportunity to learn to make their own decisions.

Learners as Their Own Evaluation Agents
> Learners should be encouraged to practice self-evaluation in an environment that is geared to provide rapid, constructive feedback.

If self-evaluation is to be learned, then the environment must be 'responsive' in giving timely and non-threatening feedback designed to help learners improve their performance. Not only the teacher, but also self-paced instructional materials with built-in assessment devices, techniques of programmed instruction, or approaches to co-operative inter-learning are vehicles for applying this principle.

Democratic Relationships in the Learning Situation
    Relationships between learners themselves as well
    as between teachers and learners should emphasize
    democratic values rather than hierarchy and
    authority.

    The social environment should be consistent with the earlier principles of flexibility, freedom to make choices, and facilitation. This does not imply that personal authority, as such, should not exist in the learning situation. In most situations demonstrated personal competence provides a kind of authority that is sufficient for engaging in constructive evaluation, help, and guidance. Authority derived from competence is not necessarily arbitrary in nature. However, it would be unrealistic to expect that all authority derived from status can or should be dispensed with for most learners. Rather, it is a matter of using authority when it is wise and necessary while encouraging individual choice and responsibility whenever possible.

Capitalizing on Intrinsic Motivation
    Learning should be organized so as to take advantage
    of the intrinsic motivation of learners.

    Berlyne (1965) has shown that learning situations structured so as to enhance curiosity elicit intrinsic motivation on the part of the learner. Discovery learning methods are one manifestation of this approach. There are also a variety of tactics commonly used by effective teachers to relate formal content to the learner's interests or goals and thereby engage motivation that has an internal, rather than external, basis.

Emphasis on Expressive Educational Objectives
    Where appropriate, learners should encounter problems
    for which there is no single path to solution and
    which are 'open-ended' in the sense that the manner
    and form of the solution are the prerogatives of
    the learner.

    Eisner's (1968) concept of expressive objectives refers to open-ended tasks or problems in which the path to the solution as well as the form of the solution is under the control of the learner. There is no single, 'right' answer to an open-ended problem or task. All avenues of expression that can legitimately be characterized as 'creative', are open-ended in this sense. Self-direction in learning is inevitably associated with the successful pursuit of expressive educational objectives.

Incorporating Learning Outside of the School
>Wherever appropriate, learners should be encouraged to use the community and its institutions as alternative learning environments.

If, during the formative years, children learn systematically only in school, then they may come to depend on that institution as the sole avenue to learning. The use of resource specialists in real-life situations outside the school has been repeatedly recommended as a means of helping children realize that they can learn anywhere if they choose to do so. Activities that occur outside of the school may also be conducive to learning of an experiential type, the central theme of at least one of the theories discussed below.

SELF-DIRECTION AND THEORIES OF LEARNING

The principles just stated were described as hypotheses. There is no fully articulated body of evidence that people become self-directed learners when they are exposed to learning environments that incorporate any or all of these principles. Still, the principles are grounded in what evidence is available and were extremely useful for focusing the case studies on aspects of the schools most likely to be related to self-direction in learning.

As implied above, current theories about human learning did not play a large part in the initial formulation of the eight principles. However, it is important to establish a theoretical basis for educational hypotheses whenever it is possible to do so. A theory provides a more comprehensive and integrated perspective on the variables that influence a given phenomenon than is provided by a more or less *ad hoc* principles for praxis. But more important, theories are explanatory. At one level, theories explain by stating the conditions under which a phenomenon occurs. At a more abstract level, theories generate and integrate constructs which communicate meaning.

Adequately defined theoretical constructs contribute to understanding and can be generalized from one situation to another.

Six theories of human learning will be briefly surveyed.
From the perspective of this book, the most important way in
which the theories differ is in the motivational principle on
which each is based. Motivation is in many respects the key
issue in the explanation of self-direction in learning. Theories of motivation specify the conditions under which a particular type of behavior is initiated and maintained. In the
case of self-direction, motivation is internal (or intrinsic)
rather than external (or extrinsic). Therefore, theories that
deal with the development or manifestation of intrinsic motivation for learning are of primary interest.

All six theories to be examined are relevant to one or
more of the principles discussed in the first section, and all
were treated more or less equally in Skager (1979). Here, it
will be apparent that one of the theories seems to be especially
powerful, conceptually, from the perspective of self-direction
in learning.

Humanistic Theory
        The ideal of humanistic psychology is Maslow's
        self-actualizing person, an individual continually
        in the process of development toward as yet unreal-
        ized potentials.

Humanistic theory in psychology has been most thoroughly
articulated by Rogers (1959), who transposed clinical, thera-
peutic principles to the relationship between teacher and student. Humanistic theory is a theory of interpersonal relationships. According to Rogers, all human motivation is derived
from a basic *actualizing tendency*. Fully expressed, this actualizing tendency moves the individual in the direction of a
state of personal autonomy in which he or she is ultimately free
from control by external forces.

The relationship between self-direction and motivation in
Rogerian theory is thus plainly evident. Certain other Rogerian
concepts are equally relevant. Rogerian theory (and its educational counterpart) seeks a state of *openness to experience* as
the polar opposite of defensiveness, which shuts out new experience. Openness to experience, in turn, is possible in situations in which the individual perceives that nothing threatening to the self will occur. Another important state is that of

positive self-regard, a self-sustaining condition based initially on positive experiences with others in a given class of situations. Positive self-regard becomes independent of the behavior of others to the extent that that individual becomes his or
her own "significant other" (evaluation agent). The *locus of
evaluation* of events becomes internal rather than external.

Rogerian theory, derived as it is from clinical practice,
seems somewhat removed from the specifics of classroom practice,
although applications described by Rogers (1969) involved the
encouragement of goal-setting and self-evaluation on the part
of students. The emphasis on empathy and understanding in interpersonal relationships that is at the heart of the Rogerian approach is certainly not inconsistent with the principle of
democratic relationships, though the two are not necessarily
identical. Certainly other Rogerian concepts relate directly
to the educational principles of *encouragement of choice,
teaching as a facilitating activity*, and *learners as their own
evaluation agents*.

At a conceptual level, Rogerian theory incorporates self-
direction in learning within its central principle of self-
actualization. The goal of both Rogerian therapy and Rogerian
education is a learning and developing human being who has attained sufficient positive self-regard to make choices briefly
and to competently evaluate his or her own efforts to achieve
the goals inherent in such choices. Unfortunately, the theory
has not been as greatly elaborated in educational practice as
it has clinically, so we are somewhat lacking in connections
between the two. Its translation of the principle of empathy
from the therapist/patient relationship into the teacher/stu-
dent relationship may be something of an overgeneralization to
a new situation, but there is no denying the overall commonal-
ty of concern between Rogerian theory and self-direction in
learning.

Theories of Modeling
Children are frequently observed to learn through
imitation, and even adults consciously or unconsciously model the behaviors of others at times.

Could the tendency to use others (presumably self-directed
individuals) as models be a factor in the development of self-
direction, especially in children? There are, as it turns out,
two different theories which incorporate modeling as an important learning principle.

Psychoanalytic theory. As Sears (1967) points out, psychoanalytic theory emphasizes the motivational principle of *identification* as basic to the imitative behavior children show with respect to their parents. The theory holds that parents foster dependency and identification by providing warmth and nurture to their children. Identification underlies imitation, including imitation of parental activities that involve learning.

Psychoanalytic learning theory focuses on the interactions of parents and very young children. Is the adult role model provided by the teacher also imitated by children through the principle of identification? Kagan (1966) has argued that this is the case for children in the earliest grades. Children at this age, according to Kagan, engage in learning because of socially-based motivation to be accepted by significant others. So psychoanalytic theory may have some relevance, although its principle of imitation is not related directly to any of the educational principles cited at the beginning of the chapter.

Reinforcement. The second type of learning theory that has incorporated modeling as an important type of learning is based on the motivational principle of reinforcement. According to social learning theory, children imitate or model behaviors for which they have seen others reinforced and avoid behaviors for which they have seen others punished. Bandura and Walters (1963) also suggest that knowledge of the life history of a model can lead to modeling at a symbolic level, and in all cultures myths about heroic or saintly figures are used in the education of the young. The result is that learners act out social roles for which they have seen others positively reinforced.

The proposition that the role of 'self-directed' learner can be learned entirely by modeling, whatever the motivational basis, perhaps seems somewhat far-fetched. Moreover, there is no research evidence, pro or con, which shows how this can be done. There is promising evidence, however, from more focused studies in which children were taught through modeling to use consistent standards in self-evaluation. Thoresen and Mahoney (1974) and Lepper (1976) and his colleagues, for example, found that children who originally observed models setting high standards for personal performance themselves maintained similar standards over time and even extended them to new tasks. Lepper and his colleagues concluded that the children they had studied set standards for themselves not simply through passive mimicry, but through active, cognitive processes resulting in the adoption of a generalized rule.

The picture is thus mixed, with little or no evidence that children can learn the role of the self-directed learner through modeling, although both the psychoanalytic principle of identification and social learning principle of reinforcement might predict this to be the case. However, on the positive side there is evidence that children do learn to apply high standards to their own performance after observing models using such standards. These findings clearly relate to the principle of *learners as their own evaluation agents*.

Reinforcement Theory: External and Self-Reinforcement
The belief that human behavior is primarily a function of previously experienced patterns of rewards and punishments underlies the largest body of empirical work on learning.

In the radical Skinnerian version of behaviorism, successfully maintained contingencies of reinforcement would achieve virtually total environmental control of the organism, a condition of learning utterly antithetical to the conception presented here.

Skager (1979) cited two bodies of work on reinforcement. One is based on the study of the effect of external reinforcements such as material or social rewards on the persistence of learning behavior itself. The other involves the use of self-reinforcement by learners. These two approaches will be summarized briefly.

External reinforcement. When external reinforcement is applied to maintain learning behavior, the source of motivation is extrinsic to the learner. The expectation of external rewards thus established may inhibit the development of attributes such as intrinsic motivation and internalized evaluation, because the nature of the situation creates dependency on the environment for both rewards and feedback.

The literature examined in Skager (1979) suggests that external reinforcement is at best a risky tool with respect to the development of self-direction. One important study by Lepper *et al.* (1973) showed that spontaneous learning behavior in children declined in frequency when external rewards for successful performance were anticipated. In contrast, spontaneous learning behavior was found to persist when rewards were not expected. However, Lepper and his associates concluded that extrinsic rewards reduce motivation for learning in children who were already intrinsically motivated when what had originally been a desirable activity becomes merely a means to obtaining a reward. But these writers also cautioned that over-generalizations about the negative aspects of external rein-forcement should be avoided. Other research has suggested that extrinsic incentives can be used for a time to heighten inter-est on the part of children whose initial interest was low. Given engagement over some period of time under reinforcement conditions, the attractiveness of an activity may ultimately become apparent.

Self-reinforcement. A second strand of research on rein-forcement seems less incompatible with the enhancement of self-directed learning. In this type of research learners monitor their own performance by keeping records of success or failure and/or by administering their own rewards when successful. In general, this approach seems to be directed at important as-pects of self-directed learning behavior, especially inter-nalized evaluation and planfulness.

One study by Glynn *et al.* (1973) is illustrative of work in self-reinforcement. This research proceeded through several stages in an investigation of how effective behavioral self-control methods might be for increasing the amount of time a group of elementary level children spent 'on-task' during read-ing periods. After observing frequency of on-task reading be-havior for several days to establish a baseline for each learner, the researchers entered a phase in which learners were given various rewards on a random contingency schedule for engaging in observed, on-task reading behavior. Then, as the experiment proceeded, behavior was gradually shaped in the direction of full self-control of monitoring and reinforcement. Ultimately, the children moved to a point where they summarized their own reading behavior on a reporting form, decided whether the result was satisfactory, and administered their own rewards. These authors concluded that in a regular classroom setting, children as young as seven years could successfully use behavioral self-control procedures to maintain learning behavior initially es-tablished through externally administered reinforcements.

Self-evaluative processes are also a promising area of investigation within reinforcement oriented research. In rela-tion to social learning theory, Bandura (1976) summarized re-search investigating how people develop standards and the degree to which 'self-administered consequences' enhance learning per-formance. Bandura (1978) emphasized that children learn to

establish personal performance standards through other means as
well, including the influence of precepts, exposure to self-
evaluative standards as modeled by others, as well as by ex-
periencing consequences of performance that are not self-
administered.

Research on self-reinforcement is primarily relevant to
the principle of *learners as their own evaluation agents*. It
does appear that important aspects of self-direction can be
systematically taught. Attributes of self-directed learning
such as setting one's own performance standards and systematic
self-monitoring persist overtime and may generalize to new
situations. Moreover, contemporary views of the role of reinforcement in human learning often avoid the environmental
determinism of early behaviorism by concentrating on how people
learn to direct their own learning processes. Still, caution
is warranted because of the seeming incompatibility of the
behavioristic goal of 'controlling' behavior with the humanistic values which underly the concept of self-direction in
learning.

Curiosity and Exploration

Berlyne's (1965) classic paper on spontaneous or
'epistemic' exploratory behavior in higher animals
and humans stimulated extensive interest in the role
of curiosity as a variable in the learning equation.

Berlyne observed that some exploratory behavior is 'intrinsic' and conducted for its own sake rather than in order
to attain some definable set of consequences. Epistemic curiosity is also reflected in spontaneous attempts to explain
cognitive conflicts induced by situations of surprise, doubt,
perplexity, bafflement, or confrontation with apparently contradictory events or information. Berlyne and others saw curiosity as a drive aroused by the stimulus conditions of the kind
just cited, resulting in exploratory behavior, and motivating
all humans (as well as other mammals).

Others, such as Maw and Maw (1964), have defined curiosity
as a personality characteristic on which individuals differ
sharply rather than as a universal motivational principle.
They have, for example, observed that highly curious children
tend to be rated as more intelligent by their teachers, formu-
late better questions during instruction, possess more general
information, and prefer complex to simple stimuli.

Finally, a third theory of curiosity proposed by Kreitler *et al.* (1974) has exploratory behavior originating in learned, cognitive belief systems rather than from a universal motivational principle or possibly innate differences in personality. In this research, school-children who demonstrated higher levels of curiosity or manifested exploratory behavior, held beliefs that were consistent with that behavior, e.g., that adults like children who ask questions, that new activities are usually entertaining, and (perhaps most significantly) that learning how to do new things is advantageous.

Whatever its basis, curiosity and its manifestations in exploratory behavior has in recent years been widely recognized as an under-used educational tool. Vidler (1977) derived several implications for the classroom for research on curiosity. Two of these principles are especially worth citing.

1. Exploratory-learning in children declines as situations become more anxiety-provoking. Classroom settings emphasizing competion and rigid conformity tend to promote such anxiety.

2. The preschool and elementary years may be the best time to encourage the habit of exploration of the environment and learning through exploration, as early learning tends to have the most profound effect on subsequent development.

Exploratory behavior directed at solving a problem or simply at gaining useful experience is, by definition, a type of self-directed learning. Moreover, the use of exploration as a deliberate strategy in the learning situation reflects five of the eight principles and is potentially related to the other three. Obviously, the situation must be organized so as to take advantage of *intrinsic motivation*, there must be *flexibility*, and *opportunity for choice*. Learning through exploration also assumes that learners are their *own evaluation agents*. In addition, it is likely that the use of exploratory-learning would require teachers to play a primarily *facilitating*, rather than directing, role. It is also likely, in the case where exploration involves solving open-ended problems, that *expressive educational objectives* will have been selected.

'Discovery-learning' is a relatively well-known tactical approach to formalizing learning through exploration. Cronbach (1966) described this approach to teaching as inductive in contrast to didactic or directive, and suggested that its potential

outcomes include the ability to solve general problems in a
discipline by acquiring search and information processing behaviors ('heuristics').

The limitations of discovery-learning have been described
by Kagan (1966). It is not appropriate with low I.Q. children,
with children who are poorly motivated, or with impulsive
learners who jump to inaccurate, early conclusions. Other work,
such as that by Werdelin *et al.* (1971), has investigated whether
or not retention and generalization are superior under discovery
as compared to didactic learning.

Exploratory-learning deriving from curiosity thus incorporates discovery-learning, but it is at the same time only one
aspect of self-directed learning. The latter, for example,
also includes systematic learning by means of predetermined
activity to achieve paradigmatic objectives that may have little
or nothing to do with curiosity. However, exploratory-learning
appears to be a logical part of a teaching/learning environment
designed to develop self-direction. Its facilitation is remarkably consistent with a number of the educational principles
stated at the beginning of the chapter.

Competency Motivation
White's (1959) reanalysis of the concept of motivation in relation to learning also accounts for exploratory behavior in the concept of *effectance*.

For various reasons, White rejected curiosity 'drive' as
an energizer of exploratory behavior. Instead, he found in
Piaget's documentation of spontaneous, playful exploration in
very young children evidence of a generalized human motivation
to deal effectively with the environment. White labeled this
motivation 'effectance' and suggested that it energizes bio-
logically significant exploratory behavior.

Unlike curiosity motivation, effectance is not conceived
as a drive susceptible to reduction through satiation as is the
case for physiological drive states such as hunger, thirst, or
oxygen deprivation. Rather, it is postulated as a continuing
disposition to control the environment through the development
of knowledge and competency. Projected on to the classroom,
effectance theory highlights the importance of learners developing positive self-esteem through the successful performance of
meaningful tasks and problems. Keifer's (1973) longitudinal
study of high *versus* low achieving school children found the

two groups becoming increasingly divergent on measures of self-esteem, self-concept of ability, and locus of control (extent to which events affecting the self are attributed to one's own efforts rather than to chance or the power of others). Keifer concluded that instruction should maximize the probability that every learner, rather than only a few learners, should feel competent. In a similar vein, Blaney *et al.* (1977) found that peer tutoring in co-operative learning groups increased the self-esteem of the learners (all took a turn at tutoring) in contrast to the usual situation in which competition allows only a few individuals to feel successful.

The connection between success and self-esteem implied in effectance theory is both conceptually reasonable and supported by empirical research. A number of the educational principles relating to self-direction in learning also seem to apply to effectance theory. Avoiding the destructive aspects of competition among learners by substituting co-operative learning strategies can readily be interpreted as an application of the principle of *democratic relationships*. Certainly the principles of *flexibility* and *opportunity of choice* would suggest using individualized instruction to make it easier for learners to work in ways, and toward objectives, that are more appropriate for them as individuals. In this kind of situation teachers are likely to play a *facilitating* rather than a strictly didactic role, since the principle of effectance implies the learner's active engagement in the learning process. Finally, effectance could also incorporate the principle of *learning outside of the school*, because learners spend most of their lives in that outside world and must develop competence in it as well.

Attribution Theory and Personal Causation

> Weiner (1972) suggested that labeling an action as 'intentional' presumes that the actor perceives himself as the cause of whatever outcome from that action.

Attribution theory, initially formulated by Heider (1958), deals with how people make causal interpretations about events that affect them. Its basic distinction is between causal attributions that are *internal*, or to the actor's own efforts and abilities. People who make external causal attributions in effect define themselves as helpless in a given situation. Those who make internal attributions consciously see themselves as responsible for events, even if those events are undesirable.

Attribution theory is the most relevant of the six theories selected for examination in relation to self-direction in learning. A strong sense of the self as the causal agent in learning must inevitably be at the core of the self-concept of people who plan and direct their own learning. Internal attribution also implies a feeling of personal competency. In this sense attribution theory incorporates the concept of effectance, since only those who are effective in a situation are likely to see themselves as causal agents. Finally, one of the most promising attempts yet reported to develop self-direction in learners at the school-level, readily fits within the general perspective of attribution theory.

Personal causation theory. De Charms (1971, 1976) characterizes the work just referred to as "personal causation training". He distinguishes between the learner who perceives himself as an *origin* or locus of causality, and the learner whose self-perception is that of a *pawn* controlled by more powerful external forces or subject to more or less capricious turns of good or bad luck.

De Charms and his co-workers conducted a four-year study of a cohort of school-children from the fifth (about age 10) to eighth (about age 13) grade levels. In the initial phase of the study, teachers were trained to

1. encourage goal-setting in their students;
2. allow students to select the way in which they were to attain goals;
3. stress realism in goal-setting;
4. develop and maintain an atmosphere in which students could take a personal responsibility for their actions; and
5. instill confidence in their students.

During the initial stage of the research the teachers were also trained to see themselves as origins rather than pawns by methods analogous and, in some cases, identical to those that they would later use with students. An apparent outcome of this work with the teachers shows how pertinent personal causation training is to self-direction in learning. De Charms (1972) reported that by the fourth year of the research, 35% of the participating teachers had advanced professionally (mainly by pursuing additional learning) as compared

to only 5% of a control group of teachers who did not receive
personal causation training.

Personal causation training was embodied in a curriculum
incorporating an ingenious variety of games involving training
in realistic goal-setting and avoidance of extreme risk-taking.
(Earlier research had shown that learners who see themselves as
pawns often set very unrealistic goals as a means of avoiding
a task altogether.) The curriculum also incorporated direct
instruction in the meaning of the origin/pawn distinction as
applied to the students' own experiences. In addition, children
were taught to use various methods of record-keeping so as to
keep track of accomplishments.

For tracking each learner's self-perception on the pawn/
origin continuum, De Charms and his colleagues analyzed stories
the students wrote in response to standard questions about
thematic picture stimuli (from the *Thematic Apperception Test*).
The stories were scored for evidence of origin type behavior on
the basis of evidence of:

1. internal goal setting;

2. internal determination of instrumental
   (e.g. goal-attaining) activity;

3. perception of reality; and

4. internal control.

In general, the research demonstrated siginificant development of origin behavior in the students as compared to a
control group. The experimental group also showed a significant
improvement in level of academic achievement.

Experiential learning. 'Experiential learning', according
to Chickering (1976), is "... learning that occurs when changes
in judgements, feelings, knowledge, or skills result ... from
living through a particular event". Chickering proposed that
this kind of learning makes it possible for learners to perceive
themselves as origins and to develop a sense of personal causation. Coleman (1976) suggests that experiential learning pre-
sumes intrinsic motivation and, when successful, contributes to
self-assurance and a sense of accomplishment.

Experiential learning is an anthropological concept developed independently from attribution theory. The school is,
after all, a recent social invention in the full perspective of

human cultural history. Earlier forms of learning often, Lee
(1967) points out, left the experience of 'finding out' to the
child. Adults arranged events, asked questions about experiences, and criticized performance, but scrupulously avoided
interfering with the intensely personal experiences that led to
learning. Modern conceptions of experiential learning, as vari-
ously presented in Keeton (1976), assign similarly active roles
to the learner, again suggesting the development of internal
attribution and the relevance of attribution theory.

Democratic climate and attribution theory. Attribution
theory is relevant to all of the other principles of the learning environment cited at the beginning of the chapter, so these
need not be cited individually in this section, with the exception of the principle of *democratic relationships.* This is
perhaps the most easily misunderstood of the eight principles
because it may, in spite of the caveat stated originally, be
taken to mean that teachers should avoid the exercise of authority and that classrooms should be organized according to a
laissez-faire spirit. This is emphatically not what is meant
by the democratization principle, nor is it consistent with
applications of attribution theory. De Charms (1978) makes this
explicitly clear in describing personal causation training. In
this approach it remains the responsibility of teachers to plan
and manage the learning process. Decision-making authority is
allocated to students only when they are mature enough to assume responsibility.

QUESTIONS TO BE ANSWERED IN THE CASE STUDIES

The educational principles and learning theories just
reviewed helped greatly to focus the case studies on a common
set of questions to be answered in the research. In addition,
Henry's (1960) cross-cultural outline of education provided a
general framework for studying schooling in any society. The
Henry outline applies both to schools and to non-formal modes
of learning. It was derived from the field experience of an-
thropologists in cultures ranging from the pre-industrial to
the technically advanced. It is especially useful as a device
for surveying the possible kinds of index that might be pertinent to a given study.

The outline is broken down into 12 major categories,
each in turn further differentiated into two or more specific
subdivisions. One of the reference documents provided to par-

ticipants prior to the initial project meeting described each
major category of Henry's outline and cited illustrative subcategories, especially those that might be judged relevant to
self-direction. Henry's complete list of several hundred indices was also provided to participants.

The 12 major categories of the outline are each defined
by a general question. For example, the fourth category is
listed under the following question:

"How does the person being educated participate?"
(What is his attitude?)

Some of the specific indicators selected from Henry's
largest list of over 50 items relating to the learner's mode of
participation are clearly related to one or another of the hypothesized characteristics of self-direction enhancing learning
environments reviewed at the beginning of this chapter. For
example:

"Through making independent decisions and suggestions"
(opportunity for choice)

"Through spontaneous contributions or other demonstra-
tions not precisely within the context of the lesson"
(capitalizing on intrinsic motivation and flexibility)

"Corrects teacher" (democratic relationships)

"Mobile-free" (flexibility).

The Henry outline proved to be useful as an aide in an-
choring the research onto more or less universal dimensions of
schooling, through from the particular perspective of the principles and theories reviewed earlier. This process of synthesis
ultimately resulted in the identification of nine specific research questions around which the case studies were designed.
These questions are listed next as they were originally stated
in the reference document on research design. Brief elabora-
tions of each question are provided here in abbreviated form.

Organization and Governance
"How was the selected school organized and
administered?"

This question is particularly concerned with whether or
not decisions about structure and policy were distributed among
participants. It deals with how flexibility may be built into

the process of governance, and how various categories of individuals participate in running the school and setting its
policies.

Characteristics of the Participants
> "What personal characteristics did teachers and
> students (as well as other participants, if
> relevant) display which might be related to the
> enhancement of self-direction on the part of
> students in the school?"

For example, this question is concerned with whether
teachers themselves provide appropriate role models by engaging
in personal learning activities in ways that are likely to be
apparent to the students. Have teachers or others had special
training or experience which might help them to create and
maintain an environment conducive to the development of self-
directed learning? Did any of the students show evidence of
self-direction in their own learning?

Decision-Making in the Teaching/Learning Process
> "To what extent were students allowed to assume
> responsibility for making decisions about their
> own learning?"

Allowing the learners, as clients of the school, to make
decisions that determine and regulate their own learning implies
flexibility as well. Without flexibility decisions are obviously not required. In particular, the case studies were to find
out if learners were at times responsible for deciding on any
of the following:

1. the amount of time to be devoted to a given
   learning activity;

2. the mode or approach to learning;

3. the place the learning occurs; and

4. the content to be learned.

How Teachers Teach
> "Did adults other than a regularly assigned teacher
> also participate in the teaching/learning process?
> Did students teach other students? Were outsiders
> representing various work roles in the society
> involved in teaching?"

Diffusion of responsibility for teaching, especially to the students themselves, presumably broadens the learners' conception of the kinds of human resources, their own included, that may be used for learning. The question asks how teachers approached the teaching act itself. For example, did teachers encourage students to evaluate their own progress? How was this done? (A set of principles developed by Sawin (1969), describing how teachers can encourage self-evaluation on the part of their students, was cited. Sawin's principles are quite concrete and suggest aspects of teacher behavior that can be measured directly.)

How Students Learn
"How did students typically engage in learning?"

In particular, this question asks the extent to which individual differences among students were considered in the selection of alternative approaches to the learning process. (This is of course another indicator of flexibility.) Did the learning process incorporate problem-solving or discovery-learning techniques? Did it emphasize early learning or experiential learning? Were there factors in the learning situations which might help learners develop a sense of themselves as active agents in their own learning as compared to passive recepients?

Influence of Goals of the School on the Curriculum
"Did the written curriculum (if such existed for the school) or people's statements about the curriculum suggest that self-direction, including self-evaluation, was deliberately incorporated in the learning process? If so, how was this done?"

Curriculum is often defined in the limited sense of formal academic content. In this project curriculum was defined more broadly in the same way that teaching was more broadly conceived. How learners go about learning, the so-called 'hidden curriculum', is generally thought to be immensely influential in the development of an image of the self as a learner.

Use of Available Materials and Facilities
"Were there any ways in which equipment, materials, space, etc., were used in a manner that encouraged self-direction?"

It would be important, for example, that students be able to work alone when appropriate. Likewise, was it also possible

for students to work in co-operative learning groups without
bothering others? Were alternative learning materials or devices available and to what extent were they used? Were there
materials and procedures, such as unit tests that can be scored
by learners themselves, available for use in self-evaluation?
In general, how were material and spatial factors manipulated
to facilitate learning, especially self-direction in learning?

What Students Learn
> "What evidence was there that students in the
> school were learning desired content, skill,
> attitudes, and concepts of the self?"

While learning academic content is obviously important,
achievement should be defined more broadly. Was there any
indication that students were developing some of the personal
characteristics of the self-directed learner (Chapter 2)? Do
some students appear to be making more progress than others,
and what might account for this phenomenon? Generally, how
did students appear to be influenced by the school, over and
beyond what they were learning in the academic curriculum?

What Various Groups Think about the School
> "What is the school's image in the community and
> country as a whole?"

Did teachers, parents, students, other participants, as
well as knowledgeable outside experts, agree on their assessments of the accomplishments of the school? Those intimately
involved in a school may often see the results of their efforts
in the light of what they are attempting to accomplish rather
than in terms of what really is happening. Outsiders may have
a different perspective. While this particular question deals
entirely with opinions rather than objective observation, opinions often reflect valid experiences and in themselves constitute factual data that reflect the degree to which the school
is seen as successful by outsiders as compared to insiders.

These, then, were the questions that the case study reports addressed in the section on empirical findings. How the
questions were to be answered was a function of the strategy
for collecting information selected by each team. This latter
information is provided in Appendix C, where the research strategy adopted by each team is described.

SUMMARY

Eight operational principles of learning environments hypothesized to contribute to the development of self-direction in learning were reviewed. The principles include:

1. flexibility in the learning situation;

2. encouragement of choice;

3. teaching as a facilitating activity;

4. learners as their own evaluation agents;

5. democratic relationships in the learning situation;

6. capitalizing on intrinsic motivation;

7. emphasis on expressive (or open-ended) educational objectives; and

8. incorporating learning outside of the school.

The principles are properly viewed as hypotheses rather than established findings. However, in lieu of the latter, they served collectively as a mechanism for focusing the case studies on aspects of the schools most likely to relate to self-direction.

In addition, six theories of human learning were surveyed for elements pertaining to the development of self-direction. The theories were:

1. humanistic;

2. modeling;

3. reinforcement, both external and self-administered;

4. curiosity and exploration;

5. competency motivation; and

6. attribution and personal causation.

All of the theories were found to relate to one or more of the operational principles.

Finally, the nine research questions on which the case studies were based were presented. These specific questions were derived from the above operational principles, pertinent aspects of the theories reviewed, and the Henry cross-cultural outline of education.

Of the six theories, attribution theory appears to be the most promising in helping to understand the origins of self-direction and guide the design of learning environments that promote it. Self-directed learners must, by definition, attribute responsibility internally for the results of their own attempts to learn. In an alternative formulation of the attribution concept, learners see themselves as origins in the learning process rather than as helpless pawns. Attribution theory also incorporates important aspects of other theories, especially in its application to personal causation training.

Finally, Henry's cross-cultural outline of schooling was used along with the foregoing material to generate a set of research questions that addressed universal aspects of schooling, but within the particular perspective of self-direction in learning. These questions dealt with the topics of

1. organization and governance;

2. characteristics of the participants;

3. decision-making in the teaching/learning process;

4. how teachers teach;

5. how students learn;

6. influence of goals of the school on the curriculum;

7. use of available materials and facilities;

8. what students learn; and

9. what various groups think about the school.

The particular research strategies by which the case studies answered each of these questions, are described in Appendix C.

Chapter 4

Participating Institutions

SELECTION

Participation in Unesco Institute projects by schools and colleges in different countries depends on local capabilities and enthusiasm. In this respect the project was fortunate. Directors of the national case studies were granted full access to the institutions selected for study. This was in no small part due to their own good relationships with staff in the participating institutions. At all four of the participating institutions, staff and students contributed significant amounts of their own time, freely provided a great deal of information, and otherwise assisted in the collection and interpretation of information.

Diversity among participating institutions was highly desirable in this research. Could a school or college in a developing Asian country such as the Philippines be adequately described in terms of the same dimensions as a school in a European socialist country such as Hungary? Would participants, including the case study research staff members, see these dimensions as relevant and pertinent? Or would they find that important aspects of the institutions studied were overlooked? As it turned out, these fears were not justified. The researchers in each country had no difficulty applying the personal characteristics and dimensions of the learning environment to the students and institutions they were studying.

Diversity of participants under a common framework of study has the potential for turning up more varied approaches to the instructional process than might be the case if the research were limited to one relatively homogeneous culture. Perhaps most important, there is even the possibility that some findings may generalize beyond a single case study. One example of this occurred in the Philippine and U.S. studies, where self-

directed learners in schools in two different countries were
independently observed to behave in remarkably similar ways
(Chapter 8).

Interest in participation and a general emphasis on self-
direction in learning were the overall criteria used in the
search for participating schools and colleges. However, letters
of inquiry written to Unesco regional offices and professional
colleagues in several countries contained more specific criteria
abstracted from the eight hypothesized conditions of the learning environment described in the last chapter. It was made
clear in these communications that no single institution would
be expected to have incorporated all of the principles in its
curriculum. Rather, schools were being sought that were explicitly committed to the encouragement of self-direction
through the implementation of at least some of the following
principles:

1. flexibility in time, place, mode, or content of
   learning;

2. maximizing opportunity for choice on the part of
   the learners;

3. emphasis on the facilitative (as contrasted to
   the directive) role of the teacher;

4. encouragement of self-evaluation on the part of
   the learners;

5. encouragement of democratic interpersonal relationships among all participants in the learning
   situation;

6. capitalizing on the intrinsic motivation of
   learners by taking into account their personal
   interests and motivation;

7. emphasis on educational objectives of the
   'expressive' type through use of open-ended
   problems or situations in which the method and
   form of the solution is under the control of
   the learner; and

8. incorporation of learning in the community as a
   means of orienting learners to life outside of
   the school.

Initially it seemed preferable to secure the participation
of institutions serving learners of approximately the same age

level. This did not turn out to be possible. However, the study of different levels of schooling provides another potentially productive kind of diversity in case studies. The case study method does not test hypotheses, so the requirement of representative sampling from a defined population does not apply. When successful case studies in contrast *generate* hypotheses and examples. Diversity may contribute more in the way of practical examples and generality of hypotheses than homogeneity. If similar phenomena are observed in schools in different national contexts serving learners at different age levels, then it is possible that some hypotheses and examples of practice will turn up that are especially interesting and generalizable.

Ultimately, three schools and one traditional institution (school to college level) were identified. The countries in which these institutions are located are diverse, culturally and geographically. Most important, each of the institutions places a high priority on the development of self-direction in its students and was interested in participating in the project.

The four participating institutions were the *Bielefelder Oberstufenkolleg* at Bielefeld, Federal Republic of Germany, the *Katalin Varga Grammar School* in Szolnok, People's Republic of Hungary, *Arellano High School* in Manila, Republic of the Philippines, and the *Canfield-Crescent Heights Community School* in Los Angeles, California, U.S.A. The remainder of this chapter will be devoted to descriptions of the schools and the local and national context in which they operate. Later the schools and their programs will be dealt with analytically; it is useful at the beginning to provide a more holistic picture of each school and the population it serves. Descriptions of the schools will be given in order of their level, beginning with Canfield Crescent Heights at the elementary level, followed by two secondary schools, the Katalin Varga School and the Arellano High School, and finally with the Oberstufenkolleg, an institution combining upper secondary school with the first two years of the university.

THE COMMUNITY SCHOOL

The National Educational Context
In the United States, jurisdiction over education is assigned by the Constitution to the 50 states. State governments exercise regulatory and financial authority, but are not assigned

administrative authority at the local level. The administration of U.S. public schools is thus under the authority of local
school districts, of which there are about 15,000 nationally.
District policies are determined by an elected school board and
carried out by an administrative staff headed by a superintendent appointed by the school board. Schools are normally headed
by principals.

The Local Context
       The Canfield-Crescent Heights Community School is located
in the Los Angeles Unified School District, the second largest
district in the nation, (600 square miles, 26,700 teachers,
558 schools and over one half million pupils). The size of
the district is important. The school in its current form is
the result of a neighborhood movement of parents attempting to
gain influence over their children's education in the face of
what was perceived as a distant and inflexible bureaucracy and
school board.

       Los Angeles schools are organized on a 6-3-3 model, with
one year of noncompulsory kindergarten, six years of elementary
school, three years of middle or junior high school, and three
years of high school. Elementary schools usually operate with
self-contained classrooms in which there is a single teacher,
often assisted by aides or parent volunteers. Administrative
authority is vested in the principal. Classes vary in size
from 25 to 40 children.

       The character of the local community from which the school
draws its students is also important. The study was conducted
during the first year of a district-wide racial and ethnic desegregation program which incorporates a variety of administrative arrangements plus movement of children by bus to areas of
the city quite distant from their homes. The school itself is
unaffected by this movement of pupils because it was already
racially balanced, enrolling about 50 per cent each of white
and minority (mainly black) pupils, respectively. In fact, the
school was organized several years before through the efforts
of parents who in part wished to achieve racial balance *before*
mandatory desegregation became district policy. These parents
managed to obtain approval from the school board for the establishment of a separate school located on the campuses of two
existing elementary schools located less than a mile apart.
The organization and curriculum of this school reflects an educational program worked out jointly by parents, teachers, and
Program Directors serving in the place of a principal.

The School

The Community School enrolls a total of 180 students, making it small in comparison to other elementary schools in the district. All students are enrolled voluntarily by their parents. Applicants are accepted in order of application within the established racial/ethnic guidelines of the district. Priorities are given to siblings of currently enrolled students, however.

The first three grades and kindergarten are located at the Crescent Heights site and the last three grades at Canfield School. Third grade students may be assigned to either site. The first three grades are self-contained and taught by a single teacher. At the upper site each of the three teachers specializes in a single academic area (math, reading, language and writing skills) and pupils spend part of the school day with each.

Parental participation in the school is intense, and decision-making on policy and expenditure is shared among staff, parents, and elected student representatives. There are monthly 'town-hall' meetings at which major decisions about budget, policy, and curriculum are discussed by these three groups. The four elected school offices are filled by parents who also chair standing committees on various aspects of the school program. All staff members, including the Program Director, are selected by a committee of Community School parents and school staff. It is especially important to note that this extensive level of parental involvement and shared decision-making stands in distinct contrast to virtually all of the other 500-plus schools in the district. The Community School is organizationally unique in its context.

The educational program of the school is built around the two core goals of individualization of instruction and multicultural education. While the curriculum includes the normal scope and sequence of content, non-traditional practices such as multi-age classes, team teaching, flexible scheduling, and use of resource labs and centers are incorporated in the instructional program. The individual abilities of students are the primary considerations in placement rather than age or nominal grade level. The multicultural program is designed to support racially integrated education through ethnic studies designed to help children learn about their own backgrounds as well as to understand and appreciate other racial heritages. There is an Ethnic Studies Co-ordinator and Ethnic Studies Resource Center to support this aspect of the curriculum.

OSTE-C*

The Community School is allocated the same resources that are provided to regular schools in the district. Additional instructional materials needed for the multicultural program and other special supplies and equipment are purchased through parent-sponsored fund-raising activities. Parents also are heavily involved as classroom volunteers.

The Community School was selected from among other alternatives because its emphasis on individualization as a basis for the instructional process implied the criteria of flexibility, opportunity for choice, facilitating aspects of teaching, and of intrinsic motivation. The unusual degree to which authority was shared by representatives of all of the groups participating in the school (rather than being invested in a principal) suggested that interactions between teachers and learners might reflect a similar trend toward democratic relationships.

THE KATALIN VARGA GRAMMAR SCHOOL

The National Educational Context
Except for a few church-sponsored schools, the schools of the People's Republic of Hungary are coordinated within a single national system under which the various types and levels of schooling are the same throughout the country. The curriculum is likewise standardized.

The great majority of children attend kindergarten from ages 3-6. A one year alternative is available for those who do not. Primary school incorporates eight grades, with the typical student completing at age 14. Secondary school adds another four years for those who go on with formal schooling, and is differentiated into academic (grammar school) and technical tracks. There is an alternative three year vocational training school. Graduates of either academic or vocational schools are prepared for immediate work or for entry into higher education. In addition, this regular system is supported by a system of adult education as well as various types of specialized training.

The most important contextual factor in relation to this research is the Hungarian academic curriculum, especially in the grammar school, characterized by very high academic standards and expectations and retaining a number of traditional elements. There has been heavy emphasis on the acquisition of 'encyclopedic' knowledge, perhaps at the expense of experience

in making responsible decisions about learning. The curriculum
has been also quite crowded with academic requirements, leaving
little room for options. Finally, Hungarian grammar schools
have been oriented towards maximizing the number of graduates
who will obtain entrance to universities.

The Local Context
        The Katalin Varga School is situated in Szolnok, a very
old city of 76,000 inhabitants, about 60 per cent of whom are
workers. The general educational level of the citizens is somewhat higher than the national average. A variety of industries
are located in or around the city, which has developed in recent
years as a tourist center because of the availability of thermal
pools and spas.

The School
        The Katalin Varga Grammar School enrolled 329 students
aged 14-18 in 1978-79, about 70 per cent of whom were female.
The building dates from the 19th century and was not originally
a school. Hence, the internal structure is less than ideal.
Classrooms are equipped according to the subjects taught in
them, the latter reflecting traditional categories of the academic curriculum. The school has a large library, although in
other respects its resources do not differ significantly from
other grammar schools in Hungary.

        The school is highly regarded for its academic program.
All students apply for admission, and since about twice as many
apply as there are spaces available, the school selects applicants based on their comprehensive school record. The subject-
matter specializations of the twenty teachers illustrate the
strongly classical emphasis of the Hungarian grammar school
curriculum (numerals in parantheses indicate the number of
teachers in each specialization): Hungarian language and litera-
ture/history (4); Russian language/history (1); Russian (1);
English and German (2); English and Russian (1); German and
Russian (1); mathematics and physics (2); chemistry and biology (2); chemistry and physics (2); geography and biology (1);
physical education (2). The school staff also includes a headmaster, a deputy headmaster, a librarian, a laboratory assistant,
and supporting staff. Regular instruction takes place in an
appropriate classroom setting, including special arrangements
for languages and laboratories for sciences.

        About 6 per cent of the students live at the school in a
students' hostel, and another 25 per cent commute daily by bus

or train from neighboring villages. Part of the budget of the
school goes to student support, including travelling expenses,
support for those needing special financial aid, and for awards
to high-achieving learners. In general, the student body is
similar to that of other Hungarian grammar schools, although
the number of live-in students may be slightly smaller, while
the number of children of manual workers (at 45 per cent of the
student body) is slightly larger.

The school is under the immediate supervision of the
County Education Department in which it is located. In addition,
it operates under the same national regulations as do other
Hungarian grammar schools. However, the regulations at the
national level are open to interpretation, and in 1970 the administration and teaching staff of the school decided to embark
on a pedagogical experiment which has differentiated the school
from other Hungarian grammar schools. Briefly, the school has
made it possible for students to select special subjects of
interest, including courses within the mandated curriculum.
Students who opt to pursue special topics are allowed to study
in small groups under the guidance of a teacher who is free to
enhance self-direction by encouraging learners to teach others
in the group what they have learned, to do experiments, and to
hold organized discussions and debates. Students may also at
any time elect to take advance examinations in one or more subjects. If the examination is passed, the student is excused
from additional regular instruction in the subject, although
he or she may decide to do more advanced work or some other
type of work such as preparation for an inter-school competition.

During the first year the school provides learners with
an extensive array of special offerings in advanced learning
and communication skills. These include practice in reading
comprehension, note taking, use of learning technology, making
sketches, organizing and quantifying data, preparing lectures,
public speaking and discussion leading, self-evaluation, and
logical thinking. The overall purpose of the special training
in 'learning how to learn' is to help learners develop the
ability to organize their own learning and to make appropriate
choices while learning.

Like the other schools described in this report, the
Katalin Varga Grammar School is an innovation within its own
context. It remains a school with a rigorous academic program
of a traditional type. Yet its staff have also managed to

mount what are generally seen as significant innovations while
at the same time continuing to fulfill the regular functions of
a grammar school in the Hungarian educational structure.

ARELLANO HIGH SCHOOL

The National Educational Context
        Although the Philippines is classified as a developing
country, its literacy rate is currently over 83 per cent. However, the country is still largely dependent on agriculture and
the exploitation of natural resources, although manufacturing
and construction industries are also part of the economy. The
Philippines has an extensive public educational system established during the American colonial period. In a country with
ten major dialects, English, also inherited from colonial
times, remains one of the languages of instruction at the
secondary level.

        In the Philippines, formulation of educational policy is
vested in a National Board chaired by the Minister of Education.
The Department of Education is divided into bureaux corresponding to elementary, secondary, and high education. Thirteen
regional offices of education, each divided into the same three
bureaux, serve political/geographic regions of the country. In
addition to the public schools, there is a large, pre-existing
Catholic educational system established during the Spanish colonial period, as well as private, secular schools.

        There are three types of public secondary schools:

1. general secondary or four-year college preparatory
   (Arellano High School being in this category);

2. '2-2 plan' schools combining an initial two years
   of academic education with two years of vocational
   education, but currently being phased out; and

3. vocational high schools which prepare students
   both for higher education and specific vocations.

These regular institutions are supplemented by specialized
schools for the gifted, the handicapped, the delinquent, or
other groups. Secondary level schools are funded from one of
five sources: the national government, a provincial government, a city government, a municipal or town government, or
by a village or 'barangay' government.

The Local Context
      Arellano High School is located in the Santa Cruz district
of Manila, an old section of the city which experienced its apo-
gee of wealth and social prestige during the Spanish colonial
period. Currently the population of this district can be described as lower middle class, with the largest single proportion of working residence (22 per cent) classified as service
workers. Other common occupational categories are sales, cleri-
cal, and craftsmen or production workers. Only about 13 per
cent of the population are classified as professional or technical. The district is quite crowded, with most of the inhabitants having been born in Manila and half in the Santa Cruz
district itself. The population is thus relatively stable for
a large city at a time when the country as a whole is experi-
encing extensive movement of people from rural areas to the
towns. The educational level of the residents of the district
compares with the city as a whole.

The School
      Arellano High School is one of the oldest public secondary
schools in Manila. Its physical facility was constructed in
1921 for a district which then incorporated a much smaller
population. Overcrowding is so extreme that four separate
sessions are run daily for morning, afternoon, evening, and
night student-bodies, with teaching staffs working in shifts.
A total of 6,850 students used the facility in 1978-79.

      The physical plant of the school undergoes continuous en-
largement in the effort to accomodate pupils. Library, science
labs, and vocational classrooms are included in the school
complex, but are as overcrowded as the regular classroom facilities. For example, the library seats 300 students, but in
high-use periods students stand about while reading or use
cabinet tops for note-taking. There is a minimum of audio-
visual equipment, and only enough science equipment for instruction of a demonstration type.

The In-School Off-School Program
      The crowding at Arellano is one reflection of the fact
that of the approximately 29,000 students who graduate each
year from Philippine public elementary schools and seek admission to public secondary schools, about 6,000 cannot be
accomodated due to lack of facilities and teachers. This situation has stimulated efforts to increase the utilization of
existing facilities through administrative arrangements such
as the four sessions at Arellano High School. However, more
innovative approaches have also been developed.

The In-School Off-School program (ISOS) was installed in
Arellano High School in 1975 on an experimental basis. This
program has national visibility as one of the principal innovations proposed by a former Director of the Bureau of Public
Schools. It is regarded as an alternative strategy that could
be adopted by other schools facing similar shortages of space
and teachers. The ISOS program, which operates within the
larger context of the regular school, is the subject of the
Philippine case study.

The ISOS program is no longer regarded by its staff as an
experimental activity, it is designed to double the number of
students who could be assigned to a given amount of classroom
space while also holding the number of teachers constant. The
ISOS program thus developed initially as an experimental approach to the problem of overcrowding due to lack of space and
staff. But it was also conceived as an educational experiment
on other grounds. The ISOS program combines formal and non-
formal education. As an experiment, the program was established
to answer questions such as how well students would achieve in
such circumstances; what the implications were for curriculum
design in a situation in which independent work outside of the
school had to be co-ordinated with formal work within the
school; and, how much such a program might contribute to the
development of self-direction in students.

Some 824 students, or 12 per cent of the total Arellano
student body, participated in the ISOS program in 1978-79.
Under the program, two sections of about 40 students each use
a classroom on alternate weeks. Regular texts are used during
the in-school week, and self-learning kits (SLK's) during the
off-school week. During the latter, students work with the SLK
modules and also visit learning centers based in the community.
Instruction during the on-school week does not differ significantly from instruction in regular school classes. However,
learning which occurred during the previous week is monitored
and reinforced. Most teachers in the program give a pre-test
just before students go off-school and a post-test immediately
after they return. The results of the post-test are used to
assign students to remedial, reinforcement, or enrichment instruction on the topics studied during off-week.

The learning centers are grouped according to whether they
will be visited by first, second, third, or fourth year students.
The following are examples:

First year: furniture manufacturing shop, health laboratory, public market, police station;

Second year: public health center, train station, community project agency, theater, bank;

Third year: medical clinic, planetarium, commercial business;

Fourth year: foreign embassy, family-planning center, construction site, offices of various types of professionals such as architects or lawyers, professional athletic teams (most of the visits during the fourth year being directed at career planning).

Students visit the centers in groups of four to eight with a prepared agenda of questions to be asked through interviews or observation. Interviews are conducted by the team-leader while other students take notes. Questions are usually provided by the teachers in the lower grades, but more often by the students at higher levels. Visits are reported during the week in school by the leader or through group presentations. Students occasionally visit centers individually.

The reasons for selecting the ISOS program of Arellano High School are readily apparent. Students must guide their own learning about half of the time without supervision by teachers. The program uses the community extensively as a resource. Students are encouraged to make choices, to explore, and to ask questions. It is perhaps paradoxical that this situation, with its potential for encouraging self-direction, arose initially out of a need to deal with inadequate facilities and shortage of staff, rather than out of primary interest in self-direction itself. But the connection between the ISOS program and self-direction in learning is clear enough.

THE BIELEFELDER OBERSTUFEN-KOLLEG

The National Educational Context

The contemporary educational system of the Federal Republic of Germany (FRG) is the outgrowth of an extended historical process which followed the 19th century unification of the separate German states. From the period of Bismarck, schools, like other German institutions, were in part seen as institutional vehicles for furthering a sense of national identity and purpose. Nevertheless, the schools themselves and their curricula remain under the authority of the various Länder (states) rather than that of the national government. This arrangement allows for significant local variation, at least in principle.

While variations do exist in the educational system between states and also between public and private institutions, the emphasis in public education in the Federal Republic of Germany (over 90 per cent of students are in public schools on achieving consistency rather than on building a climate of diversity and experimentation, as evidenced by the important planning role of the joint "Federal Government / Federal State Commission for Educational Planning" (Wilhelmi, 1979). This influence is especially apparent at the secondary level, where students planning to apply for university entrance must pass a uniform school leaving examination (*Abitur*) after completing studies at the secondary level. This examination has assumed great importance for university-bound youth and has a comparable influence on the secondary level curriculum. While other paths to a university education do exist, the Gymnasium and *Abitur* remain pre-eminent as means for gaining access. There is thus a fairly strong centrist movement in education in the Federal Republic of Germany which tends to work against the variation which is possible structurally.

The Local Context
The town of Bielefeld is a medium-sized city of approximately 300,000 with various industries and, in addition to the university, technical schools and a college of education. However, for the Bielefelder Oberstufen-Kolleg (OSK) the most salient contextual factor is its location on the campus of the University of Bielefeld. The latter institution incidentally serves as the administrative agent for the Ministry of Science and Research. But it is the university climate rather than any administrative arrangements that is closely related to the nature and intended function of the college. The OSK is a research institution in a way that traditionally has been true only for universities. Its campus location reinforces an emphasis on inquiry that is basic to the OSK curriculum.

The College
The Oberstufen-Kolleg can be examined from two perspectives: institutional and curricular. It is a unique institution in its national context because it integrates secondary

school and university level work. The last years of the former
and the first two years of the latter are incorporated in the
OSK curriculum. These two levels of the educational pyramid
are intentionally integrated in a way that enables most graduates to enter at the third year of the university, having
covered five years of work in four years, although graduates in
some fields enter the university at the second year level. All
students who successfully complete the OSK curriculum go on to
universities, otherwise their experience at the college would
have been in a significant sense "wasted".

Also, from the institutional perspective, the OSK has
been striving to pose a viable alternative to the *Abitur* examination system which has had a profound influence on the school
curriculum of the Federal Republic. These school-leaving examinations are under state (rather than federal) control, although
the various states have agreed on a common examination mode and
set of criteria for gaining admission to the universities. At
the time of the study the OSK was attempting to implement a requirement of the state of Nordrhein-Westfalen, where Bielefeld
is located, by developing an examination whose format would be
consistent with the principles on which the college operates
as well as those of the interstate agreement. Until this examination is approved by the other states, temporary regulations
give graduates of the OSK access to universities in Nordrhein-
Westfalen.

From the perspective of curriculum the OSK incorporates
a radically innovative program, not only for the Federal Republic, but even at the international level. This report will
focus on the program of the college which, due to its complexity
in organization and process, need only be described in general
terms at this point.

The OSK is housed in a modern structure without enclosed
classrooms. This open-plan setting was selected so as to allow
flexibility, especially for small group and individual work
with or without the presence of teachers. The building is multi-
level, with other areas assigned to the library, science laboratories, sports activities, photography, printing, films and
musical activities. It is significant that teachers' personal
work spaces are not enclosed, and that desks and files (except
for personnel files) are not equipped with locks. These and
other structural factors reflect the open processes and democratic relationships which will emerge in the findings of the
case study.

Admission is by application, with about 600 prospective students applying for 230 places for Fall, 1979. The total student body averages about 850 over the four year program. Applicants are expected to have completed their tenth year of full-time study in a *Hauptschule*, *Realschule*, or *Gymnasium* (three different branches of secondary schooling in the Federal Republic). Selection among applicants is random within prescribed stratification categories. The categories reflect demographic characteristics of the surrounding area and include

1. sex (equal representation);

2. social class (6 per cent upper or university trained parents, 44 per cent middle, and 50 per cent working, including 10 per cent migrant laborers);

3. vocational experience (33 per cent with, and 67 per cent without); and

4. prior schooling (about 33 per cent coming from each of *Gymnasien*, *Realschulen*, and other types of schools including vocational).

Some applicants are also accepted who have finished only their elementary schooling, so long as they have also completed an apprenticeship program.

The philosophy of the college is best summed up in terms of the principle of *integration*, including that of social classes, subject matters, and school with work. Learning is seen as equally valid whether it occurs in the classroom, in a workshop on an aspect of the curriculum, through participation in self-government, or in the community. The manner in which attempts are made to achieve these types of integration are the subject of the analytical treatment which comes later. In a general sense, the fundamental integrative principle is participation by students and staff in all areas of college governance as well as in curriculum development and the instruction process. At the OSK, *process* is at least as important as *content*. Process is participation in the planning and execution of a personal plan of studies, in setting policy for the institution, or in evaluating courses and other types of learning activities.

The college has considerable visibility in the Federal Republic of Germany and, because of its unusual character, has been the focal point of some controversy. It was selected because of its emphasis on participation by students, both in

planning and carrying out their own program, as well as in the
decision-making process of the school as a whole. Students are
expected to engage in individual study and in small group learning activities without a teacher. They are also encouraged to
practise self-evaluation and to participate in course evaluation. There is great flexibility as to the manner and place of
learning. In general, expectations built into the school environment appear to place emphasis on the development of self-
direction in learners.

SUMMARY

The four institutions that participated in this research
were in part selected simply because their respective staffs
were interested in participating. Local motivation to participate was a fundamental precondition, since it implied interest
in the topic of self-direction in learning as well as an open,
non-defensive attitude.

Diversity, a second precondition, was achieved reasonably
well at the national level. The four countries as a group incorporate differences in level of development, in cultural history to a considerable degree, and in social systems. Within
the group of four countries, control over the public educational
system also ranged from full centralization to extensive diffusion of authority to local districts.

The participating schools also differed in level, a type
of diversity not originally planned, but one which contributed
another dimension to the research. Self-direction in learning
is presumably a characteristic which develops over time and
which is likely to be encouraged in different ways for learners
at different levels of development. Comparisons of the manner
in which schools at the elementary, secondary, and transitional
secondary/university levels go about encouraging self-direction
may have much greater potential for generating both practical
examples and research hypotheses than would the study of schools
at only one level.

All of the schools selected have attempted to implement
several, though certainly not all, of the instructional and
organizational principles for encouraging self-direction listed
in the previous chapter. At the same time, the schools differ
not only in level and national context, but also in the motiva-

tions underlying the kinds of innovations they have introduced.
Each school has responded to its own type of challenge.

The Community School is a community response to a perceived need for greater democracy in the form of shared decision-making among parents and staff, for a curriculum that dealt
directly with the issue of racial and ethnic integration, and
for an instructional process that emphasized individualization
of learning. Staff of the Katalina Varga Grammar School recognized a need to provide students with experience in making their
own educational choices against the background of a highly prescriptive national curriculum, and also a parallel need for the
development of generalizable learning skills. At Arellano High
School, shortages of space and teachers resulted in an experimental program in which students spend half of their time working outside of the school, alone or in small groups. ISOS students are encouraged to make use of the community as an educational resource. Finally, as a part of its attempt to create a
model for integrating secondary and higher education in the
Federal Republic of Germany, the Bielefelder Oberstufen-Kolleg
has evolved a program which places great emphasis on participation by students in both personal and organizational decisions.
It also emphasizes the value of learning in environments other
than the classroom. Originating in response to different needs,
each of the four institutions thus attempts in its own way to
encourage self-direction in learning.

Chapter 5

School Governance and Decision-making in Teaching and Learning

The organizational and governance structures of educational institutions are of little significance in the abstract. Elaborately conceived organizational charts with carefully drawn lines of authority often reflect ideas rather than reality. Formal aspects of organization and authority become important only insofar as they affect the everyday activities of teachers and students. For example, the principal of a school in the United States of America is usually reckoned to be the ultimate authority in all aspects of school life. Yet, the study of schools in the U.S.A. conducted by Goodlad *et al*. (1970) concluded that most principals do not define their own role in terms of instructional leadership and thus generally have little or nothing to do with the learning process in the schools for which they are ostensibly responsible.

This chapter analyzes the findings of each case study in regard to the way decisions are made about school-wide program and policy and in the teaching and learning process. Opinions of participants about governance and decision-making in the school will be examined where relevant. Findings concerning each topic will be dealt with separately, and opinions about these two facets of the school will be incorporated in each section.

THE COMMUNITY SCHOOL

During the 1960's many groups of parents in the U.S. actively sought to participate more meaningfully in the education of their children. An especially important goal of this movement was participation in decision-making about curriculum and the educational process. The Community School concept emerged

68

nationally as an articulation of this mood. Parents who had
grown to be disenchanted with the judgement of educational professionals, found the concept particularly appealing because of
its emphasis on shared decision-making. They also saw involvement in school governance and the classroom itself as the only
way to achieve their goals relating to the curriculum. The
parents who founded the Community School were quite representative of this movement and worked energetically to put their
ideas into practice.

   A second factor identified entirely with the local community was a desire on the part of the founding parents to
achieve voluntary racial and ethnic integration before it was
imposed by the courts on a city-wide basis. It was hoped that
by establishing "neighborhood" control over the integration
process, the movement of significant numbers of white families
out of the neighborhood in which the school was to be established could be prevented.

   The Canfield-Crescent Heights area at the founding of the
Community School contained two schools, one enrolling mainly
white students and the other predominantly black. The successful unification of the two racial communities in 1974, based on
the plan to establish a Community School, brought into existence
a single integrated "school within a school", physically located
on both of the original school sites. However, in spite of the
importance of the voluntary integration theme, the case study
findings reported below testify to the overriding influence of
the concept of parental involvement in governance and decision-
making about school program.

Decisions about Program and Policy
   Interviews with parents and staff produced a reasonably
clear picture of the evolution of the governance structure of
the school into its configuration at the time of the case study.
Initially, all major decisions about policy and program were
made by an elected Board of Representatives composed of at-
large parent officers, chairpersons of various committees of
the school, teacher and student representatives, and the Program
Director.

   During the school's first year of operation dissatisfaction with this representative governance structure rapidly
emerged. Parents in particular felt that power was concentrated
in the hands of a few elected individuals rather than distributed throughout the school community. It appeared that initially

less vocal and active individuals (especially among black parents) were not becoming involved in school governance, thus frustrating full implementation of the community concept itself.

These initial difficulties resulted in the abandonment of the initial representative structure in favor of a "Town Hall" concept in which elected officers of the school merely presided at regular evening meetings. (1) Any member of the Community School attending a meeting, whether parent, teacher, or student, was given the right to vote. This principle of operation persisted and was unanimously approved by the parents interviewed in the study. As one formal officer of the school suggested, "Even if you come to only one meeting a year you have as much of a vote (*sic*) as someone who comes to every meeting." This governance structure was also seen by parents as providing maximum flexibility.

Participants in the Community School also complete an annual *evaluation questionnaire* on which they are asked to specify those aspects of the school that are working well and those which need improvement. The process of internal evaluation resulting from the questionnaire findings, brought about the change from a representative governance structure to the Town Hall format. Formal evaluation is thus a data source for school governance at the Community School.

By way of further example, evaluation information gleaned through systematic poling of participants also produced a significant change in structure in the curriculum. Initially, the ethnic studies curriculum called for the students to be separated into three primary ethnic classifications several times a week in order to study the history and culture of their own group as well as to discuss their personal conceptions of their racial identity. Many Community School parents and teachers felt uncomfortable with separate approaches, feeling that it was antithetical to the school's goal of integrated education. Black parents in general tended to support separation, while white parents preferred integrated ethnic instruction. This issue was a potentially divisive one along racial lines, and accordingly a threat to the concept on which the school was founded.

This potential impasse was avoided through compromise. During the first year of the operation of the Community School the Ethnic Studies curriculum was revised so that children spent less time separated by ethnic groups. While there is still

separation for about one hour per week, for much of the time devoted to this important topic the different groups work together.

Decisions about Teaching and Learning
  The governance structure of the school has also been directly involved in shaping the nature of the learning process.
The strongly humanistic orientation of the group of parents who
founded the school placed great emphasis on the individualization of instruction. The original proposal called for an "open
structure" concept in which students would have considerable
freedom to pursue their own interests, e.g., to engage in self-
directed choices. Many parents and some teachers were quickly
dissatisfied with the seeming disorganization which resulted
from the implementation of an open structure. This dissatisfaction was initially most manifest among black parents, who expressed concern on evaluation questionnaires and at school meetings about what they perceived to be a lack of discipline, lack
of direction on the part of the teachers, and inattention to
basic skills.

  In response to their concerns the school modified some of
its idealistic, student-centered goals. A behavior code approved by parents, faculty, and students was established.
Students currently have less unscheduled time, and engage in
more activities directed by teachers. Time devoted to basic
skills has been increased significantly. In the words of one
parent in favor of these changes, "We want a very strong and
very structured academic program with enough flexibility and
opportunities for kids to learn how to make decisions and
choices for themselves, but with direct guidance from the
teacher ... We are demanding the basics in education and we
want to see evidence of it."

  The development of the behavioral code and the more
strict accounting of the way in which students spend their time
are responses by the school community to disagreement among
groups of parents about the orientation of the school. At the
time the Community School was founded parents strongly disposed
toward an emphasis on educational "process" goals were clearly
dominant. This group of parents, predominantly white and ethnically Jewish, still wishes to maintain the humanistic orientation of the school in addition to its commitment to integrated
learning. These same parents consider educational goals relating to individual self-growth to be especially important. They
also continue to emphasize the importance of learning to get
along with people from diverse backgrounds as a necessary part
of the curriculum.

Black parents, in contrast, have usually been more interested in concrete learning outcomes than in fostering humanistic processes in the classroom. This group, of course, shares a concern about intergroup relations. The views of black parents have influenced the instructional process especially through the evaluation questionnaire. The case study report indeed noted that *all* major changes in the school program were traceable to this evaluative mechanism and concluded that it has been a key factor in the stable continuation of the Community School.

The school governance procedures continue to affect the teaching and learning process directly. Most recently, the evaluation questionnaire revealed that parents were concerned about student accountability for individual work, remediation for lack of skills, and follow-through by staff for special student needs. In response, the staff has developed an *individual student profile* which will be used to provide continuous evaluations of individual student mastery of specific skills and competencies. The anticipation is that this instrument will allow teachers to monitor student progress more closely and deal more effectively with the academic needs of individual students.

But what about the *classroom*? Here the case study found that in both the lower and upper grades, teachers created and maintained the overall structure of the program. In general, observations revealed that teachers also provided direction for moving through the content of school work by specifying the books to be used and by allocating the amount of time to be spent on individual tasks. Teachers, or sometimes aides, would suggest to students what to do when they had completed assigned work. Sometimes they did this verbally, sometimes they did it by means of written communications deposited in message boxes set up for each student.

Observations also revealed that opportunities for choice varied little between classrooms. Irrespective of whether a classroom was at the upper or lower grade level, students were free to sit wherever they wished and with whoever they wished, as long as they did not disrupt the work of others. They were also free to select whatever activity appealed to them once they had finished assigned work.

In the case of the lower three grades, students were generally given assignments in blocks of time, either individually or in groups. For example, during a given activity segment some children would work on assignment sheets, others in workbooks, others with the aide, and still others with the teacher. These younger students for the most part had very little choice about either the content of the activity or the mode of learning. Choices which did arise were mainly confined to free time situations when assignments were complete or when no homework had been assigned. The most frequent choices of activity involved playing games. The second was the classroom listening center which had been designated as an activity area for free time.

These observations were confirmed by interviews with the children. Thus, when asked about the choices that they made in school, the younger children said, "If we finish our work, we can choose whatever we want, but we can't go ahead in our book." Other younger children indicated that their choices were limited to selecting a book for individual reading or doing art work after their assignment had been finished.

Opportunities for choice were more frequent in upper level classrooms. Here older children rotated among three classrooms each morning for mathematics, reading and language arts. But assignments were still made by the teacher who explained the assignment and then assigned a period of time in which it was to be completed. For longer assignments especially, the students used their own discretion as to how and where they would get their work done. They were free to choose among physical possibilities, e.g., they could sit or sprawl on the floor, sit at a table, or talk with others. There was a general acceptance of the fact that students could choose to work together. They could also choose how much of the work was to be completed in school. All of the work could be done in the classroom or all of it could be done at home. But these choices were restricted somewhat by the content of the assignment and the date that it was to be handed in.

In general, the observations of Community School classrooms revealed that three patterns of activity were engaged in during choice periods:

1. selecting an activity and working alone;

2. selecting an activity and being joined by another student or coached by the teacher or an aide; and

3. wandering about the room and possibly getting into trouble.

The following two extracts from classroom vignettes written by observers for the third and sixth grades summarizes the flavor of the overall findings just reported.

> Student choice about time, mode, place, or content of learning was not evident during the observation period. Most of the time in the morning was taken up with regular assignments. Available choices were of a more social type, especially choosing other learners to be participants in activities, such as telling a story to the class about a topic pulled randomly from a set of cards provided by the teacher. Or learners could choose to leave the room by writing their names on the large blackboard. Because of the relaxed ambiance in the room, learners could (within limits) choose to work, daydream, interact socially, or move about. The teacher generally gave learners time to terminate their own off-task behaviors, reminding a talking or wandering child of the task or the behavioral rule only when the off-task behavior had become distracting or had endured for some time. Learners could also choose who they wanted to work with when the teacher was not present, or they could choose to work alone. (*Grade 3*)

> Student choice of content of learning was minimal. However, choice regarding time, place, and mode of learning was manifest. There seemed to be an acceptance of the fact that students could work together and that students could choose the amount of work to be completed at the school. That is, they could decide for themselves how much they would complete in the classroom and how much would be finished as homework. (*Grade 6*)

On the topic of governance and decision-making the case study concluded that the school "works" because there are mechanisms available to all parents for retaining control over their children's education. Community School parents thus enjoy a level of responsibility and authority in decision-making that does not exist in more traditional U.S. schools, locally or nationally. The division over process *versus* product orientation still exists, with parents holding the former philosophy significantly more active in the daily affairs of the school. But the school's open governance structure, plus the regular evaluation survey, provide for parents who are less active to make their feelings known and to establish policy through the direct voting privilege.   This openness and responsiveness appears to preserve unity in a diverse community.

ARELLANO HIGH SCHOOL

The ISOS program at Arellano High School and the regular instructional program of the Katalin Varga School both operate within traditional educational institutions. Their organizational and governance structure in relation to the learning process more or less reflect familiar hierarchical patterns of school organization and decision-making. As a result, decision-making processes were somewhat less salient than other factors in the case studies of the two schools. This was in striking contrast to the case studies of the Community School and the Oberstufen-Kolleg. The latter institutions, by virtue of sharing a strongly humanistic orientation, inevitably place heavy emphasis on governance and decision-making, especially in the distribution of such authority among various categories of participants.

During the period of the case study the 38 teachers in the ISOS program at Arellano High School were responsible for over 800 students. Because these students were in their regular classrooms only half of the time, an ISOS teacher handling the same number of classes per day as a regular teacher (four classes of approximately 40 students each) would be able to deal with 320 students as compared to 160 for the latter. While in practice most ISOS teachers took only three classes per day, the greater efficiency of the ISOS arrangement, assuming the same learning outcomes, was readily apparent. However, these kinds of numbers would presumably leave little time for participation in governance on the part of teachers or students, even if the climate of the school encouraged such participation. The environmental emphasis at Arellano is on efficiency, that is on dealing with the largest number of students possible in an inadequate, though constantly expanding, school facility.

Decisions about Program and Policy
The basic structure of the ISOS program was laid out by its founder, Dr. Miguela C. Alarcon. The program functions as a separate administrative unit under the Principal of the regular school. While ISOS students interviewed usually named the Principal as the person in charge, teachers reported that the Assistant Principal had been assigned direct responsibility for

the ISOS program. However, many administrative details are delegated to Department Heads, these being teachers with administrative responsibilities who work closely with the Assistant Principal.

ISOS teachers reported that they were not involved in decision-making beyond the classroom level, though they recognized that teachers were initially responsible for selecting learning centers in the community. Still, there was nothing in the findings of the case study to suggest that organization and governance *per se* involved anything other than the usual pattern of locating program and policy decisions among purely administrative personnel.

An opinion questionnaire answered by five component groups in the school community (ISOS teachers, non-ISOS teachers, ISOS students, administrators, and parents) showed that ISOS teachers ranked third (behind non-ISOS teachers and ISOS students) in terms of their relative satisfaction with the way in which the program was governed. Sample items on this section of the questionnaire include the following:

"The program is rigidly structured by the organizers and no changes are allowed." (negatively scored)

"The administrators/organizers of the ISOS program are open to suggestions." (positively scored)

It was not clear from the questionnaire results whether teachers in the ISOS program were actually *dissatisfied* with the governance structure, or merely somewhat less satisfied than the two other groups. Parents were even less satisfied than ISOS teachers. This is not surprising, as the study uncovered little evidence of parental involvement in decision-making of any kind in the school or ISOS program. However, the possibility that there was dissatisfaction among ISOS teachers is evidenced by the fact that only 25 per cent indicated that they would stay in the program if given the choice, and even those qualified their willingness to remain by indicating that certain changes were needed to improve the program. The case study, in this regard, concluded with a set of recommendations, one of which was that means should be found to eliminate the feeling on the part of ISOS staff of being left out of program and policy decisions. In other words, one might conclude that the traditional governance structure of Arellano High School was accompanied by equally traditional complaints by teachers working in that type of structure.

Decisions about Teaching and Learning

The ISOS approach requires teachers to be more concerned about placement of students than would be the case for regular classrooms in which there is day-to-day contact between teacher and students. The case study reports that pre- and post-tests are given by most teachers immediately before and after each out-of-school period. Depending on performance, students are placed by teachers in remedial, reinforcement, or enrichment lessons during the in-school portion of their work. This important type of decision-making goes on throughout the year.

Teachers also assign students to off-school learning centers in groups of four to eight. While the list is prepared by a head teacher, other teachers have the option to choose learning centers of their own. Students assigned to each group ordinarily select their own leader, although sometimes the teacher makes this selection. Occasionally a student may decide to attend a learning center alone if it is close to his or her home.

When the group visits the assigned learning center during its out-of-school week, the leader interviews employees and asks most of the questions. Other team members are expected to listen and take notes. The leader keeps a log of individuals interviewed and obtains their signature as verification. The leader also reports in class, although sometimes the members of the group may do a skit or a role-playing exercise to dramatize their findings.

The picture is mixed on the source of questions asked by students at the learning center. At the lower grades, it is usually the teacher who prepares the questions to be asked in the interviews. At the higher grade levels, the situation is generally reversed, with the students framing the questions. Younger students are also assigned centers near to the school, with older students expected to go further afield.

The original plan for the ISOS program set one room aside at the school as a special learning center for advanced students. Students were supposed to use this room for consultation on selecting additional units beyond the level of his or her class. The study found, however, that space problems had caused this room to be preempted for regular instruction.

Interviews identified certain additional choices open to students. They decide whether to join in certain activities, indicate their preference for electives beginning in the second year, and take on responsibilities voluntarily. While questions written by teachers must be asked first during the visits to centers, students may pose their own questions later. Students also decide on all scheduling matters related to visits to the learning centers, including where and when to meet and who is to ask the questions (e.g., function as leader for the week).

In spite of the independent work that the ISOS student does at home with the self-learning kits (SLK's), the in-school instruction was found to be class- or group-paced. The loss of the on-site learning center room eliminated the only significant opportunity for self-pacing during the regular school program.

The SLK's, like the entire ISOS curriculum, are based on the standard curriculum for the school as a whole. In most curriculum areas, the kits are produced through group work in which teachers participate. In some areas supervisors and department heads do most of the work, although teachers are contacted through meetings or brainstorming sessions in which ideas on coverage in the SLK's are solicited.

In general, questionnaire findings confirmed that for both teachers and students involvement in decision-making is almost entirely confined to the teaching/learning situation. Teachers make most of the decisions in the classroom. Students are able to make pacing decisions about work on the SLK's and organizational scheduling decisions relating to visits to the learning centers. One of the major recommendations of the case study report was that greater efforts should be exerted to enhance independence and individuality in students through the provision of more varied opportunities for making decisions.

THE KATALIN VARGA GRAMMAR SCHOOL

It has already been observed that Arellano High School and the Katalin Varga Grammar School have in common traditional governance structures not markedly different from other schools of the same type in their respective countries. In both, the emphasis has been on changing the curriculum and to some extent on the way in which learning is carried out, rather than on altering the manner in which the school is governed.

Decisions about Program and Policy
   The School Regulations issued by the Hungarian Ministry
of Education vest full authority in the Headmaster as the "individually responsible leader of the school". The Headmaster
is the head of the staff in the pedagogical as well as the administrative sense. The findings of the case study made it
clear that the Headmaster of the Katalin Varga Grammar School,
Mr. János Páldi, used this authority to become the primary
catalyst in the emergence of the school as an experimental,
innovative school within the Hungarian system. This conclusion
was apparent not only in information collected from staff and
students in the school itself, but also from statements made
by authorities in the Education Department of the County Council,
a school inspector, and others interviewed in the research.

   The national School Regulation charge teachers with direct
responsibility for the development of the curriculum and the
methods by which it is taught, though within the constraints of
an integrated set of requirements. Teachers are expected to
work in subject-matter teams.

   The school, or more specifically its teaching staff, may
carry out formal experimentation with the approval of authorities in the Ministry of Education (rather then the Headmaster
or County Council). Authority for the Katalin Varga experiment
was obtained in 1970. As an institution engaged in experimentation, the school has been visited by the Head of the Grammar
School Department of the Ministry and receives regular visits
from inspectors of the County Education Department.

   The Headmaster, Deputy Headmaster, and Staff of the
School collectively articulate policy through documents
dealing with

   1. rules for operation of the school;

   2. a code covering expected work and behavior
      patterns for students; and

   3. a basic annual plan of work for the school.

The case study found these documents to be quite important in
the life of the school as the means by which basic policies
are communicated and applied. Thus, the code for student work
and behavior contains the standards by which the former are to
be evaluated. Principles pertaining to the way in which students are expected to work, include being active in lessons,
showing interest and, especially, perseverance of effort.

Principles of behavior emphasize taking responsibility for
one's own work and that of one's schoolmates, showing initiative, being self-reliant, and engaging in activities likely to
benefit the community.

The *plan of work* for the 1977/78 school year, for example,
emphasized giving learners responsibility for making "... their
own decisions on matters concerning themselves". Teachers were
urged to develop learning tasks which "... demand self-directed
observation, collection of data, and research work". Master
lessons within each form level were to become forums of debate.
Gifted learners were to be encouraged to take advance examinations in areas in which they learned more quickly than others,
and so on.

In addition to interviews, the case study surveyed
teachers' perceptions of the specific areas in which the administration of the school (in the person of the Headmaster)
had the most significant impact with respect to self-directed
learning. This was done by means of a formal questionnaire in
which the impact of the leadership of the school on each of the
eight characteristics of the learning environment associated
with the enhancement of self-direction (Chapter 3) were rated
on a 7 point scale. All eight of the ratings averaged above
the midpoint of the scale, suggesting the teachers perceived
at least some impact in all areas. However, the relative importance of leadership was seen as especially high in the areas
of

1. encouraging choices on the part of learners;

2. teaching as a facilitating activity (meaning
   that lessons are to be organized so as to
   require active participation by students and
   self-learning); and

3. encouraging democratic relationships between
   teachers and students as well as between Headmaster and teachers.

All Hungarian secondary schools incorporate a Youth Parliament which convenes every second year. The Parliament is an
open forum in which the Headmaster presents issues of his own
choosing and in which students may request the opportunity to
speak out on aspects of the school. In the record analyzed in
the case study, student presentations touched on such diverse
areas as:

1. needed improvements in equipment and facilities;

2. the need for greater student self-evaluation in certain types of lessons;

3. student choice of themes for outside speakers (from a university);

4. the role of teachers in helping students prepare for inter-school competitions; and

5. student responsibilities with respect to orderliness and other traditions of the school.

The Youth Parliament is a complementary element in the governance structure of the school, serving as a channel for direct communication between students and administration.

At the level of decisions about policy and program, the Katalin Varga Grammar School thus maintains a traditional type of organization, with authority and responsibility for policy clearly assigned to the Headmaster of the school, but with various paths open for communication and suggestions. While the leadership and staff of the school are accountable to the Ministry of Education and the Education Department of the County Council, the school has been formally assigned a role as an institution engaging in educational experimentation within the general guidelines of the National School regulations.

Decisions about Teaching and Learning

The Katalin Varga experiment was founded on the principle of allowing choices in the teaching and learning process. Its most essential characteristic is thus the building of choice points within a curriculum which is specified with considerable detail in a set of national regulations and in the context of a traditional type of school organizational structure.

Students and teachers are encouraged to make four kinds of choices as a part of the experimental program of the school:

1. First year students may choose either one or two subjects for additional study at a deeper level. Any combination of two subjects is permissible. If the student is not satisfied with the initial choice, other subjects may be selected at the end of the term or year. While the core curriculum is studied in regular, intact classes, optional subjects are studied in small *facultative groups*.

2. Subject-matter teachers freely develop teaching
   material for the extra lessons based on
   (a) student interest and
   (b) the requirements of the entrance examina-
       tion for higher education.

3. The facultative groups in which students study
   optional subjects allow the teacher to be
   flexible in choosing the method of study.
   Self-direction on the part of students is emphasized through the encouragement of exploration and by allowing students to take on
   teaching responsibilities in giving short lectures or engaging in discussions and debates.
   There is also flexibility in the choice of
   instructional materials.

4. At the time of the study, learners at the Katalin
   Varga School were the only students in the nation
   allowed to take advanced examinations in one or
   more subjects. Combined with the facultative
   grouping system for optional subjects, the advanced examination option allows students to
   progress more rapidly, depending on their ability
   and motivation. Once an examination has been
   passed under this system, the student no longer
   has to attend classes in the subject-matter, but
   may pursue individual study under a teacher's
   supervision or do research work in the library,
   perhaps in preparation for one of the inter-
   school competitions that may substitute for the
   regular university entrance examination.
   Occasionally students, engaged in this type of
   independent study, may report orally or in
   writing to classmates and the subject-matter
   teacher.

The annual plan of work for the school, in effect during
the case study, stressed the importance of personal decision-
making on the part of the students. Teachers were urged to
develop tasks which "... demand self-directed observation,
collection of data and research work". The experimental status
of the school program was seen as an opportunity to allow able
students, especially, to learn to pace themselves and to complete required work more quickly. However, healthy self-con-
fidence and self-evaluative skills were goals for all students
in their interactions with the experimental program.

Related to this emphasis within the school, the case study report noted that students could also choose to use educational facilities of the town, such as libraries, museums, archives, etc. A check was made in the case study of student use of the county library. This survey showed that 171 of the student body of 329 had participated during the school year in one or more library programs offered by the largest library in the city. During a one-month period in the fall of the year of the study 165 students borrowed 710 books, about 70 per cent of which were directly related to school subject matter.

A separate survey of a sample of 106 students found that, while the majority of the learners make extensive use of the various opportunities provided by the school and community, the early examination option was selected by only a minority of students at the time of the case study. Questionnaire and interview data revealed that those who did elect to take early examinations, in addition to indicating they wished to make faster progress, often expressed a desire to be able to study the subject on their own, without having to attend classes. Some saw the examination as a chance to test themselves and their capacities.

Students who took one or more examinations early, appeared to have fared especially well in the school environment, doubtless in part because of their personal characteristics. These students tended to treat learning as a kind of hobby. They expressed a high level of aspiration, both within the school program and for careers later. They also reported receiving a high degree of encouragement from adults, including regular classroom teachers, from masters, and parents.

Students who had not elected to take early examinations most often cited as the reason a personal need for regular, systematic instruction from teachers. Smaller numbers of students cited their own lack of diligence or lack of definite academic goals. A few were concerned that they might do badly and thus endanger their chances for entrance to the university.

Although parents of students in the Katalin Varga School do not participate in decision-making in the teaching and learning process, they do decide whether to enroll their child in the school with its experimental program instead of a regular secondary school. A brief questionnaire on reasons for choosing the school was sent out to parents under the Headmaster's signature as part of the case study. The parents, who responded anonymously, most frequently cited the facultative system with small group study of topics chosen by the learner as the primary reason. Other factors cited were the general reputation of the school, the advice of the primary school headmaster, and the emphasis placed by the school on developing all the learner's potential talents.

At the level of teaching and learning, then, an important aspect of the stress on self-direction at the Katalin Varga School involves giving learners the opportunity to make choices. Consistent with the organized structure of the school within a strongly academic system, the choice points are clearly specified and invariably involve decisions to achieve beyond what is ordinarily a high level of expectation. As will be apparent in the next chapter, there is also a noticeable emphasis on "learning to learn", beginning with the *studium generale* curriculum and articulated in the use of discussion, debates, and student responsibility for part of the instruction, especially in the voluntarily selected facultative groups. As an organization, the school is especially interesting, not because it is unusual, but precisely because its headmaster and staff have managed to build strategies for enhancing self-direction within a traditional academic structure.

THE BIELEFELDER OBERSTUFEN-KOLLEG

From a purely organizational perspective the Oberstufen-Kolleg is unquestionably the most unusual institution studied in this research. Organizational issues and their relationship to decision-making in the teaching and learning process merge in their own right, irrespective of which aspect of the institution is under scrutiny.

At the OSK, governance if anything is the "real" curriculum. This assertion may overstate the case, but it does serve warning that, whatever aspect of the college is described, organizational and decision-making processes will emerge as part of the story.

Arbitrary topical distinctions are made in this report in order to preserve parallelism in the characteristics by which the four institutions are described and compared. Nevertheless, the way in which the institution is organized and the manner in which decisions are made, must be weighted more heavily than other facets in the case of OSK. Admittedly, this was

partly true for the Community School, which also placed great
emphasis on democratization. But the Community School, serving
elementary level children, emphasizes parental involvement.
The OSK, as a transitional institution bridging the upper secondary and early university period, involves students in decision-making more than it does parents. This allows participation in the decision-making process to become an all-pervasive
aspect of the curriculum and associated teaching and learning
processes, and to be fully reflected in the governance structure of the college.

Decisions about Program and Policy

From a national perspective, the OSK combines two official
functions (Harder, 1978). (2) As an experimental school approved by the state, it is responsible to the Ministry of
Culture and Education. As a research institute focusing on
curriculum development, it is likewise responsible to the
Ministry of Research and Science. If two distinct governmental
authorities are not sufficient, it may also be noted that the
OSK is an administrative unit of the University of Bielefeld,
to which the governance of the college is directly responsible.
The Scientific Administrator of the college (Professor Hartmut
von Hentig) is both a member of the faculty of the University
and the originator of the concept of the college. As director
of the research and development program, the latter has only an
indirect influence on the educational program, e.g., *via* the
original college concept and the on-going research program.
However, it should be noted that the OSK is a very rare breed
among schools, in that "R & D", instead of regular school administration, has a logical dominance in the affairs of the
institution.

Ordinarily, the intricacies involved in the above lines
of authority would be of little interest in a report on research
primarily concerned with the real world of teaching and learning. But the fact that the OSK, as such an innovative research
institute and as a school, must continually justify its policies
and existence on two different levels having different priorities and standards, illustrates the restraints under which the
college must operate and why it is unique within its national
context. Other comparable experimental public institutions
have not been able to emerge, given the current public mood
vis-à-vis educational reform and the traditionally regulatory
stance of governmental bodies in the Federal Republic. In this
regard, Harder (1978) reports that frequently "... applications
from the OSK for special permission or exceptional rulings are

dismissed with the note that there is nothing comparable anywhere else (and) ... the application is inapplicable to the
norm and (therefore) cannot be reconciled with the operating
official rulings".

The OSK must meet challenges to its legitimacy and at the
same time fulfill its dual functions of

1. educating students within an experimental
   framework; and

2. producing curriculum innovations that might
   ultimately be exportable to the system of
   public education at large.

This dual function is evident, in part, in the current organizational structure of the college. But the importance of careful
planning and adequate justification for policies and programs
in the face of external pressures is everywhere apparent in
the way in which the decision-making bodies of the college conduct their work.

It has already been noted that the OSK has a dual and in
some respects contradictory mission. On the one hand it admits
students who have been educated in the conventional system and
ultimately delivers them back to that mass system, though at a
higher level. In other words, the OSK must comply with the
basic conditions and regulations of the larger educational
establishment. On the other hand, the OSK is expected to develop new curricula, new modes of teaching, and new organizational patterns as potential solutions to educational problems.
This requires the freedom to deviate from established regulations, standards and procedures.

The organizational chart for the OSK shows the functions
of school management, and research and development, as separated, and future development of the college may accomplish
this separation. (3) Clearly, the legitimacy of the college
and the validity of the credentials it confers, could easily
become the main concern of regular administrative leadership,
with innovation and research under a second level of authority
a potential threat to hard-won institutional legitimacy. So
far this remains only a potential conflict.

The governance of the college is based on the principle
of distributing decision-making authority among participants -
teachers, students, technical and administrative staff, and

parents. The largest of the three governing bodies is an
Assembly (*Konvent*) consisting of 80 members, 50 per cent being
elected teachers, and the other 50 per cent distributed among
staff, parents, and students. This group meets two or three
times a year, ordinarily with about 60 members present and
approximately 30 observers.

The Assembly deals with basic policy issues relating to
organization and structure. For example, issues which arose
during the period of the case study included the question of
whether the administrative team should be elected from the participants in the school and serve on a rotating basis, or be
appointed by the Ministry of Culture and Education to permanent
positions. As a large body that meets relatively infrequently,
the Assembly deals with broad policy issues that may be of concern to participants over a relatively long period of time.

The potential separation between school administration
and the research and development function, at least on paper,
is continued in the two smaller school organizations with direct
authority to implement policy. The first of these, the College
Conference, is the unit responsible for what are usually classified as purely administrative functions. Its membership is
composed of seven teachers, five students, and one member from
parents and staff, respectively. This committee has the power
to allocate funds. However, it also makes decisions concerning
personnel along with the second of the smaller governing boards,
the Curriculum Committee. This latter body represents the systematic research and development focus of the college, and is
composed of the Director, six teachers, three students and
three staff members.

The Curriculum Committee meets weekly in open session.
Its authority derives from the basic premise that educational
research and pedagogical practice must be combined and mutually
carried out by the students and teachers involved. Hence,
authority for approving courses, teaching methods, learning
projects, and research itself are vested in this single committee. This committee reviews proposals from participants for
research and teaching activities, usually integrated, according
to criteria established by its membership in the light of the
basic policies of the school.

It was readily apparent that the potential separation between the two committees was considerably mitigated by deliberate efforts at exchange of information and the open meeting

system. The important principle here from an organizational
perspective is that these two groups, representing the school
community, especially teachers and students, carry out decision
functions that are normally assigned to individuals in administrative roles. They are not merely advisory to authority,
rather are the groups themselves assigned authority.

The organization of the research and development work
within the college is carried out through a separate structure
under the basic plan of work adopted for the experiment as a
whole. At the time of the study, there were 28 Research, Development and Planning (RDP) groups each composed of 3-6 teachers
and students. Each teacher in the OSK normally works on two of
the RDP groups. A major function of these groups is to integrate research and teaching. Groups are divided into two sets,
one dealing primarily with organizational and administrative
matters, and the other with curriculum topics. Among the former,
for example, various RDP groups deal with admissions, counseling,
the constitution of the college in relation to student and
teacher representation and participation, and the system of
assessment and final examinations. On the curriculum side there
are groups dealing with alternative goals, new subject matter,
improved arrangements for teaching and learning, and criteria
for assessing achievement, or with scientific method in diverse
fields such as social sciences, arts, humanities, and natural
sciences, or with special subjects corresponding to broad academic disciplines such as social science, and finally with
teacher training.

A concrete example presented by Harder (1978) for the
group dealing with assessment and final examinations reveals
how the RDP groups manage to combine research with pedagogical
functions. The OSK is unique in the Federal Republic in its
authorization to assign grades on a pass-fail system rather than
according to a more differentiated grading and marking system.
In addition, every student must submit two written and two oral
pieces of work for each course, all of which have to be passed
if the student is to receive credit. (Completion of studies at
the OSK is based on having passed a predetermined number of
courses.) This grading system is both a regular element in the
operation of the OSK as well as an aspect of the experimental
program.

The members of the assessment R & D group have the following major responsibilities in the area of assessment and final
examinations:

1. They must maintain scholarly interest and activity in the assessment of achievement by being familiar with current theoretical discussion and by making their own contributions to this discussion through publication.

2. They are responsible for conducting evaluations of the assessment system for the college as a whole by regularly collecting pertinent information. Their evaluations of the system should include suggestions for changes or further development.

3. They may be required to act as advisors in situations involving conflict over the results of assessment before an arbitration committee.

4. They are expected to be able to communicate the nature of the assessment system in written form to new students and teachers or, verbally, to visiting groups.

5. They are responsible for preparing an evaluation report on the assessment system for the Ministry of Education as well as applying for an extension of the time limit extended for this use of the system as an experimental device.

While other activities may also be required of this and other groups, the way in which the RDP group structure manages to combine research with practice while at the same time making sure that there is an organizational entity responsible for each operational/experimental aspect of the program of the college, should be evident as a general principle. This division of labor incidentally meets the reporting and justification needs brought on by the status of the college as an experimental entity reporting to multiple governmental authorities. But its most important function is the integration of research and practice.

With the major elements of decision-making at the organizational or policy level now described, it is necessary to make a somewhat artificial transition to decisions in the teaching and learning process. Here it will be seen that the R & D groups are involved as well, at least at the most general level.

Decisions about Teaching and Learning
    The curriculum at OSK is divided into several types of
course. While these will be dealt with in the next chapter,
one will be selected here to illustrate how the RDP groups
function in the process of making decisions about the curriculum. It will be quickly apparent that in this domain the second
set of RDP groups work in a fashion that is exactly parallel to
the groups dealing with organizational and administrative
issues.

    The basic plan on which the college operates requires
that students participate for the final three weeks of each
semester in a *project* course that is designed to put theory and
practice together in the form of some type of interdisciplinary
project. This type of course is an especially important part
of the OSK curriculum because of its integrative nature.

    The RDP group dealing with project courses operates under
the framework of the plan approved by the Ministry of Culture
in carrying out the following tasks (Harder, 1978):

1. determine the criteria for what constitutes
   appropriate interdisciplinary projects and
   develop methods for planning, approving, and
   carrying out such projects;

2. organize the regular "project day" on which
   teachers and students suggest themes and form
   planning groups;

3. present planned projects to the Curriculum
   Committee for approval;

4. be involved in the evaluation of completed
   projects; and

5. prepare a summary report to the Ministry of
   Education and a section of the annual report
   on research of the University of Bielefeld.

    The needs-assessment and planning process in 2. and 3.
above represent the first level of decision-making about teaching and learning at the OSK. RDP groups dealing with other
aspects of the curriculum have similar responsibilities.

    The RDP groups represent formalized, organizational de-
vices for decision-making about the curriculum. Another way
of looking at this issue is to ask about the kinds of decision
that individual students make as a result of the participation

in the programs of the college. While this question also
touches on activities to be described later, a listing of types
of decision is appropriate at this point.

Choice of course of study. The first semester for every
student at the OSK is devoted primarily to orientation through
exposure to different subject-matter disciplines. This arrangement reflects a basic premise of the OSK program - that students
matriculating from ordinary secondary schools are not prepared
by experience to make final decisions about their professional
field(s) of study at the time they enter the university. Thus,
after a five week initial orientation period the new OSK student
chooses four orienting courses which constitute most of the instructional time for the semester.

At the end of the orientation semester the student is expected to choose the two subjects that will consititute his or
her program of study for the remaining three and a half years
of enrollment in the college. Ordinarily this decision is made
primarily on the basis of formal experience gained during the
initial orientation period and the four orienting courses.
Counseling by tutors and less formal meetings and individual
discussions are also likely to contribute.

The two courses of study selected by the student are from
the broad disciplinary categories of Social Sciences (history,
geography, legal science, sociology, sports, theology, social
economy, educational sciences, and psychology); Language and
Fine Arts (German, English, French, Latin, Russian, arts, and
music); and Natural Sciences and Mathematics (biology, chemistry, geology, technology, physics, mathematics, and health
studies). Not all combinations of subjects are possible, especially in the natural sciences. Students may change these
choices later, although the program of studies is likely to be
extended timewise if the change is not made sufficiently early.
At the end of the courses the student is expected to be sufficiently acquainted with the fields of study to make an informed
choice of profession at the university level. A variety of
other types of choice about the program of studies are also
made by the student, as will be apparent later.

Choices in the learning process. In two of the four types
of course conducted on site, students have the freedom to choose
specific *content*, the *mode* that learning will take, the *place*
where learning will occur, and the *time* of learning. For those
students who are taking their *Praktikum* during a particular

semester, a brief course is also conducted which normally involves off-site activities. The specific content selected by
students is limited to the overall subject matter of the course.
Time is also predetermined for organizational and planning activities involving all participants in the course. But within
these general limitations significant latitude for choice is
left to the student.

The case study reported observations of course meetings
in order to illustrate part of this decision process. One
course, meeting as a committee of the whole in plenum session,
dealt with mathematical models. The session began with discussion and voting on subject matter for future work. One of
the topics selected involved developing a model for calculating
the amount of government support grants for students. The
plenum session proceeded to set

1. the date for the first meeting of smaller working
   groups;

2. the subject matter goal (developing of a formula
   for calculating grant amounts);

3. the specification for resource materials to be
   used; and

4. the dissemination goal (producing a leaflet to
   inform the OSK student body of the result).

This process was repeated for a second topic selected for study.

The decisions in the example just cited were group decisions, consistent with the highly democratic approach of the
institution to organization and decision-making. However, peer
groups can dominate individuals just as firmly as can arbitrary
authorities who have been allocated power within a hierarchical
system. The case study reported at least a few informal observations in which individual students appeared to be "controlled"
through social pressures from the groups in which they found
themselves (by choice, it should be pointed out). However, the
system does allow individuals to choose to work autonomously if
appropriate to the task.

Learner evaluation. The evaluation system at the course
level is most appropriately described later in the section on
curriculum. Suffice it to say here that both oral and written
achievement criteria must be passed, and that the activities
themselves are both individual and group in nature. Part of
the work of the student participants involves identifying types

of indices of achievement that are consistent with the theme
of the particular course.

Selection of advisor. Each students selects a faculty
advisor after completing the initial period of seventeen weeks
of general orientation and four orientation courses. The advisor acts both in an academic as well as in a personal counseling role, and this choice is a potentially important one for
many students.

Committee work. Students, as already noted, sit on the
governing committees of the school. They are also members of
the RDP groups which carry out the process of planning evaluating, and reporting on courses and projects. These activities
inevitably mix the specific topic of decision-making with the
more general topic of *participation*. The latter is necessarily
a key theme of the teaching and learning process to be described
in Chapter 7.

The interrelatedness of governance and curriculum at the
OSK was illustrated by a question raised during the discussion
of the case study report at the closing workshop of the project.
After the description of the two governing committees of the
OSK, one of the participants at the meeting asked where authority for maintaining order and discipline resided in the organizational structure of the college. The answer turned out to
be that no single body or individual had such authority. Rather,
problems of inappropriate conduct falling within the category
of what would usually be thought of as disciplinary action would
instead be treated as a situation requiring research into causes.
In other words, the problem would be defined as either a pedagogical one (i.e., a student needs help, advice, or information)
or as something caused by factors within the institutional environment, rather than simply one of apprehending and punishing
guilty parties.

By way of example, during the case study concern about the
appearance of wall *graffiti*, presumably the handiwork of members
of the student body, had surfaced. A teacher in response, developed and submitted a project proposal for the study of the
content of the wall scribblings. The research study was approved
by the Curriculum Committee and in due course the investigative
team reported that there did appear to be a pattern in the
anonymous messages. The problem was defined as one of poor communication involving certain administrative arrangements. As a
part of this project a second analysis of messages exchanged

between staff was conducted, tending to confirm the findings of the study of *graffiti*. Appropriate actions, it was reported, were taken to remedy the causes identified in the report. (4)

It is readily apparent that openness and participation are the key principles underlying decision-making at the OSK. Participation of the whole college community in decision-making is also consistent with:

1. an open door policy to parents and members of the community; and

2. an open floor plan in the building itself which renders even formal instructional activities accessible.

In the latter regard, it can be noted that even the working space assigned to teachers is accessible, as are all files with the exception of those on personnel.

The diffusion of authority within an institutional structure means that time must be devoted to various types of decision process. Teachers, for example, spend about six hours per week in committee work, although this is a relatively small figure when compared to twelve hours of actual contact hours in teaching and approximately twenty-four hours in course preparation. The case study report estimated that teachers worked close to sixty hours per week during the regular term. Yet, despite a demanding work load, teacher resignations were reported to be very infrequent. This low attrition rate is probably in part due to self-election among teachers who apply for positions at the OSK, and in part to the criteria applied by a joint selection committee (Curriculum and College Conference).

Students also spend considerable time in work which is administrative and organizational rather than directly academic. The report of the students in a regular secondary school, who visited the OSK as a part of the case study, noted that there appeared to be a fairly widespread opinion among OSK students interviewed informally that committee work was time consuming and inefficient and hence to some extent frustrating.

Descriptions of decision-making processes at the OSK do reveal meticulous processes that are significantly more time-consuming than is decision-making under the usual hierarchical structure of authority. Democracy takes time, especially in its original form where all participants in the institution are allowed to participate in any governance meeting and when those who were not present at a given session are entitled to information about the decisions taken. In addition, conflicts at the school are resolved by debate and discussion rather than by administrative fiat.

There is a parallel here with an observation made early in this book with respect to school organization and the encouragement of self-direction, that freedom in itself does not ensure that productive choices will be made, or indeed that any meaningful choices will be made at all. From the institutional perspective, choice has to be organized within a structure that helps make it productive. If that structure is to be democratic and open to all participants, then appropriate organization is required along with the willingness to spend significant amounts of time on decision-making processes of all types.

SUMMARY

It is readily apparent that the Community School and the Oberstufen-Kolleg manifest significant similarities. Both have succeeded in implementing open processes of decision-making that encourage participation by various groups. This is rather surprising in view of the differences in the level of institutions (elementary vs. secondary/university), national contexts, and basic educational objectives of the founding groups (one to achieve voluntary racial/ethnic integration and individualization in the instructional process, the other to develop a model for integrating secondary school and university and educational research and practice). These underlying similarities between the two schools were not anticipated.

Both the Community School and the Oberstufen-Kolleg are in part reactions to over-controlling bureaucracies administering excessively prescriptive and standardized educational curricula. Both must justify their existence within larger institutional contexts that, if not hostile, are at least quite skeptical. In these kinds of context the two institutions have, independently, developed modes of governance that de-emphasize the vesting of administrative authority in individuals while setting up structures involving full participation by groups such as teachers, students, staff, and parents. The detailed differences between the modes of operation of the two institutions are very great, but the principles of openness of process and multi-group involvement reveal a remarkable degree of commonality.

At the level of organizational decision-making, the ISOS
project at Arellano High School, and the Katalin Varga Grammar
School, are traditional structures that have managed to incorporate and promote innovations at the level of teaching and
learning. At this level, the programs provide choices for students and teachers. For the Katalin Varga School, this has
been accomplished by developing alternatives which supplement
and extend a regular instructional program that is much like
that of other academic grammar schools in Hungary. In the ISOS
program, the choices open to teachers relate to the development
of self-learning materials for students and the selection and
organization of learning activities outside the school. For
their part, students are responsible for working entirely on
their own on the materials prepared for the out-of-school period,
and for organizing and reporting on their out-of-school activities in the community.

NOTES

1. The "Town Hall meeting" is an open governance structure in
   which all citizens of the village or small town in attendance
   have the right to vote directly on issues confronting the
   community. The Town Hall evolved in New England in colonial
   times and is still used in parts of that region.

2. A very useful additional source on the OSK is the article by
   Wolfgang Harder, "The Oberstufen-Kolleg in Bielefeld", in
   Nissen, G. and Teschner, W.P. (eds.), *Curriculum Research
   and Development*. Kiel: Institut für die Pädagogik der Naturwissenschaften, 1978. (IPN Report-in-Brief).

3. A communication from Professor von Hentig received shortly
   before this book went to press reported the appointment of a
   new and separate administrative leader.

4. A report on the school by a group of visiting students from
   a regular secondary school conducted as part of the case
   study expressed surprise at the cleanliness of the college,
   citing the complete lack of "... wastepaper, cigarette ends,
   or litter inside or outside the building".

Chapter 6

Curriculum in the Four Schools

In order to *evaluate* schools in terms of their effectiveness, it is ordinarily appropriate to stress the outcomes of schooling, e.g., "what" or "how much" students have learned. But to *understand* schools as dynamic institutions, it is necessary to look at the process of teaching and learning. Of the questions dealt with in the final case study reports, those assessing how teachers teach and how students learn are in this sense the most fundamental questions that can be asked.

But teaching and learning as processes are acted out in categories that are specified by the curriculum, both implicit and explicit. Curriculum has been separated from teaching and learning processes in this and the chapter that follows, although in practice 'curriculum as content' and 'curriculum as process' are usually not easily distinguishable (Skager and Dave, 1977).

The four schools were found to vary considerably in the extent to which they incorporated teaching and learning practices different from typical practices for schools of their level. For example, at the Community School the emphasis on participation in decision-making was seen in the previous chapter to be sharply at variance with what is usual for the surrounding community and for the country as a whole. The aspect of the curriculum dealing with multicultural education is also atypical. But the remainder of the curriculum, as well as the way in which teachers go about their work in the classroom at the Community School, differs from typical schools in degree rather than in kind. At the Katalin Varga School, the situation is more or less similar with respect to curriculum, while for the ISOS progam at Arrellano High School, curriculum innovation is apparent in the off-school activities more than for the in-school portion of the program. In contrast, the Oberstufen-

Kolleg differs radically in all three categories (curriculum, teaching, and learning processes). Each of these aspects at each school will be described at a level of detail which re- flects the emphasis devoted to it in the original case study.

THE COMMUNITY SCHOOL

The Community School embodies a rather harmonious co- existence of traditional, progressive, and radically innovative practices. Its most radical aspects have already been ident- ified in the real power held by parents in the governance of the school and in the way in which decision-making is shared among parents, teachers, and the school administration.

Other aspects of the school can be classified as liberal and progressive, or even as fairly traditional in character. These aspects, mainly associated with the curriculum and the process of teaching and learning, will be described in this and the following chapters. It is important to recall, though, that the Community School case study incorporated the most systematic observations of the teaching and learning process that were done in the project as a whole. Given the special focus of those observations on self-direction in learning, an interesting qualitative observation about how teachers may foster self-direction resulted. This will be discussed in the last chapter.

Multicultural Education
Without question the school's emphasis on multicultural education is a highly distinctive feature of the curriculum. Based on an approach to integrated education developed by the San Francisco Multicultural Institute, the ethnic studies pro- gram at the Community School endeavors to help children learn about their own ethnic backgrounds and to instill in them an appreciation for all racial heritages.

The multicultural curriculum separates learners by ethnic group (e.g., Black, Jewish, polyethnic) for one segment of time each week. Teachers are of the same ethnic group as their stu- dents in these sessions. Students learn about their own cul- ture and group history and have the opportunity during informal discussion sessions to express attitudes and feelings about their own ethnic status and background.

In addition, the curriculum contains cross-cultural units

developed by the teachers themselves and studied by all students. There is an Ethnic Studies Coordinator on the staff and one of the resource centers is devoted to this topic. Instead of ignoring racial and ethnic differences, as is often the case in integrated classrooms in the United States, the Community School emphasizes such differences in positive ways through systematic teaching and exploration.

Observations of classrooms conducted during the case studies revealed a careful policy of ethnic and racial balance for all activities except ethnic studies, where separation was deliberate. There was also a deliberately maintained parallel distribution of responsibilities among black and white students. Not a single instance of friction associated with differing ethnicity was noted in the classroom observations. Voluntary associations among children during play or other types of activities were almost invariably integrated.

The school is not at all unusual in terms of the content of its regular curriculum of reading, math, social studies, etc., except as these (especially social studies) interact with elements of the multi-cultural curriculum. Observations of the high and low self-directed learners showed *reading* to be the most common learning activity at both lower and upper grade levels (36 and 31 per cent of the instructional time, respectively). "Skill" subjects, such as language arts, were next most frequent (25 and 21 per cent). *Math* and *science* accounted for relatively small amounts of time at the lower grades (12 and 3 per cent), but for somewhat more time at the upper grades (22 and 14 per cent).

The above reflects the fact that the school is a public elementary school obliged to teach basic subjects under standards established by the state of California. The strong parental support for "basics" was noted in the previous chapter. In these respects it is like any other school in the Los Angeles district. Likewise, its physical plant and equipment were indistinguishable in kind or quality from any other school randomly chosen from the second largest school district in the nation.

Individualization
The liberal or progressive aspects of the Community School are associated with its emphasis on individualization of instruction. Interviews and observations of teachers revealed the individualization theme to be, along with multicultural education, a major preoccupation of the staff. As a matter of fact, the case study concluded unequivocably that individualization,

rather than self-direction, was the primary organizing principle
of the curriculum. Self-direction was perceived in practice by
teachers as more of an outcome of individualization rather than
as the object of a conscious program of instruction in its own
right.

From the perspective of curriculum, individualization
provides the rationale for the schools' use of small groups and
individual study, multi-age classes, team teaching (mainly upper
grade levels), flexibility in scheduling, and extensive use of
resource centers. For example, age and nominal grade level are
de-emphasized in placement of students within the curriculum,
while individual ability and level of development are primary
considerations. At upper grade levels the teachers specialize.
One teacher provides mathematics instruction to all students,
another teaches reading, and a third concentrates on language
and writing skills. The "departmentalized" approach, with
students spending some portion of the day with each teacher,
tends to make optimal use of the individual teacher's talents
and abilities.

Resource centers are an important curricular adjunct of
an individualized program because they make alternative study
and resource materials available to individual students within
the regular classroom situation. Observations conducted during
the case study revealed these centers to be extensively used.
Other aspects of the individualization theme will be considered
in relation to the sections on teaching and learning in the
next chapter. But individualization itself is a basic principle
of the Community School curriculum.

ARELLANO HIGH SCHOOL

Those aspects of the ISOS program at Arellano High School
which are the more pertinent to self-direction occur mainly outside the school. Teachers influence this out-of-school activity
by developing and assigning the self-learning kits (SLK's) and
by arranging visits to community learning centers. In contrast,
the in-school portion of the ISOS program does not differ substantially from the instructional program for the regular school
except by being interspersed with periods of student activity
outside the school. Teachers take the latter into account by
incorporating out-of-school experiences into the regular classroom program through the mechanism of student reports and other
activities. But the innovative aspects of the curriculum at

the school involve out-of-school activities either directly or indirectly.

The ISOS student is supposed to learn all of the regular secondary school curriculum content. This is evident, for example, in the fact that he or she takes the same subjects and reads the same textbooks as do students in the regular school. The subjects include five required academic courses each year (two languages, social studies, science, and mathematics). Beginning with the second year a sixth academic subject is added as an elective. In addition to this regular academic program, the student takes pre-vocational work, civics, and physical development courses.

Interviews with Teachers
        Seventeen ISOS teachers were interviewed about various aspects of teaching and the curriculum. When asked to diferentiate between learning objectives associated with in- as opposec to out-of-school activities, these teachers saw the in-school part of the program as most effective in developing knowledge of subject matter and communication skills, especially writing and speaking. The out-of-school program was associated with development of practical skills, social skills, and self-confidence.

Self-Learning Kits
        The research team surveyed all currently available SLK's for the following academic subjects: Language (English and Filipino/Tagalog), Science (General, Biology, Chemistry, Physics, and Environmental), Mathematics (levels for first three years), and Social Studies (four years). The survey took the form of a documentary analysis in which each SLK was examined for evidence of characteristics pertinent to lifelong education in general and self-direction in learning in particular. Each SLK was reviewed from the perspectives of objectives, teaching methods and learning activities, and evaluation. Characteristics judged to reveal an emphasis on self-direction included provision for

1. self-learning;

2. inter-learning;

3. guided learning;

4. educability (development of skills for future learning);

5. participating in planning and implementation;

6. self-evaluation; and

7. learning alternatives.

The results of the analysis of each kit were recorded on an checklist.

The findings of the documentary analysis were presented in narrative form in the Philippine case study report. For a more concrete picture of the nature of the SKL's, specific descriptive statements from the report of the analysis are provided for each of the above characteristics:

1. *Self-learning*. "Objectives are behaviorally stated and addressed to the learner" (Communication Arts: English I-IV); "... material is presented in a manner that makes possible individualization of learning ... activities can be performed by individual" (Communication Arts: Filipino I-III); "Objectives are stated in terms of behavior expected of the students" (Mathematics I-III).

2. *Inter-learning*. "A variety of activities are suggested, some of which provide opportunities for inter-learning with other students or with adults" (Social Studies I-III).

3. *Guided learning*. "... (activities are) so structured that learning is guided, cues and instructions are given" (Science I-IV); "Most SLK's provide sufficient guidelines, pointers, and cues for guided learning to take place" (Social Studies I-III).

4. *Educability*. "The following skills are included (in third year Filipino): deriving main ideas from paragraph selections, verifying main ideas through use of details, identifying sentences irrelevant to a paragraph, rearranging sentences to make a coherent paragraph, listing cause and effect relationships" (Communication Arts: Filipino I-III); "Skills they tend to develop include ability to read with comprehension, to compare and infer from statistical data, read graphs and maps" (Social Studies I-III).

5. *Participating in planning and implementation*. "In a few instances (e.g. Environmental Science)

the student is involved in planning and implementing projects" (Science I-IV).

6. *Self-evaluation*. "Self-assessment exercises
with corresponding feedback are provided at
appropriate points" (Communication Arts:
English I-IV); "Evaluation items are intended
to help students assess themselves" (Filipino
I-III).

7. *Learning alternatives*. "There is a great
variety of pencil and paper type of activities,
with students encouraged in some instances to
use magazine selections (in the study of
grammatical forms)" (Filipino I-III);
"Additional activities in year II provide for
flexibility/creativity (write skits, poems,
or draw), additional activities included in
year III are for fast learners" (Social
Studies I-III).

The individual SLK's were found to vary qualitatively in
the extent to which they incorporated the above characteristics.
The relative adequacy of individual examples of SLK's is not the
issue here, however. What is important is the composite picture
of the fully-developed self-learning kit. The latter is a self-
contained set of instructions, learning materials, exercises,
and self-assessment tests that is fully transprotable from
school to home. The SLK, or at least parts of it, may incorporate group activities deliberately designed to encourage co-
operative or inter-learning. Ideally, it should provide for
alternative ways of doing problems or exercises. It should not
only address specific skills and competencies, but should also
provide for practice in generalized learning skills that transcend a particular content subdivision. In its most developed
form, the SLK is an educational tool which makes it possible
for learners to be responsible for much of their own learning
within the context of an overall instructional program in which
classroom activities account for only part of the student's
learning time.

Classroom Observations

Classrooms at each of the four grade levels were observed
for a period of approximately two days. At the conclusion of
the observations each classroom was rated for the extent to
which each of 12 descriptive statements about learning goals
were applicable. The intent was to assess the extent to which

general skills and competencies were addressed. Specific subject matter content was ignored except in relation to the
generalizable skills.

Results suggested that across all four grade levels there
was a stress on communication and expression in all courses
rather than just in language courses, and that across three of
the four grade levels attempts were apparent to encourage
problem-solving and "thinking things through". Somewhat surprisingly, classes during the first and fourth year tended to
be oriented to the basic disciplines composing the curriculum,
with second and third year classes more oriented toward the
physical and social environment and practical topics useful in
daily life.

Student Interviews
Sixteen students, distributed approximately equally among
the four grade levels, were interviewed on the advantages and
disadvantages of the ISOS program. Their responses to the two
open-ended questions were categorized and compared across grade
levels.

In response to the question on advantages of the program
the students typically referred to what they had learned. Three
responses were common to all four grade levels:

1. "Students learn to interview."

2. "Students learn to study by themselves and
   independently."

3. "Students learn about government agencies,
   private establishments, institutions, and
   people (by) visiting different places."

Each of these common responses reflect a different aspect
of curriculum content, and one (studying independently) is obviously indicative of self-direction. The other two are unusual
skills from the perspective of ordinary school learning. Interviewing, for example, is a complex communication skill that has
broad application in work and everyday life.

Disadvantages cited by the students pertained more to how
students went about learning, and will be cited in the next
chapter.

THE KATALIN VARGA GRAMMAR SCHOOL

It has already been noted that, of the four schools studied, the Katalin Varga Grammar School would probably appear to the visitor as most like other schools of its type within its own national context. But the Hungarian school is also an academic rather than a general high school. Its program is oriented towards sending graduates to the university. In this second sense it has already been described as similar in mission to the Oberstufen-Kolleg, despite the great differences between the two institutions in many other respects.

The Hungarian case study report stresses that in the traditional view of education schools were expected to impart subject-matter knowledge in a manner that approached the encyclopedic. There was correspondingly less emphasis on schooling as a way of fostering attitudes, generalized skills and capabilities, and even values. This traditional, classicist conception of the function of the school considers admission of a maximum number of graduates to universities and colleges as the primary criterion for assessing the effectiveness of any innovation. Moreover, the school final and university entrance examinations have helped significantly to maintain traditional curriculum goals through an emphasis on the measurement of knowledge of primarily verbal nature. Whether or not students, through the curriculum, developed the ability to make responsible choices in relation to learning would presumably have been dismissed as irrelevant. This familiar view of the purpose of the academic secondary school is currently giving way in a climate which in various ways makes innovation possible and in which there is a growing appreciation of schooling as a way of developing generalized skills and attitudes. This climate is illustrated in the support for experimentation and in greater flexibility in school regulations.

Within this transitional context of changing beliefs about many of the most important goals of schooling, the Hungarian case study conducted in-depth research on the content of the curriculum at the Katalin Varga School. Several approaches were used, including content analyses of syllabi and textbooks, qualitative review of final examinations and form master lessons, and biographical reports from students on their learning activities outside the regular curriculum. As already indicated, these empirical studies emphasized criteria relating to self-direction in learning.

Content Analysis of the Syllabi

Like many other nations, Hungary has a uniform national curriculum which specifies subject-matter content and provides relatively detailed guidelines about the methods by which each aspect of content is to be taught. Syllabi for Hungarian language and literature, English language, history, Marxist philosophie, biology, chemistry, geography, physics, and mathematics were analyzed. The analyses included only those words and phrases which involved either

> a. elaboration of the curriculum materials in terms of purpose, method of elucidation, etc.; or
>
> b. descriptions of the role of the teacher.

Elements of the syllabi which reflected pure subject-matter content were judged not relevant to this analysis. In all, the total number of elements that were included in the analysis numbered 1,391.

Each of the elements identified was classified using a six category system, each category being elaborated by means of several subcategories. The six general categories were:

> I. The role of the subject in developing self-direction.
>
> II. Method(s) for elaborating material in the curriculum.
>
> III. Learning materials and media.
>
> IV. The use of reference materials.
>
> V. Guidelines on difficulty and complexity.
>
> VI. The role of the teacher.

The subcategories under each of the above can be interpreted as either favoring or not favoring the development of self-direction. For example, two of the subcategories under VI (The role of the teacher) were: VI. (1) "Demonstration or imparting knowledge" as against (2) "Developing ability and capacity through application". Elements classified under the former would not reflect an emphasis on self-direction, whereas those classified under the latter obviously would.

The results of this content analysis of syllabi were summarized by the percentage of such statements classified under each subcategory. Admittedly, this type of analysis poses a problem with respect to interpretation of the findings. What

percentages for each subcategory would be most desirable? A
suitable theoretical basis for determining ideal proportions is
lacking, and comparative data of a normative type do not exist.
In spite of this limitation, it still is possible to identify
those categories which have only token representation as well
as those that receive relatively more stress.

It was apparent that subcategories reflecting an emphasis
on self-direction received an uneven degree of emphasis in the
school syllabi. Four of the subcategories associated with self-
direction and identified relatively frequently were (the figures
refer to the percentage of the total number of elements classified under each):

1. "Developing ability and capacity through application" (subcategory VI.2; 19.5%).

2. "Elaborating the curriculum through analysis,
   expounding, or evaluation" (II.3c; 7.8%).

3. "The role of the teacher as motivator -
   mobilizing, heightening interest or attention,
   making content relevant to learners, identifying problems" (VI.6; 7.1%).

4. "Elaborating the curriculum through use of observation, study, examination, or experimentation"
   (II.3.c; 6.2%).

Examples of elements of the syllabi identified under the
first category or "capacities and skills" follow. The first is
for chemistry, the second for history.

"Our most important task is to put into practice
the dialectical way of thinking and the elements
of logic; to study the relation of cause and
effect consciously; to raise problems; to put
forward hypotheses on the basis of experience and
realities and those of the results of experiments;
to verify the above, and to make the necessary ...
generalization."

"The task of the training courses ... is to develop
capability and skills enabling learners themselves
to draw conclusions and lessons on the basis of the
knowledge of facts and coherences; to connect
recent knowledge with earlier; to discern the
similarities and dissimilarities between individual
historical phenomena."

While the problem of what degree of emphasis is most desirable for each category remains unresolved, it is apparent
from the above that considerable attention is given in the syllabi to analysis, evaluation, observation, and experimentation
as modes of learning on the part of the student, and to application of knowledge and motivating students on the part of the
teacher. These practices were judged to be consistent with
the development of self-direction.

On the other hand, the report noted that relatively little
stress was given to the use of other modes of learning that presumably enhance self-direction, including debate and argumenta-
tion, independent work, developing strategies for efficient
learning (learning skills), and team work or inter-learning.
Overall, it was concluded that the syllabi placed relatively
too much emphasis on the teacher (43% of the elements were classified under subcategory VI) and correspondingly less on what
learners might do to develop their ability to function in a
self-directed manner.

Content Analysis of Textbooks
A similar analysis of content was made of the first and
last chapters of 31 textbooks representing all academic subjects
in the Hungarian curriculum. The texts surveyed were required
in all grammar schools.

In Hungarian schools the text is the primary medium for
communicating instructional content. Teachers and to some extent students may introduce material that supplements or expands
on the text, but the latter comes first in importance.

A second system of classification was developed for the
textbook analysis. The major categories of this system were:

  I. Motivational elements (conveyance of purpose
     and function of subject, use of devices to
     enhance interest).

 II. The mode of presentation (factual, use of ex-
     planation, presentation of conflicting ideas
     and theories).

III. The guidance and organization of study (ques-
     tions and study tasks).

 IV. Guides for review and summary by learners
     themselves.

  V. The use of supplementary sources.

Two of the above subcategories and one category were
judged particularly relevant to self-direction in learning.
The findings for these will be summarized here.

Category III, dealing with how the texts guided and organized study through questions and tasks, was differentiated into
two subcategories. The first comprised ten different types of
questions with which the student might be confronted - cause
and effect, similarity as opposed to difference, etc. The
second subcategory consisted of five types of tasks recording
data or facts, using outside cultural sources such as period-
icals, museums, etc. As in the content analysis of syllabi,
elements of the texts relating to each of these questions or
tasks were identified and classified. Summary data again refer
to the percentage of elements for the category as a whole that
were classified under each subcategory.

Dealing first with the breakdown for 683 elements involving questions to the student, the content analysis determined
that the largest single proportion (21%) was represented by the
subcategory of "practical application or example". Close behind
was "recording data or facts" (20%). Other illustrative findings for subcategories included "determining cause and effect"
(13%), "evaluation" (6%), "finding a rule, law, or principle"
(4%). The case study report concluded for this first part of
category III that any type of question to the student might
conceivably facilitate self-directed study. However, there did
appear to be a relatively heavy emphasis on simple production
of data or facts as compared to other subcategories of questions
which require higher levels of functioning.

The second analysis of textual elements defining tasks
showed similar results. Recording data or facts turned out to
be the primary activity required in a substantial proportion
(26%) of the 658 tasks identified. However, an equal percentage
of the elements involved analysis of pictures, diagrams, tables,
data, etc., normally a higher level of cognitive activity.
Overall, the findings of this particular aspect of the analysis
were considered positive, as all categories were represented by
significant proportions of elements. The least frequently observed type of task (use of cultural sources such as museums,
media, general reference books, etc.) still accounted for a
substantial proportion (10%) of the elements.

Category IV, dealing with guides for review and summary
by students themselves, was the third category judged to be

especially pertinent to self-direction. This category was comprised of the same subcategories of questions that were used for the first part of Category III above. In this case the subcategory, "practical application or example", accounted for over half (54%) of the total of 1931 elements identified and classified. Somewhat less emphasis was given here to simple recording of data or facts (13%).

The report concluded with respect to the last analyses that some types of questions, often judged to be important within a contemporary perspective about secondary education received, appeared with low frequencies. These included the production of explanations (6%), determining cause and effect relationships (5%), and evaluations (3.4%). However, these elements were present to some degree.

Finally, when texts from different subject-matters were compared, it was readily apparent to the Hungarian researchers that some texts did not address self-direction at all. These included texts in mathematics, biology, and literature (the latter for three of the four form levels). However, there was some degree of relevance for the largest group of texts, the latter representing virtually all areas of the curriculum. Likewise, there was a relatively high degree of support for self-direction in other texts, some of them from the same disciplines represented in the first group of texts.

In a curriculum that is common for schools of the same type over a nation as a whole, content analysis of documents such as syllabi and texts is a potentially valuable strategy of curriculum evaluation. The analyses conducted for the Hungarian study in many respects paralleled, for the topic of self-direction, an earlier Swedish study by Fredriksson and Gestrelius (1975) on lifelong education criteria.

Final Examination

On completing work at the Katalin Varga School the student takes a final examination that is virtually identical to that administered to other grammar school students throughout the country. (Vocational school students take a different examination.) The examination has two obligatory subjects (Hungarian literature and grammar, and mathematics) and two optional subjects to be selected from a list of six possibilities (history, foreign languages, physics, chemistry, biology, or geometry). The examination combines written and oral assessment.

Final examinations sum up the student's development at the end of the secondary level including

1. knowledge of facts and related thinking skills;

2. ability to organize and apply knowledge;

3. awareness of contemporary issues and problems in various fields; and

4. general erudition and possession of capabilities sufficient for self-education in the future.

In addition, the examination is used to determine whether the student would continue to be eligible for admission to a college or university, which is based in part on a separate entrance examination.

The Hungarian study established through qualitative evaluation of oral and written portions of the examination that preference was still given to verbal knowledge and memory. Students were not confronted with new situations and applications, especially instances in which improvisation, originality, or dealing with the unexpected would be necessary. The examination was in part found to be less than adequate with respect to 4. above, but more importantly was found to be ill-adapted to the innovative goals of the Katalin Varga curriculum, especially in relationship to self-direction in learning. It was suggested in the report that the same kind of criticism could be made of university entrance examinations.

The final examinations are administered by an expert from outside the institution assigned by the County Council. This individual works with the Headmaster at the school in directing the examination and evaluating and summarizing the results. To accomplish this, the examiner prepares a summary of the final examinations, five of which were examined as a part of the case study. The conclusion from this inspection and less formal observation lent further support to the conclusion that the experimental curriculum at the school was not taken into account in the preparation or evaluation of the examinations. Again, the emphasis was on firm grounding in the disciplines with the demonstration of factual knowledge the primary goal.

The case study detected little emphasis in the examination on "the learner's self-acceptance, planfulness in knowledge acquisition ... curiosity, openness to experience, willingness to deviate from (established) patterns, or individual development of personality". Aspects of the curriculum of the school

designed to facilitate the development of self-direction seemed
to be ignored in the final examination as well as the university
entrance examination.

Form Master's Lessons
      Students at every grade level of the grammar school have
one lesson from the form master each week. Such lessons at the
Katalin Varga School usually incorporate discussion and conversation in addition to an oral presentation by the form master.
The syllabus prescribes 60 per cent of the themes, and the rest
are chosen by participants in the school. Qualitative examination of the themes for these lessons at each of the four grade
levels revealed an emphasis on values, personal development,
and social issues. Illustrative themes from each of the four
grade levels included:

Form I.   learning methods in grammar school, self-
             knowlege, the individual and the community;

Form II.   the communal personality, individual apti-
             tudes and motivation, dealing with failure,
             internationalism;

Form III.   choice of profession, the learner of today,
             accepting responsibility and dependability;
             and

Form IV.   discipline and freedom, personality develop-
             ment, life goals.

Generally, these topics and others suggest an orientation toward
life and learning outside of the school.

Learning Skills Program
      As indicated briefly in Chapter 4, the Katalin Varga
School is unique within the Hungarian system in its general
course on learning skills offered to all first year students.
The *studium generale* program incorporates a variety of activities that involve "learning how to learn", especially in relation to making choices about the organization of learning. The
topics covered in the *studium generale* program and the relative
emphasis given to each are as follows:

- using the library (10 hours);

- exercises in reading comprehension and understanding (8 hours);

- using learning technology (8 hours);

- taking notes and making sketches (8 hours);
- making excerpts and arranging and qualifying data (4 hours);
- composing short lectures (4 hours);
- preparing bibliographies (4 hours);
- communicating information logically in a speech or as a leader of a discussion (6 hours);
- self-knowledge and awareness (12 hours); and
- concept formation and analyzing and synthesizing information (4 hours).

These topics also make readily apparent the expectations of the school with respect to student performance.

Additional School and Non-School Activities
Almost 90 per cent of the students at the school reported involvement in some sort of school learning and organizational activity outside of the regular lessons. In terms of learning directly relating to the curriculum, additional study in mathematics and the sciences, especially physics, appeared to be most frequent.

A majority of the students (62 per cent) reported attendance at political courses sponsored by the youth organization, with a further small segment (14 per cent) studying historical and socio-political issues relating to the labour movement. Others involved themselves in courses in sports (21 per cent), technical drawing (15 per cent), singing in a choir (21 per cent), engaging in individual or group problem-solving competitions sponsored by a mathematics journal for secondary school students (13 per cent). Additional activities reported by smaller numbers of students included a film club, theatrical group, Red Cross circle, etc.

There is thus a voluntary curriculum within the school which extensively supplements the regular curriculum. In some cases it may relate directly to regular work - as in the example of the mathematics problem-solving groups - while in other cases it may add elements that are not present in the regular curriculum.

Out-of-school activities reported by students were tabulated according to frequency. There was such a wide variety of these extracurricular activities listed that all need not be repeated here. The most frequent (reported by 79 per cent of the students) was reading in the library. Listening to music and reading books at home were a close second. Cultural and scientific programs on radio and television were mentioned by approximately half of the students. Activities engaged in by 15-30 per cent of the students included sports clubs, lectures, preparing for national learning competitions, and theater. A variety of other activities were reported less frequently.

THE BIELEFELDER OBERSTUFEN-KOLLEG

Curriculum development, research on the curriculum, and the teaching and learning process at the OSK are meant to be complementary activities. In fact, it is possible that at times they are indistinguishable. This is consistent with the perspective of *action research*. Harder (1978) points out that action research, as compared to the classical experimental method of the scientific laboratory, reflects a belief common to participants in the college that the classical research paradigm has served only to separate educational practice from scientific pedagogical investigation. From the perspective of its participants, especially the teaching staff, the OSK is more than anything else an institution experimenting with ways of breaking down the barriers between research and practice.

The action research strategy adopted by the OSK has a direct effect on the definition of the roles played by teachers and students. They are participants in an institution which is both an accredited school within a large state system and at the same time a research and development enterprise continuously involved in self-study. Harder (1978) reports, "The division of roles into researcher and research object which is a dominant trait of empirical social research work is thus done away with at the OSK. All of the people who take part are involved in planning and carrying out tasks of research and documentation."

It was clear in the case study that this duality of role for participants has a major impact on the curriculum of the college. This impact is evident whether one considers the content of curriculum or the process by which it is communicated. Harder (1978) reports that the duality at times creates conflicts. On the one hand, there is pressure to run the college efficiently by rapidly adopting pragmatic solutions to problems. On the other, there is the programmatic desire to isolate problems scientifically to identify underlying causal factors.

The study of wall graffiti cited in Chapter 8 is representative of a scientific rather than a pragmatic approach to
problem solving. The action research paradigm explains much of
what is to be reported next. Participation, in fact, is the
key concept in understanding the way in which the teaching and
learning processes are carried out. However, in order to be
able to understand how participation works, it is first necessary to have a clear picture of the way in which the OSK curriculum is organized.

By its own definition of mission, the college is obliged
to equip students with a general education as it is imparted
during the last three years of secondary school and a specialized education as it is imparted during the first two years of
university. Students study sciences, mathematics, languages,
social sciences, literature, and related fields, as they would
in any other academic secondary school. However, the way in
which this familiar set of academic disciplines is divided up
and recombined and the use that is made of it, is unusual by
any standard and certainly unique within the Federal Republic.

Optional Courses
This first type of course covers the longest block of time
during the semester. Optional courses are series of seminars
in the student's two chosen (or "major") fields of study, each
of which lasts twelve weeks. One emphasis in these courses, in
addition to the basic knowledge and systematic methodology of
the subject, is on the relation between the field and professional roles in society. Optional course seminars account
for 30 per cent of the student's total time and are held daily
during the twelve weeks in which they are offered.

Complementary Courses
Also using a seminar format, complementary courses are
selected by the student from among four to ten such courses
offered by each of the three major subject-matter sections
cited earlier (Social Sciences, Language and Fine Arts, the
Natural Sciences and Mathematics). Each semester the student
selects two complementary courses from different subject matter
sections. These courses run for twelve weeks (concurrently
with the optional (major) seminar courses) and jointly account
for 25 per cent of the coursework during the semester.

The complementary courses have an important role within

the general integrative approach to curriculum taken at the OSK.
The courses stress interdisciplinary knowledge and methods, and
treat themes that recur in various branches of systematic inquiry. The courses are "complementary" in the sense of being
designed to broaden and integrate the specialized subject matter
knowledge of the optional (major) courses.

Students select complementary courses on the basis of need
or interest. For example, a student might select a particular
complementary course in mathematics because of its application
to his optional coursework in the field of paleontology.

Project Courses
The final three weeks of the semester are devoted entirely
to the project course mentioned in the previous chapter. (1)
Here the students attempt to apply what they have learned by
participating in a large group project dealing with some type
of social question that requires solution. Students from different optional course specializations work together in interdisciplinary teams. The projects are usually designed to result
in a product such as an exhibition, a film, a model, or some
other means of conveying information and concepts. The intent
is that students gain concrete experience with the interdependence among categories of specialized knowledge by having to
deal with problems that do not fall within the domain of a particular discipline. This type of course occupies 15 per cent
of the semester.

The following illustrations of problems suitable for defining project courses are partly drawn from Harder (1978),
(whose examples were taken from the original proposal for the
OSK) and partly from the discussion of the final project meeting:

- communicating with foreign workers;

- prices of agricultural and dairy products;

- libraries, bookshops, bookstalls, and their
  various publics in (the city of) Bielefeld;

- the conditions of the OSK environment (warmth,
  light, heat, acoustics, building structure); and

- how to measure the lead content of drinking water.

Intensive Courses
The semester at OSK lasts twenty weeks. Except for the
first semester which begins with an orientation period, students
begin each semester with five weeks of study devoted entirely

to intensive courses. This study is individualized and designed
to enable the student to keep abreast of regular secondary level
(first four semesters) and university requirements (second four
semesters) in content areas such as languages and mathematics.
To meet external standards thirteen out of sixteen possible intensive courses are obligatory, the remaining three courses being electives. Although some of the same subject matter may in
part be covered in other types of courses, the intensive phase
allows for a period of concentration entirely on standard academic requirements determined by individual needs.

Praktikum Courses
        A final type of course accounts for about 5 per cent of
each semester and occurs during a portion of the period devoted
to longer seminar type courses. This short *Praktikum* course
(lasting two weeks) is devoted to planning, arranging, and
analyzing outside employment experiences in industry or some
other type of outside job. The required work experience is to
be gained during vacation periods. The *Praktikum* course-work
is designed to integrate that experience with the student's
formal studies. Part of the work experience may be of any type.
The other part is to be tied to the student's specific course
of study, e.g., a student of psychology working in a psychiatric
clinic.

        Integration, flexibility, and the opportunity for choice
are thus dominant themes in the OSK curriculum. At the same
time, students in the OSK must meet the same academic requirements that are met by students enrolled in regular secondary
schools and universities. The curriculum structure just described requires that each student should experience and apply
a variety of approaches to formal learning and its application.
Above all, the curriculum works against the development of
narrow disciplinary specialization and the concomitant insula-
tion of academic learning from social problems and issues.

SUMMARY

        Analysis of the curricula at the four institutions has
revealed consistent themes underlying the programs of each.
Abstractions can be misleading when they are used to oversim-
plify, but a great many of the practices observed at each of
the schools can be understood as manifestations of these basic
themes. The themes are general, organizing principles, which
not only explain why particular types of content are emphasized,

but also serve to prepare the ground for the analysis of teaching and learning processes which follows in the next chapter.

Both classroom observations and interviews of teachers, for example, established that the individualization of instruction and multicultural education were the dominant themes at the Community School. Self-direction was more or less assumed by the teachers to be a natural outcome of a successfully individualized program. The major tactics built into the curriculum for promoting individualization were the use of resource centers within the classrooms, small group and individual study, and multi-age grouping.

The multicultural education theme focused on racial and ethnic integration and, laudable as it is, had nothing to do directly with the enhancement of self-direction. Interestingly, the term "integration" describes underlying themes at all four of the schools. At the Community School, however, integration has a meaning that is peculiar to the Community School and to the national context of the U.S.A.

The dominant theme of the Arellano High School ISOS program is unquestionably independent study. Integration is a second theme, perhaps equally important, but one which devolves from the emphasis on independent study. The latter is articulated through the out-of-school portion of the program, specifically in the learning kits which students use at home. The kits are designed to be fully self-contained, although they may incorporate group activities. Content analyses revealed that many of the kits incorporated features that may be identified with the enhancement of self-directed learning. These included provisions for self-evaluation, independent or self-learning, inter-learning, and provision for alternative approaches to learning. There was also some effort to promote skills relating to general educability and planning.

In the case of the ISOS program, "integration" refers to the incorporation of community resources in independent learning activities. Various sources, especially teachers, suggested that this aspect of the program related closely to the development of self-direction, not only because learning occurred outside of the school and independent of the teacher, but also because students developed skills and competencies useful for gathering information in the social world. Interviewing was stressed by both students and teachers as an example of this type of skill. Thus, integration of school and community, a

principle of lifelong education, may also facilitate self-
direction when students develop skills of inquiry and investigation which are not ordinarily stressed by the school.

The concept of "learning to learn" summarizes that aspect
of the curriculum at the Katalin Varga School which relates
most closely to self-direction. The primary role of the school
as a strong academic institution preparing students for entrance
into the university requires traditional emphases in many aspects of the curriculum as well as in the examination system.
These emphases were extensively documented in the content analyses of syllabi, textbooks, and examinations conducted in the
Hungarian case study. However, the *studium generale* course
taken by all students in the first year is the major purely
curricular element reflecting an emphasis on self-direction.
This course emphasizes learning to use resources of all kinds,
as well as organizing and communicating information by a variety of means.

In addition, the Katalin Varga School emphasizes and fa-
cilitates learning activities of a less formal nature at the
school itself as well as in the surrounding community. Virtually all of the students were found to engage in one or more such
activities. So here again the principle of integration, in
this case between school and community and between formal and
informal learning activities within the school itself, emerges
as an important theme underlying the activities of students.

Without question, the integration principle is deliberately applied by staff and students to virtually all aspects of
the curriculum at the Oberstufen-Kolleg. Certainly the adoption
of the action research paradigm conceived as it is to break down
the barriers between social science research and educational
practices, is one aspect of the theme that is highly salient to
the observer. The institution itself becomes a subject of study
in the curriculum. This mode of implementing the integration
theme will be even more apparent in the following chapter on
teaching and learning processes.

In addition, the way in which the OSK curriculum is organized, incorporates the principle of integration in the regular
use of project courses which require the application of academic
knowledge, in the interdisciplinary combinations of optional and
complementary courses, and in the way in which project courses
make it possible for students with different academic fields of
study to work together on a common enterprise. Finally, the

Praktikum course combines school and work, with planning and analyzing outside employment experience covered as a part of the school experience.

Each of the four institutions thus incorporates some aspect of the integration concept in its curriculum, although each does so in its own way. Each also has its own particular theme in relation to self-direction: individualization in the case of the Community School, independent learning for the ISOS Program, learning to learn for the Katalin Varga School and action research - the school and the community as objects of study - in the case of the Oberstufen-Kolleg. The ways in which these themes are expressed in the teaching and learning process is the focus of the next chapter.

NOTE

1. The English titles selected for the last three types of courses convey, at best, only rough approximations of the meaning of the German course titles. These are: *Wahlfachunterricht* for optional course; *Ergänzungsunterricht* for complementary course; and *Gesamtunterricht* for project course.

Chapter 7

Teaching and Learning Processes

The case studies scrutinized teaching and learning processes by a variety of methods. The intention was to answer,
insofar as possible, parallel questions about how teachers
taught and how students learned. These questions had been
agreed upon in the initial project meeting as of fundamental
importance to the case studies.

This parallelism will be reflected in the material which
follows. The section on each school is divided into subsections
on learning processes and teaching practices. In each case,
the dominant themes identified in the previous chapter on curriculum will be related to the findings on teaching and learning.

THE COMMUNITY SCHOOL

For the Community School, the guiding theme in relation
to self-direction was individualization of learning. Tactics
such as classroom resource centers, small group or individual
learning, multi-age grouping, and flexibility in the curriculum
were found to be means for implementing this larger theme. The
U.S. research team approached the investigation of teaching and
learning practices mainly by searching for empirical evidence
as to whether the individualization provided for in the Community School classrooms affected self-direction in learning.

Learning Processes
It was reasoned that the emphasis on individualization in
the goals of the Community School should be manifested in the
fact that relatively little time is spent on whole-class instruction. Fortunately, the observations of high and low self-
directed learners reported in detail in the next chapter can be
used to test this prediction. These two groups of students

were found to be engaged in the same types of activities as most other learners at all six grade levels. Four learners at each grade level (two high and two low in self-direction) were observed twelve times each. The percentages of time devoted to various types of grouping during learning shown in Table 7.1 are thus based on a total of 144 observations for the three lower and three upper grade levels.

Table 7.1

Percent of Observations of Four Grouping Patterns
for High and Low Self-directed Learners in Community School

Type of Group	Grades 1-3	Grades 4-6
Whole class	22.9	11.8
Large groups	4.2	20.8
Small groups	52.1	37.5
Individual	20.8	29.9
TOTAL	100.0	100.0

It is clear from the table that the dominant mode or modes of learning involved grouping patterns other than whole-class instruction at both upper and lower levels. Younger students worked in small groups a little over half of the time, with whole-class instruction only slightly more frequent than individual study (23 per cent as compared to 21 per cent). Large group instruction (10 or more students) was more frequent for upper than for lower level students, but so was individual work. Another way of summing up the table is to conclude that all types of grouping patterns were used, but with small group and individual instruction accounting for by far the largest proportion of time at both upper and lower grade levels (73 per cent and 67.4 per cent respectively).

In the lower site, student learning groups usually combined boys and girls of mixed ethnicity. In this situation, the children were consistently observed to exchange interests and ideas in informal conversation while they developed joint working strategies and shared materials. The general impression among observers was that the children enjoyed being together.

At the upper site, the working groups were not always in-tegrated ethnically to the degree that was apparent for younger children. The extensive use of workbooks and exercises was re-flected in the amount of time these learners spent in checking and comparing answers with one another.

In the lower grades, instructional content was usually transmitted at the teaching center where a small group of children read or did math under the teacher's direction. Part of the time would be spent going over material the students had already worked on, the other part in explaining the next assign-ment. These learners, on leaving the center, would use work-books or single exercise sheets developed and reproduced at the school. A photograph of the entire classroom would ordinarily show some students working with the teacher, some using work-books or exercise sheets individually or in loosely formed groups, and others working with the teaching aide assigned to the classroom, usually because they needed extra assistance.

The pattern of work in upper site classrooms was quite similar, with frequent co-operation in checking answers and procedures. At both levels this type of activity was supple-mented by work done at home, although to a somewhat greater extent for the older children. It is readily apparent that the dominant mode of learning at the Community School involves working with materials, exercises, problems, etc., alone or in small groups, and after preparatory orientation and teaching, in moderate sized groups. This conclusion is evident in Table 7.2, which shows *written response* materials to be the type of learning material most frequently observed in the study of high and low self-directed learners (see next page).

The students were encouraged to work with each other through appropriate grouping. There was also considerable tol-erance for verbal interaction. This tolerance by its very na-ture permitted a certain amount of irrelevant play, social inter-action, or aimlessness on the part of some students. Teachers continually had to monitor this behavior to keep it to a reason-able minimum. This is evident, for example, in the excerpt taken from an observer's description of the third grade class-room:

> There was more freedom of movement about the class-room than would be the case in a more structured approach. Rules allowed movement only for a purpose, but these were frequently violated, even to the ex-tent that a child might leave his or her table and

approach the teacher who was working with another
group ... The teacher generally gave learners
time to terminate their own off-task behaviors,
reminding a talking or wandering child of the
task or the behavioral rule only when the off-
task behavior had become distracting or had
endured for some time.

Table 7.2

Percent of Observations Using Different Types of
Materials for High and Low Self-directed
Learners in the Community School

Materials	Grades 1-3	Grades 4-6
No materials present	15.0	6.0
Textbooks	25.3	24.4
Written Response	50.0	54.7
Supplementary	0.0	2.0
Other	9.7	12.9
TOTAL	100.0	100.0

The previous chapter reported that students in Community
School classrooms were not confronted with extensive opportunities for making choices. Younger children were encouraged to
make choices primarily in free time situations rather than as
a part of formal learning. Older children were allowed to make
more choices directly related to learning, particularly of the
mode of learning and distribution of learning time between home
and school. Aspects of individualization potentially related
to the enhancement of self-direction thus incorporated relatively little opportunity for choice, although somewhat more for
older children.

Pertinent aspects of individualization that were commonly
observed in student behavior at the Community School were thus
an extensive use of materials for individual work (instead of
didactic instruction), students working alone or in small
groups, and a generally relaxed classroom atmosphere which required students to be responsible for their own self-discipline

while working. How teachers carried out their own role in promoting these kinds of processes is considered next.

Teaching Practices

All observers of the grade 1-3 classrooms noted the relaxed and informal nature of student-teacher interactions.
Students typically addressed teachers by their first names, a
quite unusual practice at any level of schooling in the U.S.,
and remarkably parallel to students' use of the familiar form
of address at the Oberstufen-Kolleg noted later in this chapter.
There appeared to be few constraints against raising questions
and seeking feedback. Teachers frequently praised children for
pro-social behaviors, verbally or by writing their names on the
blackboard.

At the 4-5 grade levels, a similar kind of informality
prevailed, although interaction between teachers and students
tended to be primarily about subject matter. A common utter-
ance among students at this level was, "I like ....
(teacher's name) because I learn a lot from her". This basis
for interaction was undoubtedly due to the fact that each classroom was devoted entirely to one subject matter area. Students
apparently perceived teachers as specialists in subject matter
rather than as individuals playing the multi-faceted, partly
academic, partly social, role of the elementary level teacher.

As already noted, all of the classrooms had teacher aides
as well as parent volunteers (except that a new aide had not
been assigned to the third grade at the time of the study).
Observers at both upper and lower levels reported very little
direct involvement in instruction in most classrooms by these
two categories of "other adults". The latter were most often
assigned tasks involving the preparation of materials and con-
sequently had relatively little contact with children in spite
of their physical proximity. A few classroom aides did take
part in instruction by conducting tutorials for small groups or
evaluating student progress on assignments.

An analysis of teacher communications to students derived
from the observations of high and low self-directed learners
broke down into three categories:

1. communications about instructional content;

2. messages about appropriate behavior; and

3. instructions about classroom procedures.

The amount of attention given by teachers to each of these
three categories of exchange differed from classroom to classroom, as did the techniques used to convey information and the
manner of indicating approval or disapproval.

An informal comparison of the observer reports classified
teaching styles as either *directive* or *supportive*. The directive style was characterized by task-oriented directives. The
supportive style of teaching contained more personal or social
remarks from teachers to students. The Community School was
much like typical schools in the U.S. in that the style of
teaching is a function of the predilections of the individual
teacher rather than the result of an institutional policy.

During each observation of a high or low self-directed
learner, the type of activity in which the teacher was engaged,
in relation to the student being observed, was recorded. It
will be recalled that each observation of a single student
lasted approximately 5 minutes. Any interaction between the
teacher and the child being observed during that period was
recorded, whether or not it was continuous throughout the
period or merely a momentary contact. A summary of these data
is provided in Table 7.3.

Table 7.3

Percent of Six Types of Teacher Student Interaction
Recorded During Observations of High and Low Self-Directed
Learners

Teacher Role	Grades 1-3	Grades 4-6
Not present	46.0	42.4
Instructor	21.5	27.9
Activity Management	11.0	12.1
Behavior Management	14.0	7.9
Social/Affective	5.4	2.4
Observer/Listener	2.1	7.3
TOTAL	100.0	100.0

The table shows that, for both levels, the teacher had
no contact at all with the student observed during almost half

of the five minute observation periods. For about one fourth
of the observations, the teacher was engaged in *didactic teaching* of the child being observed, with this role slightly more
frequent for the upper than the lower level (28 per cent to
22 per cent respectively). For a similar proportion of the
observations, the teacher engaged in some type of *management
activity* (behavioral or learning) with the student being observed, though to a somewhat lesser extent for the older learners (about 20 per cent for older students as compared with 25
per cent for younger). *Social/affective* interactions and simply
observing or listening accounted for the small remaining proportions of observations.

Similar data for aides and other adults revealed no interaction at all with the student being observed during approximately 90 per cent of the observations in grades 1-3 and 74
per cent in grades 4-6. Other adults were thus not a significant factor in the active teaching and learning process in the
Community School.

The above data are another way of showing that the role
of the teacher and other adults in Community School classrooms
is defined in a way that leaves students alone to work on their
own for a significant portion of the time. This is even more
apparent when it is recalled that even very brief contact between teacher and student during the observation period is represented in Table 7.3. This allocation of responsibility to
the student for maintaining his or her own level of work is
probably the single factor that is most highly related to the
enhancement of self-direction in learners in the instructional
program of the Community School.

ARELLANO HIGH SCHOOL

The dominant theme of the ISOS Program, from the perspective of self-direction, was found in the study of the curriculum
to be the development of independent learning. The Philippine
case study investigated the expression of this theme in learning
and teaching by means of observations of learning activities
and interviews. The relatively open and unstructured approach
to the interviews produced some useful evaluative information
from both students and teachers on the strengths and weaknesses
of the ISOS Program.

Learning Processes
        Students learning in the ISOS Program were assessed
through observations in classrooms and at learning centers, as
well as by means of interviews of teachers and students.

        Observations. Observations of student learning were the
basis for completing a rating schedule which assessed each of
the eight conditions for facilitating self-direction in learning listed in Chapter 3. Each condition was measured by several
specific items (e.g., for *flexibility*: "Some in-school classes
are informal, unstructured") which observers rated on a seven
point scale ("strongly agree/disagree"). Three of the conditions observed dealt with teacher behavior and will be discussed in the next section.

        Observers worked in two teams, each of which observed

    1. two whole day, in-school sessions for each
       grade level;

    2. two sessions of the homeroom class for each
       year level; and

    3. activities of several small groups at various
       learning centers.

These experiences were treated as a composite in making the
ratings. In a few instances, ratings of particular items were
facilitated by talking informally to students or inspecting
materials such as logbooks. Finally, the ratings for each
level were pooled and averaged for each item.

        The analysis concentrated mainly on items which averaged
in the "strongly agree" or "disagree for negatively phrased
items" categories for all four grade levels. Examples of one
such item for each category will be given.

        a. *Flexibility.* This category contained items referring
to alternative approaches in time, place, mode and content.
Three out of sixteen items were rated as applicable to all
three grade levels. These included,

        "Much interlearning takes place in the out-of-school
        situations and in the learning centers".

Other items characteristic of all grade levels related to the
availability of materials in addition to the learning kits and
to the informal approaches to learning at the learning centers.

b. *Opportunity for choice.* The eleven items in this category referred to various types of opportunities which might be
given to learners to make choices about their own learning.
Five of the items were rated as characteristic of all four
grade levels, among them,

"Students plan their own individual learning schedule".

The other four items referred to choosing another student to
work with, using informal modes of learning such as mass media,
choosing the time to complete an assignment, and choosing between school and home for completing work.

c. *Learners as their own evaluation agents.* Of the seven
items in this category, five were rated as characteristic of
all grade levels. These items described aspects of self-evaluation that occurred in situations in which feedback on effectiveness was likely to be available. One example was,

"Students use self-assessment tests/tools".

Two of the items referred to the availability and quality of
instructional objectives for students. The other two dealt
with feedback on periodic teacher-made tests and the extent to
which learning materials made it possible for students to check
their own accuracy.

d. *Capitalizing on learners' intrinsic motivation.* Four
items described ways in which the interests of students might
be taken into account. Only one item was judged to be true
for all levels.

"Students are encouraged to do activities on their
own, for example, experiments, reports, investigations, projects, surveys".

However, at three of the four grade levels, observers reported
opportunities to choose according to personal interest and the
use of techniques to promote curiosity, surprise, or perplexity.

e. *Incorporating learning outside of the school.* Given
the nature of the ISOS Program, it is not surprising that each
of the five items referring to learning outside of the school
was rated as descriptive of all four grade levels. For example,

"Learners use community resources (human and
physical) for learning".

Other items dealt with relating learning content to real life
situations, learners being helped to understand that learning

can take place in environments other than the classroom, and encouraging students to find answers through work in outside learning centers. These were also judged to be descriptive of learning at each grade level.

f. *The learning climate*. Another category dealt with learning climate in general and, more specifically, with the four subcategories of climate described below.

Five items assessed *student responsibility*. Three of these were judged to be characteristics of three of the four grade levels. One of these was,

"Students are assigned tasks over a long period of time (e.g., weekly or more)".

Students were also observed to take responsibility for class- work, materials, and the classroom and to take turns performing various routine duties at three of the four levels.

Two items assessed the extent to which the school climate created *expectations of success*. One of these was rated as characteristic of three of the four grade levels,

"Students are willing to try a task even when there is risk of failure".

All three of the items measuring *conviviality* were judged to describe three of the four grade levels (grade 2 being ex- cluded for each). One of these was,

"There is an absence of teasing, sarcasm, humiliation".

The other two items on this subscale dealt with interpersonal warmth and teacher attention to student responses and comments.

Finally, *interlearning* was assessed by two items, one of which was judged to apply at all four grade levels.

"Students accept leadership of peers in group/ class work".

The second item of this type was judged to be true for three grade levels (again excluding the second year) and dealt with the willingness of students to seek help from other students or adults.

Overall, the observers found the ISOS Program to have in- corporated at most or all grade levels at least some aspects of each of the proposed characteristics of environments designed to enhance self-direction. Characteristics that were most

frequently emphasized were opportunity for choice, learners as
their own evaluation agents, and incorporating learning outside
of the school. This positive picture undoubtedly in part reflects the fact that a significant part of the students' learning must by definition occur out of school. In other words,
some characteristics are virtually inevitable concommitants of
having to learn at home or in the community.

Interviews with teachers. Sixteen teachers, four from each
grade level, were interviewed about advantages and disadvantages
of the ISOS Program from the point of view of students, parents,
and teachers. Pertinent here are aspects of the responses relating to students. (Note that this is a different sample of
teachers than that interviewed about teaching and the curriculum).

On the positive side, the ISOS Program was seen by
teachers as

1. giving students more time to study;

2. making it possible for some students to be
   employed and study at the same time;

3. teaching students about institutions and agencies
   that might be useful in the future; and

4. demonstrating to students that they can learn
   from many sources.

It was also suggested that various affective characteristics
such as self-reliance and responsibility were developed through
the program as well as related skills including interaction with
adults, independent study, interlearning, etc.

On the other side of the coin, it appeared that most
teachers saw the ISOS Program as beneficial to average and
above average learners. They felt that the lack of supervision
during off-school days allows slow learners to neglect their
work and to use time inappropriately. These learners were reported to show poor patterns of attendance and frequently to
miss both "makeup" classes and regular school classes.

It appears that students who benefit most from the program
must be prepared to assume responsibility and be able to organize their own time. That is, they must have some of the characteristics of the self-directed learner before they begin the
ISOS Program. This opinion on the part of the teachers was

echoed in *essays* on the ISOS Program written by two of the students identified as high in self-direction, and studied for this reason. One, for example, writes,

> "Why are below average students grouped with the average and above average? ... They slow down our pace of study. Perhaps we will be able to cover more subject matter and learn more if (different) groupings were made".

Another suggests,

> "It's just that those in the Office or the Registrar should choose those students with high grades and those that are industrious in studying their lessons ... I can see that those lazy students are becoming more lazy ..."

But in relation to his or her own learning, this same student reports the following:

> "I have learned to make my time more worthy and use it wisely. During off-school, I always go back to school to get some of the kits ... I also have to attend some of my classes even if I'm off-school to catch up with our new lessons so that it won't be hard to understand when discussed in our class ... We have to do interviews and research work. In these interviews, my shyness was removed. They helped me a lot in talking to people. I am learning to mix with different kinds of people - from the slum areas to high ranking officials ... We are trained to study by ourselves without our teachers' help."

If there is a truism with regard to educational praxis, it is that no approach works equally well for all types of learners. It should therefore be no surprise that this is also true for the ISOS Program. The comments from teachers and students in the program suggest that students who need a high degree of structure and supervision to maintain on-task behavior do not do as well. Selection of students for the program is therefore an important practical consideration.

Interviews with students. The sixteen students interviewed almost unanimously cited various types of learning as advantages of the program, as was noted in the preceding section on curriculum. When asked about disadvantages, they tended to focus either on other students or on specific issues of logistics, scheduling, materials, etc. The latter are not pertinent here because they refer to administrative details that reflect on local institutional content.

Reactions to other students from students interviewed at three of the four grade levels echoed the conclusions of the previous section. Some students were absent too frequently or in other ways failed to participate. These and sometimes other students could not do the SLK's without special help, usually from the teacher. Clearly, the ISOS Program is more appropriate for students who are ready to assume responsibility for making and carrying out constructive choices with respect to their own learning. This type of student may be able to develop under the ISOS Program in ways that would not have been possible in a regular, structured classroom.

Teaching Practices
The interviews with teachers and classroom and learning center observations cited in the two previous sections also produced information relevant to the topic: "How teachers teach". The following material relates primarily to the way teachers in the ISOS Program behave in their formal roles as teachers.

Observations. As noted above, the rating schedule used in the classroom observations incorporated three dimensions which referred respectively to the behavior of teachers.

a. *Teaching as a facilitating activity.* There were fourteen rating items describing various ways in which a teacher might act as facilitator or helper, rather than as a judge or evaluator. Three of these items were rated as characteristic of all four grade levels by the observers. Most of the remainder were noted at three of the four levels. One example was,

"Teacher encourages participation in discussion of as many students as are willing".

The other items rated as characteristic of all four grade levels referred to the availability of teachers for counseling and the willingness of teachers to provide help to learners individually or in groups. These generally positive results suggest that the facilitator role may be a dominant model for ISOS teachers.

b. *Democratic relationships.* The five items in this group referred to relationships in which authority is used only when

necessary within an atmosphere that encourages individual choice
and responsibility. Three of these items were characteristic
of all grade levels, one was,

"Teachers are approachable to students".

The other two items in this category which were rated as high at
all four grade levels reflected the extent to which leaders of
learning teams sought opinions of student members and the degree
to which leader versus follower roles were accepted readily by
students working in groups.

c. *Emphasis on expressive objectives*. Expressive objectives confront learners with problems or tasks which are open-
ended, e.g., have more than one correct solution and/or means
of solution. None of the six items in this category was observed at all grade levels. One item noted for three grade
levels was,

"Teacher encourages students to answer their own
or fellow students' questions".

However, this item does not necessarily imply an expressive objective, nor for that matter do the other two items rated as
characteristic of three grade levels (encouragement of problem
solving, and encouragement of student questions). These items
do reflect teacher behavior or attitudes which are generally
relevant to self-direction. But other items in this category
more pertinent to the use of expressive objectives were noted
at fewer than three grade levels.

In summary, the observations revealed that teachers in
the ISOS Program played facilitating roles in a number of ways.
They also maintained democratic relationships which encouraged
responsibility on the part of students. They did not, however,
make much use of expressive objectives.

Interviews with teachers. The seventeen ISOS teachers interviewed in depth about characteristics of the program,
answered several questions about teaching methods in addition
to the questions relating to curriculum content discussed
earlier. These questions were open-ended, e.g., "How do you
teach values?", and as a result, elicited a variety of responses. In some cases there was no clear pattern noted in the
case study report. In others, most of the teachers gave similar answers, suggesting consistent features of the teaching
process.

When asked, "Who teaches other than the teacher?" virtually all the teachers interviewed cited other students. Specific
examples of how students engage in teaching were: giving reports, helping slow learners during off-school periods, conducting demonstration and group experiments, role playing in
class, teaching remedial groups during in-school, leading discussions in enrichment groups, and presenting dramas or skits.
Interlearning appears to be a commonly used way of organizing
learning in the ISOS Program.

Most of the teachers also reported that adults in learning
centers fulfilled a genuine teaching role. Parents and other
family members were also reported to engage in teaching, though
only by about one third of the teachers interviewed. It appears
that the students take responsibility for a substantial proportion of the teaching in the ISOS Program, and more so than any
group other than the teachers themselves.

The self-learning kits are seen by teachers as the primary
means of teaching students to *learn on their own* and to *be responsible*. The kits, in the opinion of the teachers, also provide *situational, real life problems for solution*. Half or
more of the teachers interviewed related the SLK's to these
goals. The SLK's were apparently not conceived merely as alternative, out-of-school devices for communicating regular curriculum content. Rather, by requiring students to work on their
own, the kits become mechanisms for teaching aspects of self-
direction as it has been defined in this research.

The remaining clearly defined pattern in the responses of
the teachers related to the community learning centers. The
centers were seen as especially useful for teaching *openness to
new experiences* and helping students to understand that *learning
is available from different sources*. Exactly half of the
teachers interviewed also cited assignment of non-formal reading
material (general books, magazines, and newspapers) and radio
listening as another means of developing the latter perception.
Teachers suggested that the learning centers also help develop
attitudes and skills that transcend specific subject-matter
content and relate directly to self-direction in learning. Together, the learning centers and SLK's are thus much more than
mere substitutes for formal instruction in the school.

The second group of sixteen teachers, interviewed about
the advantages and disadvantages of the ISOS Program, cited
more disadvantages than advantages from the perspective of the

teachers! In fact, most of the advantages this group mentioned pertained to students rather than to themselves, the former having been summarized in the previous section.

Among the disadvantages of the ISOS Program reported by the teachers, a significant portion reflect the need for administrative support commensurate with the much larger number of students assigned. In this regard, teachers cited additional record-keeping and other paper work associated with the program, plus an increased number of academic duties such as preparation of experiments and additional classroom activities. Problems of logistics loomed large in these responses. Handling twice as many students increases the administrative load associated with teaching, even though the total number of hours in the classroom remains constant for each teacher.

One disadvantage cited by more than one teacher related to student learning. The lag time between the end of lessons during one in-school period and picking up those same lessons two weeks later was judged to be too long. The SLK's may not always be extensions of in-class learning activities, as would presumably be desirable. Without integration of the in- and off-school curricula, retention on the part of students over the two week off-school period is likely to be weaker.

The teachers associated the development of the ability to study and learn independently with the out-of-school portion of the ISOS Program and specifically with the learning kits and community resource centers. Adults in the learning centers, students themselves, carry out teaching activities in significant ways. These findings are quite consistent with those based on the analysis of ISOS curriculum materials.

THE KATALIN VARGA GRAMMAR SCHOOL

Given the emphasis on "learning to learn" in the curriculum of the Katalin Varga School, the task in studying teaching practices and learning processes was to determine how such principles were put to work outside of the *studium generale* course. The latter, after all, is confined to the first year of study. Moreover, the facultative group system and regular classes provided a potential contrast of approach in which stress on self-direction might be much more emphasized in the former than in the latter.

To investigate teaching and learning processes, the
Hungarian team used a variety of methods and sources, including
interviews and questionnaires of students, teachers, parents,
and even former students. To this was added the results of
classroom observations by members of the case study staff.

Learning Processes

Several of the findings reported here are based on information about virtually all the students in the school. In addition, for investigations in which resources did not permit
assessing the entire student body, the Hungarian researchers
selected a target group of 51 students. This sample was representative of the four grade levels as well as of high, average,
and low achieving students.

Student self-descriptions. The target learners were administered several questionnaires requiring self-reports or
ratings on personal characteristics such as approach to study,
life goals, and aspirations. These questions were based on the
eight hypothesized characteristics of the self-directed learner.
Some of the resulting information was simply descriptive of
what the student respondents were like. Aspects which reflect
directly on how students typically approached learning activities will be summarized here.

When asked questions relating to their self-concept as
learners, the students reported positive feelings about their
personal capabilities and their performance in at least some
areas of school activity. When asked about possible dissatisfaction with themselves, most students referred to some aspect
of perseverance, e.g., diligence, persistence, self-discipline,
or attention span. The report made note of the fact that very
few of the target learners thought that they might pursue self-
education more effectively by placing greater emphasis on areas
of personal interest or by adopting new modes of learning.
Rather, working even harder than they were already working was
almost invariably the path to self-improvement.

When asked about their use of resources other than the
standard texts, all but three of the target learners responded
in the affirmative, listing school and town libraries, their
own books and journals, teachers on an individual basis, peers,
and informal sources such as radio and television. Teachers
were explicitly mentioned as counselors or advisors in organizing learning or selecting among alternative sources. In addition, the older learners reported significantly more frequent

use of high level sources such as journals, technical books and manuals, and other systematic reference materials.

An especially interesting questionnaire approach presented seven paragraph length portraits of different philosophical and political orientations to individual life goals. The target learners were asked to rank the seven portraits according to how closely each described their own life goals. The life goals represented were: Stoic, Epicurean, Christian, Socialist, scientific/Promethian, egocentric/individualistic, and opportunistic/pragmatic.

Only the last category was not selected by any of the respondents. Otherwise, there was considerable diversity in the goals selected. The largest number (18) selected the Socialist goal. This particular goal emphasized hard, honest work, communal struggle for a better future, loving others who are deserving and avoidance and firmness with those who are unworthy, and importance of ultimate ends over means. It also stressed the importance of individual happiness if it does not work against the interests of society as a whole.

Almost as many respondents (15) selected the scientific/ Promethian portrait. This goal stressed action and technology in contradiction to an orientation toward feelings and meditation. The exhilaration of successful struggle was emphasized, e.g., "The greatest joy in life is to solve a problem by overcoming difficulties". Risks can and should be taken in order to make discoveries and be remembered by future generations.

Even the Stoic and Epicurean goals were selected by a few students (three and four, respectively). The Christian goal was third, being selected by ten students. (This goal portrait did not mention belief in the deity, but emphasized values, especially relations with other people.)

There are two interesting observations that might be made about these results. First, there is the diversity of response students showed when asked to identify their own life goals. Alternative value systems are represented in the students in the Katalin Varga School, and this to some extent may reflect relative openness of the school's curriculum.

Of greatest interest to a writer from a different society is the ability of the Katalin Varga students to discriminate among concepts with which most secondary students in his own

society would be completely unfamiliar. The Stoic versus
Epicurean distinction would be unknown to the great majority of
U.S. students of similar age and level of schooling. It is
questionable whether most U.S. students would be able to respond meaningfully to this distinction and to others that would
be equally unfamiliar (although the hedonistic flavor of the
Epicurean portrait might draw some responses). That Katalin
Varga students could make such a distinction probably reflects
the classical emphasis in the Hungarian curriculum as well as
an explicit consciousness about the role of the individual in
different types of societies.

Students were interviewed informally about how they ad-
justed their approach to learning when confronted with frustrating situations such as material that is highly complex.
The majority reported various emotional reactions such as anger
or discouragement. A smaller proportion described systematic
problem-solving strategies (rest, change in method, analysis of
errors, etc.). Both of these groups felt free to turn to peers,
teachers, or parents for help. There was a general sense of
individual responsibility for accomplishment supplemented by
informal, co-operative relationships.

The importance of individual responsibility was generally
confirmed in a qualitative analysis of 329 written statements
by students on their approach to study outside of the school.
The great majority of the students beyond the first grade level
had formed more or less stable approaches to learning on their
own, one of which is illustrated in the following excerpt:

> "I always begin with the new material. I then
> continue with my written homework. If I feel
> like it and have enough time, I practise the
> material by solving problems (exercises) or
> reading special (relevant) literature. For
> biology, history, geography, and Hungarian
> literature, I always go through the whole
> chapter or lesson. Then I begin to think by
> developing an outline that will help me recall
> the material. If necessary, after dividing the
> material into parts, I read it through again,
> sometimes twice. While doing so, I use the
> outline."

The excerpt gives the flavor of how a mature student described
his or her own approach to work. The case study report also
incorporated examples of less systematic strategies.

Opinions of senior (4th grade) students. When asked how
they had profited from attendance at the school, virtually all
the 166 students replied in a positive vein. Individual responses after grouping in categories reflecting self-direction
in learning, emphasized self-acceptance and confidence, enhanced
intrinsic motivation, openness to experience, and the ability
to work autonomously.

When asked what aspects of the learning process they would
change or develop, the largest single group of respondents recommended increasing the participation of learners in teaching.
An approximately similar number recommended increasing opportunities to conduct experiments or do other types of research.
Much smaller groups mentioned more specific topics such as en-
larging the library, decreasing class size, etc. The two most
frequent responses thus referred to activities related to self-
direction, such as student responsibility for teaching and
student research.

Anecdotal records. Each of the 52 target learners was
observed by one of the research group in at least three different situations, including regular lessons (accounting for
about half of the total observations), youth organization programs, facultative (optional) lessons, and the *studium generale*
course. In all, some 938 separate observations on the target
learners were recorded. Each of the anecdotal records described the behavior of the learner in terms of his or her activity, verbal reactions, and non-verbal gestures.

All of the behaviors were subjectively classified as appropriate or inappropriate to the situation observed. A total
of 797, or 79 per cent, of the behaviors were in the former
category. The nature of the activities gives an indication of
how students at the Katalin Varga School engage in learning.
Taking *appropriate* activities first and going from most to
least frequent, the content of the students' activities was as
follows:

1. presentation in a formal lesson;

2. paying attention (watching or listening);

3. working or searching for information;

4. inquiring, showing curiosity;

5. discussing some relevant theme with a schoolmate;

6. answering a question or otherwise responding;

7. participating in a debate or discussion;

8. planning; and

9. solving a problem of some type in a self-directed manner.

These activities progressed from quite frequent to infrequent.

The smaller number of activities judged to be inappropriate read like a similar list that might be compiled in virtually any school, probably including the other schools in this research. Again going from most to least frequent, these were:

1. lack of concentration or attention;

2. lack of interest, or indifference;

3. talking with another student about an irrelevant topic;

4. reading inappropriate material; and

5. making a presentation characterized by lack of confidence and uncertainty.

The case study report noted that the three groups of students (academically high, average, and low) differed in relative frequency and type of activities. The patterns were much as one might predict. High academic students commonly showed curiosity or engaged in debate. Low academic students accounted for most of the inappropriate responses.

These data shed significant light on the nature of the learning process. The most common types of activity judged appropriate, such as reciting, attending, or simply doing research work with textual material, were what one would normally observe in the well-organized traditional classroom. Less frequent, but still relatively common, were behaviors associated with participatory modes of learning such as inquiry, discussion, debating, or planning. The facultative groups provided for these types of learning activities. The picture that emerges is of a learning process which incorporated innovative, participatory forms of learning into a context which also made full use of traditional modes of study.

Classroom observations. Eight members of the research team observed three regular lessons each and recorded their impressions on six evaluative dimensions. Each of the latter was defined by a seven point rating scale, briefly named and elaborated as follows:

1. *Original problem-solving* - rarely or never versus frequent.

2. *Learner questions* - learners answer questions versus learners pose questions.

3. *Use of learning resources* - teacher and textbook versus teacher and text plus full range of alternative sources such as journals, films, etc.

4. *Debate in the classroom* - debate or discussion of issues rarely or never occurs versus debate or discussion integral part of lesson.

5. *Use of reference books* - reference books such as encyclopedias, dictionaries, etc. used only incidentally versus reference books integral part of learning process.

6. *Classroom climate* - climate uneasy, hostile, embarassed versus friendly, interested, open.

The classes observed were in nine different subject fields scattered over the four grade levels. Since the total number of classes observed was only 24, it was not possible to observe each subject at all four grade levels. However, there was no systematic bias favoring one grade level. Mathematics classes were observed most frequently (six) and philosophy least (one).

The results showed a significant degree of variation among the six rating scales. The highest average rating (5.3 on the 7 point scale) went to 6., *classroom climate*, revealing a generally friendly, positive atmosphere in the classroom. All of the ratings on this dimension were at scale point 4 and above. Second and third were 1., *problem-solving* (4.7), and 3., *learning resources* (4.5). The other three dimensions were all rated below the mid-point of the scale. These included, 2., *learner questions* (3.5), 5., *reference books* (3.45), and 4., *debate* (2.9).

The above are average ratings, and even the three dimensions with low averaged ratings received ratings at the high end of the scale for at least a few lessons. In other words, there was considerable diversity on all scales except for *classroom climate*, rated highest. These results were interpreted in the case study report in terms of relationships among the dimensions. The friendly, democratic classroom atmosphere found to be typical was conducive to learning through independent problem-

solving. To learn in this way, a variety of resources need to
be available.

   On the less favorable side, the perceptions of teachers
of limitations in time available for instruction may have contributed to the relatively low ranking for questioning by
learners. (However, students did have opportunities to ask
teachers questions outside of the classroom.) A shortage of
general reference books prevented their full integration into
the instructional process. Most important, teachers (as independently confirmed in the next section on teaching processes)
did not place great value in the benefits to be gained through
debate and confrontation of ideas.

   Problem solving task. A large number of students were
asked to describe the approach they would take solving one or
more problems selected from a set of open-ended problems in
various subject matter areas. The problems were formulated so
as to allow for creative or original approaches to each task,
and altogether 470 responses were collected. The solution itself was not required, only a description of how the student
would go about finding it. The objective was to assess the
ways in which students approached open-ended problems. Examples of problems for history and physics were:

   "Describe the primitive communal society on the
   basis of the results of excavations in the county
   of Szolnok."

   "There is a condition of weightlessness in a space-
   ship moving through space. We would like to measure
   the mass of an object. The instruments available
   are as follows: a spring dynamometer, a chrono-
   meter, and a one meter length of string. Explain
   in detail the method of measurement. Several
   solutions are possible, but no instruments other
   than the above can be used."

   A great variety of solution strategies were proposed to
the fourteen problem situations. Many of these were specific
to certain types of problems, e.g., using a museum for the ar-
chaeological question above. The case study report noted that
57 per cent of the respondents would go to subject matter
teachers as one step in solving the problem. This was taken as
evidence for an open and facilitating relationship of teachers
with students. But it was also interpreted as a sign of insufficient self-reliance and independence, especially since the

proportion of students who would go to the teacher for advice
was as high in the upper grades as in the lower.

Parent meeting. Parents of third year students were in-
vited to a meeting to discuss how their children approached
learning. This meeting generated informal information mainly
confirming findings from other sources. For example, virtually
all of the parents reported that their children had developed
a regular system of study, although individuals differed widely.
(A common habit of listening to background music while studying
was reported in what must be a cultural universal for adolescents.) Parents also noted that their children used a wide
variety of learning materials. Books were described as an important item among the students' personal possessions according
to parents;   teachers were highly appreciative of knowledge or
experience gained from sources other than the regular textbooks.

When asked how the family helped the students learn, there
was consensus that the curriculum had changed so much since the
parents were in school that it was often difficult for them to
be of assistance, except in instances where the subject matter
coincided with their own work. This was reported to be especially the case in mathematics (another common finding). It
was agreed that the most effective action that parents could
take would be to establish conditions that were conducive to
learning, thus indirectly influencing achievement.

Teaching Practices
The role of teachers in the learning process was assessed
by several means. Teachers were observed during lessons;   they
described themselves in various ways, and were also described
by current students of the school. Finally, former students
contributed retrospective evaluations.

Characteristics of teachers. Students (n = 665) completed
a personality rating instrument on their form masters and one
other teacher. The instrument used was based on a typology developed originally by Leary, which classifies the person rated
into one of six categories. In terms of the teacher role,
three of the categories were judged to be positive and the
other three negative.

Tabulation of the results revealed that the form-master
teachers were classified in one of the three positive categories
by about 60 per cent of the students. The category most frequently used (about 35 per cent) described an individual who is

powerful and dominant in interpersonal relationships, but who
is also constructive, systematic, and competent. About one
fifth of the students saw the form master as a different positive type - responsible, facilitating, sympathetic and co-
operative. The most frequently used negative category (selected by a little over 30 per cent of the students) described the
form master as overly concerned with status and manifesting an
attitude of personal superiority. It was noted in the interpretation of the latter finding that, by nature of their position, form masters must apply sanctions more frequently than do
regular teachers.

In a second approach, teachers were asked briefly to characterize each of the fifty-one learners, giving special attention to the development of attitudes and capabilities relating
to self-direction. It was assumed that this open-ended cat-
egorizing task would reveal the teachers' own evaluative categories as applied to students. In turn, it was reasoned that
what a teacher judges to be important in the behavior of students not only establishes the criteria that the latter must
meet to gain recognition, but also reveals a good deal about
the teacher's own standards of self-evaluation.

The teachers' characterizations of each of the target
learners were based on observations in three situations: regular
lessons, working in the library, and debate or discussion activity. All teachers' characterizations were classified as either
positive or negative.

A significant majority (65 per cent) of the characterizations were positive. The most commonly applied characteristics
were capacity, interest, diligence, and ambition. Three of
these characteristics (with "capacity" being in somewhat un-
certain status) clearly relate to self-direction in learning.
However, terms such as "independence" and "flexibility" were
not used to a significant degree by the teachers. Rather,
their evaluative categories emphasized characteristics associated with high achievement.

The teachers were asked in a moderately structured interview to describe their own strategies for the development of
self-direction in students. They were also asked about factors
that facilitated or inhibited their efforts in this regard.
If the initial responses were incomplete, follow-up questions
about specific topics such as "encouraging choice" or "self-
direction" were added to the interview.

All of the teachers interviewed were convinced that they could have a significant impact on the development and reinforcement of self-direction in their students. They cited several aspects of the school as facilitating appropriate roles, including its democratic atmosphere, receptivity to novelty, and the facultative system, as well as the settled family backgrounds which supported achievement by the students.

Negative influences were attributed to the students themselves, e.g., excessive concern with marks and unawareness of potential for the co-operative relationship between teacher and student, or to work load factors such as class size and the number of lessons for which the teacher is responsible each week.

"Mainly the facultative lessons provide an opportunity to arouse the learners' interests and encourage their self-directed learning. Here there are fewer constraints than in regular lessons in which we are tied to obligatory material, and in which it is not possible to linger over an interesting subject."

The attitudes and opinions of the teachers about specific ways of encouraging self-direction acknowledged both possibilities and limitations.

a. *Flexibility in time, method or content* was identified by the teachers with opportunities given to students to deliver short lectures, to dramatize readings of a descriptive type, or to contrast original and adapted texts. Outside, non-formal learning activities were considered important. These included going to the theater, museums, and using communication media. The specificity of the curriculum, the stress on standard textbooks, and the importance of the university entrance examination were named as factors which inhibited flexibility. The latter were influences beyond the control of the school.

b. *Encouragement of choice* was explored in the previous chapter. The teachers saw student choice as mainly expressed through reports, learning supplementary or voluntary material, the facultative lessons, and the preparation of themes, essays, and exercises for competitions. For example, one teacher cited the regular practice in English language classes of having each learner organize one of the lessons according to an individualized theme which often would involve singing and music, situational games, or giving accounts of personal experiences in English.

c. *Teaching as a facilitative activity* was recognized by the teachers as a strategy, although there were at least some who felt their primary role to be directive in nature. Others felt that time limitations made it difficult to use strategies such as discovery learning. There appeared to be doubts among several teachers about adopting the role of organizer or facilitator in view of constraints and possibly because of reluctance to give up the familiar directive role.

d. *Self-evaluation* by learners was looked on in diverse ways by the teachers. A substantial proportion suggested that third and fourth year students have absorbed standards sufficiently to be able to evaluate themselves effectively. One teacher, who appeared to provide an alternative model, regularly had students themselves evaluate their peer group. Students were also asked, "What would you do differently if you were the teacher?"

e. *Relationships between teacher and students* were described by the teachers as democratic, although this impression might not always be shared by the students. A common theme was that the relationship between teachers and students should be based on the former's competence and humane characteristics, including respect for the self-concept of the student.

f. *Reinforcing curiosity* on the part of the learners was associated by the teachers with a wide variety of experiences mainly *external* to the regular classroom. However, teachers did see relating their own experiences as important in stimulating curiosity (e.g., "personalizing" the material) and making it clear that questions by the student are appreciated or valued. Relationships between teachers and students outside of the classroom were also thought to be important.

g. *Knowledge obtained outside of the school,* as might be expected from the variety of student activities already reported, was valued by all teachers. However, the teachers could be separated into two groups. The first were willing to make use of anything learned outside of the school situation if such learning occurred *spontaneously*. The second group planned learning activities *deliberately* to include a role for outside learning. One teacher articulated what must be an ideal attitude in the context of this book.

"I had a student in one of my classes who was very much interested in number theory. First, I helped

solve the problems. Then, I gave him technical
literature to read, and we talked over some of
it. At the end, I could no longer help him because he knew more on this theme than I did.
But this did not ruin my reputation."

In general, the studies just described portray a teaching
staff which has been sensitized to the possibilities for the
development of self-direction in a flexible school curriculum
that is coordinated with learning resources outside of the
school. But this staff also is responsible for delivering a
rigorously academic curriculum in an atmosphere of high expectation about student performance. A didactic, expository teaching
style is therefore thought by most teachers to be necessary in
the regular classroom because of limitations in time. In contrast, the small facultative groups formed for the study of
optional subjects allow a different style of teaching in which
conditions presumably facilitating self-direction could be maintained more readily.

Teaching styles. More direct information on how teachers
at the Katalin Varga School engaged the act of teaching was
derived from interviews of the targeted learners, observations
of the teachers in the classroom, and from reports by former
students who completed their work at the school during the 1975-
1978 period. The latter information was obtained by means of a
mailed questionnaire.

The interviews of targeted learners took the form of a
conversation which began with a question on how the approaches
to teaching used by the teachers might contribute to the encouragement of self-direction in students. Depending on the
student's first answer, this question was followed by a list of
seventeen specific questions on topics such as the types of
problem teachers assign, the choices left to students, the use
of cooperative group work, and the degree of tolerance by
teachers for complex or difficult questions from students.

Virtually all the interviewed students described one or
more ways in which their teachers attempted to develop self-
direction. Of these, the largest single group (22 students)
cited the opportunity to present reports and short lectures as
the most facilitating. Here the opinions of students appeared
to coincide fairly closely with those of teachers. Other teaching practices the students thought relevant to self-direction
included tasks involving research such as library work (13),

efforts to enhance the interests of students (12), the facultative groups for optional subjects (10), and a variety of specific practices involving independent work on the part of students such as doing experiments, observing and data-collecting activities, and other individualized activities.

It thus appears that students did not identify efforts to encourage self-direction with teaching style *per se*, but rather with the extent to which teachers allocated responsibility to individual students for organizing and carrying through learning activities. One exception to this generalization might be efforts by teachers to enhance student interest.

Responses to some of the specific questions reflected more directly on how teachers engaged in the teaching process. For example, there was substantial agreement (41) among the 51 targeted students that teachers appreciated *difficult or complex questions* from students as evidence of thought and intelligence. While students agreed that the ability to answer a question of this type gained respect and prestige for the teacher, they also felt that a frank admission of inability to answer a specific question would not damage a teacher's reputation. This was not true for the teacher who attempted to avoid a difficult question, however.

When asked about the extent to which teachers allowed or promoted *discussion and debate* in the classroom, an almost equal majority of the students interviewed (41) responded that this did occur. However, the students associated this type of participation with social science subject fields such as Marxist philosophy, literature, and history, and not with the natural sciences. The weekly form master lessons were also described as encouraging discussion by students. It was qualitatively apparent in the interviews that students enjoyed debate and argument and looked with something less than favor on a few teachers who adhered too strictly (in the students' view) to conventional teaching styles.

When asked if they had been encouraged to deal with topics through *systematic or scientific research* (clarify goals, collect and classify information, etc.), most students (39) replied in the affirmative. For example, one student describing work on a competition wrote the following:

"Last year, I wrote a competition essay in history ...
As we had not dealt with the era in regular lessons,

I first reviewed relevant material in the 3rd
year textbook. Then I read portions of several
technical books that dealt with the era. After
this, I searched through a newspaper originating
at the beginning of this century, writing down
notes about pertinent pieces of information on
slips (of paper). Next, I arranged the slips
in categories and wrote the competition essay."

The above is representative of the kinds of responses
made by students. At the Katalin Varga School, self-direction
in learning is closely identified with the activities of formal
scholarship. However, the school is unconventional (in comparison to the traditional, academic secondary school) in the
extent to which students make use of resources and learning
contexts outside, as various sections of this report make clear.

The students were also asked whether or not the teachers
advised them on *how to learn*. Here the responses were somewhat
mixed, with most of the students (33) indicating that advice on
how to learn was given some of the time, and a smaller number
(13) reporting that this kind of help was provided very frequently. According to students, guidance was provided mainly
in certain subjects, in this case literature, physics, mathematics, and foreign languages, as well as in form master lessons.

Finally, one of the specific questions dealt with the
extent to which teachers engaged in *self-evaluation* in the
presence of students or described as a possible model their own
acquisition of a skill or competency. Here the majority of
students responded only "occasionally". It was apparent that
students greatly appreciated this type of behavior on the part
of teachers. Those teachers who did describe their own learning experiences, generally referred to study at the university,
a topic considered quite useful by the students interviewed.
Again, the strongly academic context of the school is readily
apparent.

In an effort to obtain an independent look at teachers in
the regular classroom, a total of fifty-one lessons given by
eighteen teachers were observed. Lessons were in thirteen different subjects, with each observation lasting approximately
an hour. Observers rated each lesson on six rating scales:

   1. *Originality*, or the extent to which the teacher en-
      couraged original or inventive approaches by students
      in solving problems and performing learning tasks.

2. *Questioning*, or the extent to which the teacher allowed, encouraged, and attended to questions put by students.

3. *Learning sources*, or the extent to which the lesson used learning resources other than standard texts and incorporated material from outside of the classroom.

4. *Debate*, or the extent to which the lesson was elaborated by means of debate and discussion of issues.

5. *References*, or the degree to which reference books were incorporated as an integral part of the teaching/learning process.

6. *Self-evaluation*, or the degree to which teachers drew the student into the evaluation of his or her work with the aim of maximizing intrinsic motivation.

In order to help the two observers define the characteristics in the same way, each of the seven-point rating scales was elaborated by descriptive statements associated with the lowest (1), middle (4), and highest (7) rating. For example, the *self-evaluation* scale was elaborated by the following definitions:

(1) The teacher informs the learner what mark will be awarded a given level of achievement.

(4) The teacher gives reasons for the mark, indicating what the learner must do to obtain it.

(7) The teacher involves the learner in the evaluation in order to achieve a maximum degree of intrinsic motivation.

Analysis of the classroom observations revealed a marked split in the ratings. Three of the scales averaged above the midpoint (mean ratings in parantheses): *Learning sources* (4.9), *Self-evaluation* (4.7), and *Originality* (4.6). Teachers thus were observed to encourage the use of a variety of learning resources beyond regular texts (almost 50 per cent of the ratings being in the two highest categories), drew the learners into the evaluation process, and encouraged originality and inventiveness in problem solving and other types of learning.

OSTE-F*

In contrast, the other three scales received relatively low average ratings. Lowest of all was *Debate* (1.9), fully confirming reports by the students that this approach to learning was mainly confined to the facultative groups. This didactic emphasis was also consistent with the relatively low average rating (2.5) given to *Questioning*. The other low rating was for *References* (2.4). In contrast to the relatively high rating for use of a variety of learning resources, the use of standard reference texts appears to have been somewhat less than optimal. However, there was a shortage of standard reference works at the school, accounting at least in part for this negative finding.

In an effort to assess the retrospective opinions of graduates of the school, 285 questionnaires were mailed to 1975-1978 graduates. About 40 per cent of the questionnaires were completed and returned. The questions were both multiple choice and open-ended and assessed the role of the school in developing attitudes and competencies associated with self-direction. The three most pertinent questions will be dealt with here.

The first of the three questions inquired as to how much the respondents attributed their current level of self-directedness to the Katalin Varga School. About 60 per cent of those responding gave the school full credit in this regard, with another 39 per cent giving the school at least partial credit.

A second question dealt with the extent to which the school had maintained an atmosphere which stimulated and supported originality, creativity, and self-reliance in thought. Here a larger proportion (about 70 per cent) regarded the school favorably, with another 29 per cent finding the school at least occasionally stimulating in this regard.

Finally, when asked about the extent to which teaching practices at the school aroused curiosity, stimulated learners to think, and placed value on knowledge and experience gained outside of the school, an almost identical proportion of respondents (about 69 per cent) replied affirmatively. Another 31 per cent saw the school as occasionally stimulating curiosity.

The evaluations of graduates of the school were thus strongly on the positive side, although a bias of an undetermined nature may have been induced by those who did not return the questionnaires. But it can at least be said that a significant proportion of the former students of the Katalin Varga

Grammar School attribute their ability to be self-directing to
the experiences they had at the school.

THE BIELEFELDER OBERSTUFEN-KOLLEG

In the areas of teaching and learning, the underlying integration theme at the Oberstufen-Kolleg can be summed up in
the concept of participation. The basic responsibilities of
participants in any school are mainly shared by teachers and
students at the OSK, rather than allocated differentially.
This will be particularly apparent in the ways in which planning,
teaching, and evaluation are carried out. In traditional
schools these realms of activity are reserved for teachers and
administrators. At the OSK they are shared with students.

Learning Processes
Because of the strong emphasis on participation through
shared responsibility, the activities of both teachers and
students at the OSK are readily described in terms of the various functions each may be called upon to fulfill. The functions
described for students are arbitrarily limited in this chapter
to activities which relate directly to "content" leaning. Administrative and organizational activities were discussed in
Chapter 5.

Instructional planning. Depending on the type of course
they were taking, students were observed to participate in instructional planning activities as members of

1. *planning groups* dealing with an entire course;

2. *adjunct groups* bringing special topics into an
   on-going course; and

3. *a class* participating in the regular initial
   planning phase at the beginning of a course.

Planning groups were observed to form spontaneously
through student initiative or at the formal instigation of a
teacher. Such groups usually do most of their work before the
course begins and may or may not include the teacher as a member. As a form of participation, planning groups were usually
associated with Complementary courses selected by students in
conjunction with their main program of study and with the Project courses occupying the last three weeks of each semester.

Students may receive course credit for participating in

adjunct groups formed around topical themes under the overall plan for a course. Adjunct groups are a mechanism for bringing additional information, ideas, or materials into a course and, like planning groups, may or may not include teachers as participants. This type of group is likely to be associated with Optional or Complementary courses.

There is a *planning phase* of Complementary courses in which all students participate. This period may last from a single day to up to three weeks. A day of planning is also reserved for Project courses. Here students generally participate as members of a "committee of the whole".

Obviously, planning implies decision-making, the subject of Chapter 5. An example of this sort of decision-making at the beginning of a Complementary mathematics course was given in that chapter. This planning process during regular class meetings was bound to result in decisions about learning goals, dates of small group meetings, a problem to be solved and a means for disseminating the findings to the student body as a whole.

Individual study. When students were questioned about experiences at the OSK that were especially important, they frequently referred to autonomous activities such as searching for materials or resources, working outside of the school, using school resources such as the library, or organizing some activity. Autonomous individual study was commonly observed at the OSK. Even time ostensibly assigned to small group work was often used for individual study. However, some types of courses were more conducive to individual modes of learning. The majority of students interviewed reported that there was little or no time available for individual study during the Intensive courses at the beginning of each semester.

Small group work. The case study found that the most frequent learning mode at the OSK involved participation in small groups of between three and five members without supervision by a teacher. Interestingly, these groups in a number of cases were composed of a more or less fixed set of members who had become accustomed to working together. Aware of this tendency for some students to coalesce in relatively long-term associations, the OSK allows students to apply formally for courses as members of groups rather than individuals.

The tendency for students to form more or less permanent

groups is probably important. It suggests a cooperative rather
than a competitive evaluation context. Permitting working
groups of more or less like-minded individuals to form allows
cohesive social forces to contribute to the learning process.
This cohesiveness may often be frustrated in the typical school
environment. This topic warrants further study, however. The
case study was able to identify the existence of long-term
working groups, but did not have the time and resources to go
into the dynamics of such groups in detail.

The small working group is of paramount importance as a
mode of participation at the OSK. Its common use as a means
for organizing people in the learning process illustrated a
major qualitative finding of the case study: students showed
relatively little rivalry or competitiveness as compared to
what was assumed to be the case for regular schools in the
Federal Republic. Groups formed spontaneously according to
the perceived mutual benefit of the members. Such groups often
divided up necessary work or discussed issues or problems that
remained unresolved after the lessons. This atmosphere of co-
operation was considered to be a direct result of the fact that
students are not graded on the basis of competitive or any
other kind of examinations at the OSK.

Evaluation. Students participate in the process of evaluation by contributing assessments of their own performance in
each course. Course grades are "pass" or "fail", in contrast
to the differentiated marking systems used in other schools in
the Federal Republic. Passing a course usually requires sub-
mitting written and oral work or, depending on the nature of
the course, some kind of project involving a tangible product,
experiment, or demonstration.

It is inappropriate to generalize about the precise criteria required for passing a course. Such criteria are in
large part determined by specific course goals. Students com-
pile what is termed a "record of achievement" for a course
which consists of passes on two oral and two written criteria,
of which not more than two may be based on work completed by a
group. A list of possible accomplishments for an acceptable
record of achievement is made available at the beginning of
such a course.

When the student has compiled a sufficient number of
courses, normally over a period of four years, he or she may
sit the final examination on which entry to the university is

based. The examination is an externally mandated certification requirement that is different in form from evaluation experienced by the OSK student during his or her four years at the College. The status of this examination was the subject of considerable controversy within the OSK and had not assumed final form at the time the case study report was being written.

Students regularly engage in self-assessment by completing a rating scale on their own performance in each course. Completed rating scales are sent for summary purposes to the RDP group dealing with evaluation. Results were regularly made available to all participants in the school for self-study purposes.

Students also evaluate courses on a regular basis, although the form of this activity varied at the time of the case study. There is group discussion of project results, for example, as well as full class discussion of sub-group efforts in seminar courses. At the time of the case study, a formal proposal had been submitted by the RDP group on evaluation for a *course documentation* procedure which would include evaluations from each student of

1. the effectiveness of the teacher;

2. the student's own activities;

3. the activities of other members of the class;

4. the usefulness of the course content;

5. the conditions under which coursework was completed; and

6. the relation of what was learned to what was planned or intended.

Students would also contribute suggestions for improvement of the course.

The critical importance of evaluation in establishing the climate in which learning takes place is fully recognized at the OSK. Students are involved in the evaluation of their own work and that of other students as well as of the courses themselves.

Teaching Practices

Harder (1978) points out that the teacher at the OSK really has three interacting roles. He or she is first of all

a *teacher* with responsibility for the various types of courses
that make up the OSK curriculum. In addition, the teacher must
also be a *researcher* who is responsible for making a contribution to education through his or her work in curriculum development. Finally, the teacher is an *administrator* as a member of
one or more internal administrative committees of the College.
This last section deals with the role of teacher, or, more ac-
curately, with three specific roles within that more general
classification.

   Advising. At the end of the first or orientation semester, each student selects a teacher who will serve as his or
her advisor, normally for the remainder of that student's stay
at the OSK. Each teacher is thus responsible for ten to fifteen
students. The latter may consult with their advisor at any
time during the year, but there is at least one required intensive conference annually between the teacher and each individual advisee. The advisor role may involve personal as well
as academic advice, and the teachers act as personal counselors
for many students. This function is especially important during
the first semester, but the teacher may at any time discuss personal or financial problems the student might have, or even
occasionally act as mediator where disagreement has arisen between the student and another teacher.

   Instructing. The role of instructor at the OSK is carried
out in a variety of ways, including, but certainly not limited
to, formal didactive activities such as lecturing. The teacher
often organizes planning activities and elicits suggestions
before the course begins. During the course, teachers often
function more as resource persons than as instructors. Teachers
frequently give individual academic assistance and make themselves available outside the regular lessons. During meetings
of the full course, teachers often serve more as moderators or
chairpersons because of the extensive use of group reporting
on projects or other activities.

   There is a strong emphasis on maintaining egalitarian interpersonal relationships at the OSK. The most striking expression of this climate of equality is evidenced in the relationships between teachers and students. For example, students
address teachers with the familiar personal pronoun, "du", a
liberty that would be inconceivable in typical German schools.
Historically, teachers have been authorities in the fullest
sense and, as such, invariably merit formal address. However,
informal interviews of students conducted in the case study

suggested that students perceived individual teachers differently. A sizeable minority of teachers were described by the
students interviewed as "equal partners". The rest (still a
majority) were perceived as acting in ways which incorporated
one or more of the traditional prerogatives of the teacher as
an authority.

When interviewed on the question of encouraging self-
direction in students, the majority of teachers at the OSK saw
themselves as active agents. Relatively few believed that the
teacher ought to wait passively for such behavior to emerge in
students, but rather should structure questions and situations
so that self-direction would be deliberately enhanced. Capitalizing on the interests of students was held to be particularly
effective.

There was agreement that instances of self-directed learning behavior on the part of students were primarily restricted
to the Complementary and Project courses. Intensive courses,
emphasizing the development of required skills and competencies
and Optional courses oriented to the development of subject
matter knowledge in the student's major field, were considered
less likely contexts for the manifestation of self-direction.

In general, case study observations of course meetings at
the College and during a two week field trip with one of the
classes, confirmed the variegated role of the teacher as instructor, the informality of relationships between teachers and
students, and the freedom that was felt by students to question,
to criticize, and to make and carry out suggestions about learning activities.

Evaluating. In an institution in which relationships between teachers and students based on authority are held to be
undesirable, the teacher's role as evaluator of student performance poses a genuinely ticklish problem. Evaluation, for obvious reasons, tends to imply authority of one individual over
another. Those with the authority to evaluate must be more
knowledgeable and more powerful. This is true at the OSK as it
is elsewhere. Teachers are more knowledgeable in the subject
they teach than are students. Teachers also assign final
grades. These realities persist even in the democratic atmosphere of the College.

One tactic extensively used at the OSK to deal with the
incongruity just noted has been to distribute the responsibility

for evaluation and to render the process more informal when
possible. Projects, whether group or individual, lend themselves to presentation in a group setting and stimulate discussion. With students participating in the evaluation in this
way, the role of teachers becomes more one of organizing the
process and recording the result. However, individual products
such as essays were much more likely to be graded by the teacher,
the case study noted. Such pieces of work do not lend themselves so readily to group evaluation.

The case study found students to be highly sensitive to
the subject of examinations. The latter are not part of the
evaluation process at the OSK, except for the examinations which
are taken at the end of the students' program in preparation for
admission to the university at an advanced level. Some students
were reported to be concerned about situations having "the character of examinations". The basis of such reports was unclear,
as at no time during the observations conducted during the case
case study were assessment procedures similar to an examination
observed. This is in sharp contrast to regular schools in the
Federal Republic at which examinations are a daily occurrence.

At the time of the case study, the role of the teacher as
evaluator remained a significant topic of discussion and study
within the OSK. There is no question that the written goals
of the College and the values of the great majority of its
participants emphasize the development of self-evaluation (as
an aspect of self-direction) in students. The teacher as an
arbitrary, extrinsic source of evaluation is perceived as a
negative influence in the development of this type of self-
responsibility. While the examination as the prime representative of traditional evaluation has been avoided in favor of
modes of evaluation which diffuse responsibility among the
students, the teacher must still function as the sole evaluator
at times. The teacher also bears the responsibility for assessing whether or not the students have passed a course. Development of this aspect of the teacher's role is undoubtedly one
of the most difficult, yet at the same time most intriguing,
facets of the work of the OSK.

SUMMARY

At each of the four schools teaching and learning processes reflected underlying themes identified in the analysis
of curricula in Chapter 6. At the Community School, the in-

dividualization theme was documented by classroom observations, which revealed didactic teaching to the whole classroom to be relatively infrequent compared to small group and individual work by students. The regular use of written-response materials and encouragement given to working in groups facilitated this individualized approach.

Teachers were found to favor and promote informal relationships with their students. This led observers to describe the classroom atmosphere as so relaxed that students often had to exercise self-discipline to avoid being distracted. Observations revealed that, during periods devoted to learning and instruction, teachers were in effect "out of contact" with any given individual student about half of the time. At these times, students were either working without adult supervision or not working at all. Conditions promoting individualized learning are thus the key to the development of self-direction at the Community School.

In the ISOS Program at Arellano High School, the independent learning theme was confirmed in the classroom as well as in the off-school program. Students were observed to be responsible for planning their own learning schedules and for choosing the time and place to work, especially whether to complete work at home or in the school. There was also a climate which promoted self-evaluation. This was accomplished through teacher-constructed tests, including those incorporated in the learning materials themselves. Both teachers and students expressed the conviction that these conditions elicited self-directed learning from some students, not from others. This point will be taken up in the concluding chapter.

Teachers acted as facilitators and encouraged choice on the part of students. Other adults in the learning centers, as well as students themselves, also functioned in the teaching role. Teachers and students alike confirmed that the self-learning kits were the primary means for encouraging independent learning by ISOS students. In using the kits, students had to choose the work without the reinforcement that a teacher provides in the regular school situation.

At the Katalin Varga Grammar School, students attributed successful achievement to their own ability to persevere. The facultative groups, as anticipated in the chapter on curriculum, were the major tactic for implementing the basic theme of "learning to learn". In fact, students wanted greater opportunity to

engage in teaching and research projects. There was more than
a hint of contrast between modes of learning in the facultative
groups as against the regular classroom.

Observations revealed the climate of regular classrooms
to be friendly and open. Independent problem-solving was encouraged. However, there is no doubt that teachers stress academic values. Their descriptions of students emphasized characteristics such as capacity and diligence rather than self-
direction *per se*. Teachers did relate self-direction to the
facultative system, but also to the democratic atmosphere of
the school and its acceptance of novelty as important factors.
They encouraged the use of learning resources other than the
traditional, including those available in the surrounding community. Finally, students believed that individual willingness
on the part of teachers to allocate responsibility for organizing and carrying out learning to the student, was the most
critical single factor in the encouragement of self-direction.

The theme of integration was concretely expressed at the
Oberstufen-Kolleg in the form of participation by students in
all major functions relating to teaching and learning. Students
helped to plan courses more or less as equals of the teacher.
They developed and presented special topics through adjunct
groups and engaged in formal learning through individual or co-
operative work in spontaneously formed working groups. Likewise, they engaged in evaluation of their own and others' work.
The latter was found to be facilitated by the common use of
projects, another reflection of the integration theme, or by
other modes of achievement that lent themselves to public presentation. Examinations as a means of evaluation, were not used
at all in the schools. Students were firm in their opposition
to this traditional means of evaluation associating it with un-
healthy competition in the learning environment.

Teachers at the OSK functioned predominantly as advisors,
planners, and resource persons. The traditional didactic role
was rarely observed. Relationships between teachers and students were strikingly egalitarian. Only with individual work
such as essays did teachers often adopt the role of evaluation
authority. So, participation of students in planning, teaching
and evaluation was found to be the consistent means by which
the integration theme was brought into operation at the OSK.

Chapter 8

Comparisons Between High and Low Self-directed Learners

THRUST OF THE STUDIES

The last three chapters have concentrated first on the nature of the institutions, and on the students secondarily. The behavior of the latter has been of interest primarily as an indicator of the effect of the learning context provided by the institutions. Two of the case studies reversed this emphasis in part of their research to focus on personal characteristics of learners identified as high or low in self-direction. The primary intent in both cases was to determine the degree to which the hypothesized characteristics of self-directed learners, outlined in Chapter 2, actually described the learners so identified in the schools being studied.

Two in-depth studies of small groups of learners who had been identified by their teachers as either high or low in self-direction were conducted by the Philippine and U.S. teams. The studies were designed and conducted independently, though both began with characteristics of self-direction in learning discussed in Chapter 2. Both chose to do these intensive studies using a variety of approaches to measurement. Both also identified the high and low groups by means of teacher nominations.

While there is reason to be concerned that teachers might bring biases to the task of identifying high and low self-directed learners, alternative means of selection were not feasible in either study. There is no valid, objective test for identifying self-direction that makes it possible to avoid dependence on the subjective views of teachers, parents, or others who have had the opportunity to observe children closely. On the other hand, teachers, more than any other group, have the opportunity to observe the behavior of their students in

situations involving formal learning. As a group, their experience is the most relevant.

The two intensive studies of self-directed learners are
thus properly characterized as research on learners whom
teachers have identified as self-directed. Both of the studies
deal with the degree to which learners so selected actually
manifest the behavior and personal characteristics that earlier
were identified with self-direction in learning.

Do learners, nominated by teachers as high in self-direction, exhibit intrinsically motivated or self-evaluative behaviors more often than do learners who are identified as low in
self-direction? Or are such learners more likely to display
behaviors associated with tractability, diligence, and high
academic ability - the kinds of traits teachers are generally
thought to value most in their students? While it will be apparent that the two investigations differed substantially in
their approach to assessment, they share a common agenda of
inquiry in the questions just cited.

IDENTIFICATION OF HIGH AND LOW SELF-DIRECTED LEARNERS

The Community School Study
The U.S. research team decided that three of the seven
characteristics of self-directed learners could not be appropriately assessed within the scope of their study. The four
characteristics selected for assessment were judged to be those
most likely to be manifested in the environment of the Community
School. Thus, they believed that *planfulness* and *intrinsic motivation* were potentially observable because learners were given
opportunity to work without direct adult supervision and were
not systematically rewarded for task-oriented behavior. Likewise, *internalized evaluation* might be observed since the students were given a variety of means for monitoring and assessing
their own work. Finally, since learning activities changed
fairly frequently in Community School classrooms, it was judged
that *flexibility* might be apparent in the behavior of learners
selected for observation.

Definitions of the four characteristics were developed
for teachers to use in nominating high and low self-directed
learners at each grade level. The definitions included a description of the characteristics plus several examples of specific behaviors that learners high on the trait would manifest

in the classroom. The definition for Intrinsic Motivation is reproduced below as an example.

Intrinsic Motivation
    The learner undertakes and persists in a
    learning activity in the absence of external
    rewards or sanctions. His/her persistence is
    related more to the nature of the learning
    activity itself than to extrinsic rewards.

Examples
    A learner demonstrating the characteristic of
    Intrinsic Motivation would probably:
    1. frequently do more than what is assigned;
    2. continue working without supervision; and
    3. be able to continue working until assign-
        ment completion, even with interruptions.

Each teacher was asked to nominate from his or her classroom the four children who were highest on the four traits and
the four who were the lowest. The teachers were instructed to
think of the four self-directed learner characteristics as behaviors which children display to varying degrees in the daily
life of the classroom. They were asked to try to separate
their estimates of a child's self-directedness from their impressions of his or her academic achievements. For each nomination the teachers were asked to specify a situation which
exemplified the way in which the child manifested each characteristic.

The above procedure yielded twenty-four target learners
across the six grade levels who were rated as highly self-
directed and twenty-four who were rated as particularly low.
From these two groups the research team selected twelve learners
in each category by eliminating students who had been interviewed in the exploratory phase of the study and by choosing
equal numbers of each sex.

The Arellano High School Study
        The selection procedure used in the Philippine study to
identify high and low self-directed learners was similar to the
one just described. However, all seven of the characteristics
of the self-directed learner were judged to be open to assessment in this secondary school population. Teachers were given
a nomination form listing descriptions of the characteristics
and instructed to nominate between three and five students

"... in your ISOS classes who exhibit many of these characteristics to a high degree. Then identify three to five students
who *do not* exhibit these characteristics".

Since ISOS students attended classes taught by different
teachers, it was expected that students who were either very
high or very low in self-direction would receive multiple nominations. This transpired to be the case. High and low self-
directed learner groups were formed by selecting students who
received the most nominations from teachers. Fifteen high and
twelve low self-directed learners were identified by this process.

FINDINGS: THE COMMUNITY SCHOOL STUDY

It will be recalled form the previous chapter that information on the twelve high and twelve low self-directed learners
nominated (high and low SDL's), was obtained from four sources:
classroom observations, teachers' ratings, parents' ratings,
and self-reports by learners. This will be dealt with in order.
In addition, material from observer summaries of their overall
impressions of one high and one low SDL at the third and sixth
grade levels will be included for purposes of illustration.

Classroom Observations
During each observation the observers rated the student
for *task involvement, planfulness,* and *adjustment to change*
(flexibility). The latter was broken down into ratings of
planned and *unplanned* change. The frequency of four types of
behavior representative of *self-evaluation* were also recorded
(e.g., the number of times the learner "sought feedback on performance, etc."). Unfortunately, self-evaluative behaviors occurred with such low frequency in the approximately five minutes devoted to each observation that the data on this dimension
of self-direction could not be used.

Average scores (on a three point rating scale) for high
and low SDL's in all six grade levels are shown in Figure 8.1
(see next page). The picture here is somewhat mixed. Students
nominated as high SDL's by teachers were rated by the observers
somewhat higher in task involvement and considerably higher in
adjustment to planned change. On the other hand, students nominated as low in SDL were rated somewhat better than those nominated as high, in their adjustment to unplanned change and in

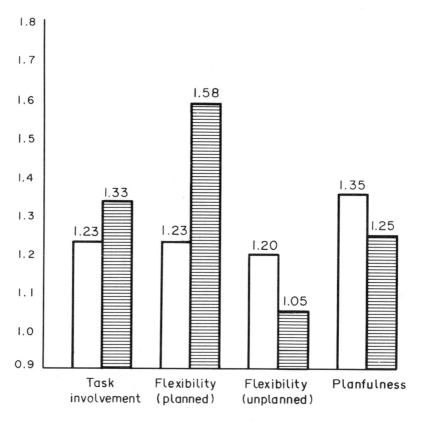

Figure 8.1

Observers' Ratings of High and Low Self-Directed Learners,
Grades 1-6
(Community School)

▦ = *high self-directed learners*

☐ = *low self-directed learners*

planfulness. By far the highest rating in the table (and the largest difference between high and low SDL's) is for adjustment to planned change on the part of the high SDL's. The high self-directed learners thus tended to be more involved in their work, but were most distinguishable by their ability to engage in a new task according to plan.

While the above finding shows high SDL's to be behaving, in part, as hypothesized, it is also apparent that the members of this group were judged to be *less* planful and *less* able to deal with unplanned changes in the judgement of the observers. These ratings are somewhat difficult to interpret. For one thing, the learners were observed during regular classroom activities for which significant planning on the part of the individual learners was ordinarily not required. The high and low SDL's were thus not observed in situations in which their own planning was a major factor in regulating performance.

The ratings of adjustments to *unplanned changes* refer to the ability to maintain concentration in the face of interruptions or other distractions occurring in the relatively relaxed atmosphere of the Community School classrooms. The low SDL's were rated as somewhat less sensitive to such interruptions, although both groups had lower ratings on this dimension than on any of the other dimensions.

This result, presumably favoring the low SDL's, may actually be a consequence of the fact that the high SDL's were more likely, at any given point in time, to be engaged in an activity from which they could be distracted by an interruption. In other words, distraction from a task would presumably be noticeable to an observer, only if the learner is actually engaged in that task at the moment an interruption occurs; hence the high SDL's were rated as somewhat more susceptible to distraction.

Speculation aside, the salient finding of this aspect of the study is the high average rating given to the high SDL's for flexibility in making planned changes. This reflects another kind of task-involvement - the engagement occurring immediately after the beginning of newly planned activity. This finding echoes the question raised at the beginning. Are students, nominated by teachers as high in self-direction, merely hardworking individuals who go to work quickly and efficiently when a new activity is begun? This is a highly appropriate behavior in the classroom, but such behavior is not solely the

province of the highly self-directed learner. Diligent, conforming students would presumably behave in the same way without being self-directing. The classroom observations, in part,
raise the issue of whether children, nominated by teachers as
high in self-direction, have all the personal characteristics
thought to be part of the concept, or rather have some attitudes
that are associated with high achievement in a given context.

Teachers' Ratings

Average ratings by teachers of high *versus* low SDL's on
each of the four dimensions (Involvement, Self-Evaluation,
Flexibility and Planfulness) are summarized in Figures 8.2 and
8.3 for students of Grades 1-3 and 4-6, respectively (see the
next two pages). Not surprisingly, teachers rate both older
and younger high SDL's as superior on all four dimensions.
Since the same teachers nominated the members of each group to
begin with, one would expect these differentiated ratings on
the four characteristics to reflect the teachers' overall perceptions about the students. What was unanticipated is that

1. ratings for both high and low SDL's were consistently higher for the 4th to 6th grade
   students, and

2. differences between high and low SDL's were
   in all cases smaller for these older students
   than for the 1st to 3rd grade students.

It is quite possible that these two findings reflect the
process of maturation. It is to be expected that characteristics relating to self-direction in learning would be more strongly apparent in older children. This interpretation in fact supports the validity of the original nominations. The very low
average ratings for the younger low SDL's show a picture, from
the teachers' perspective, of lack of interest in school work,
lack of self-awareness, distractability, and lack of organization. Figures 8.2 and 8.3 suggest that such learners are still
behind high SDL's at higher grade levels, but have nevertheless
shown some relative growth.

Parents' Ratings

Parents rated their children on the same behavioral dimensions as did teachers, but without knowing anything about
the child's nomination as either a high or low SDL. It is especially interesting, then, to see whether the parents' ratings
could confirm or disconfirm the ratings by teachers. These
ratings are summarized in Figures 8.4 and 8.5 (see pp.171-172).

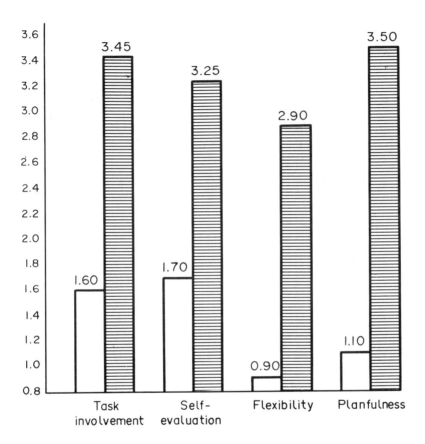

Figure 8.2

Teachers' Ratings of High and Low Self-Directed Learners,
Grades 1-3
(Community School)

▦ = high self-directed learners

☐ = low self-directed learners

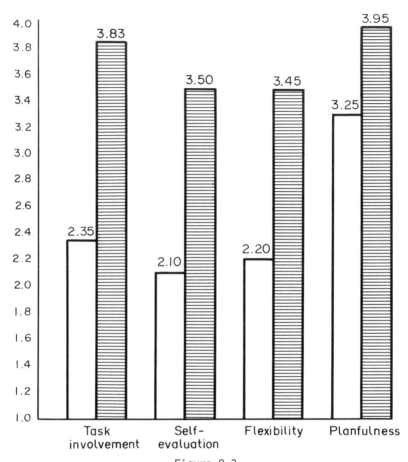

Figure 8.3

Teachers' Ratings of High and Low Self-Directed Learners,
Grades 4-6
(Community School)

▤ = *high self-directed learners*

☐ = *low self-directed learners*

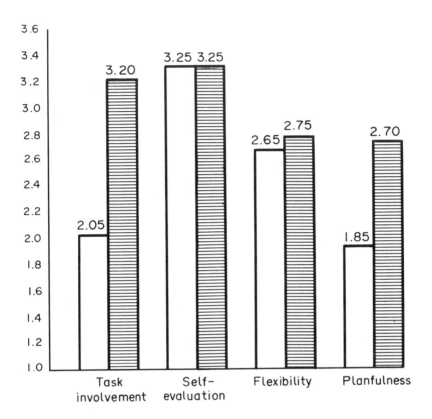

Figure 8.4

Parents' Ratings of High and Low Self-Directed Learners,
Grades 1-3
(Community School)

▤ = *high self-directed learners*

☐ = *low self-directed learners*

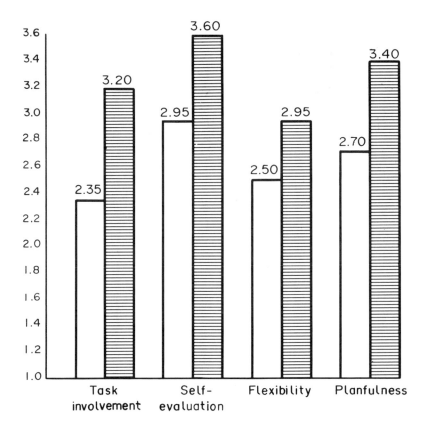

Figure 8.5
Parents' Ratings of High and Low Self-Directed Learners,
Grades 4-6
(Community School)

▤ = *high self-directed learners*

▯ = *low self-directed learners*

In the case of the younger children, Figure 8.4 reveals that parents rated the high SDL's as higher in *Involvement* (largest difference) and in *Planfulness*. Ratings of *Self-Evaluation* were identical for the two groups and virtually identical for *Flexibility*. So the teachers' ratings are partially confirmed for the younger children, although parents did not distinguish between high and low SDL's on two of the scales.

Parents' ratings for the 4th to 6th grade learners as shown in Figure 8.5 were consistently higher for the high SDL group, fully confirming the teachers' ratings. It appears that parents and teachers see the same things in children, as far as characteristics relating to self-direction are concerned, especially as their children grow older. Probably parents of upper elementary children are more likely to have had an opportunity to see their children perform in situations which might elicit all four of the characteristics. As a result they may have a more differentiated picture of the child's characteristics in relation to self-direction than do parents of younger children. Finally, the tendency noted in teachers to give higher ratings to older children on all four dimensions was true as well for parents, but only for the high SDL group. This finding presumably also reflects changes in the learners that can be attributed to maturation. Generally, it can be said that children who manifest characteristics of self-direction to teachers in the classroom show the same characteristics in the home, especially in the case of older children.

Self-Ratings

Responses to the self-rating questionnaire in general agreed with observer ratings. In addition, high SDL girls tended to give the highest self-ratings on each of the four characteristics. However, there is reason to question the validity of these data. There was relatively low variability in the responses, especially among the low SDL students. In fact, the clearest trend was for the low SDL's to rate themselves consistently higher on the four characteristics than they had been rated by their teachers and parents. This, plus the low variances of the responses, suggests that the low SDL's either had an unrealistic view of themselves or displayed a "set" to give socially desirable responses. Although these possibilities are worth exploration in the future, the self-ratings were judged to be of questionable validity in the Community School case study.

Observer Summaries

The observers were asked to write structured summaries of their field notes on the high and low SDL's. The summaries covered four topics: *Interaction with Teacher, Interaction with Peers, Task Concentration,* and *Managing Interruptions.* To illustrate more vividly how low SDL's behaved in the classroom, observer summaries for *Interaction with Teacher* and *Task concentration* are included for one high and one low SDL at the third and sixth grade levels. The students were chosen randomly. The descriptive material which follows differs in detail, rather than in substance, from the descriptions of the learners who were not selected. (Names are fictitious.)

Grade 3, high SDL (Mark, male, white, 9 years old)

Interaction with teacher: Was something of a teacher's favorite, being obviously good academically and generally non-disruptive. Mark was the only child who was observed to be assigned tutoring responsibility for a group by the teacher. He had his hand up for virtually every question or task, so interactions with the teacher were frequent and often spontaneous on his part. He was in no way dependent on the teacher, however.

Task concentration: Concentration was quite high. Mark always seemed to have homework done. He was able to work with others or alone without being bothered by other activities underway in the class room. He did engage in some socializing during periods in which the teacher worked with some other groups, but it never appeared to be to the detriment of his own work, since he was always able to complete assignments in less than the time required.

Grade 3, low SDL (Leah, female, black, 9 years old)

Interaction with teacher: The interactions of this child with the teacher were virtually continuous wherever the teacher was located with respect to Leah. It was clear from the outset that the teacher centered her attention on Leah as a child to work with rather closely. Leah was given special attention in the teacher's effort to keep her on task. Leah also approached the teacher freely, touching her person, or even half sitting

on her lap during one small group working period.
Leah also drew much attention from the teacher
with her frequent movement about the classroom
and tendency to moderately disruptive behavior.
The teacher's spontaneous comments to me about
Leah confirmed her special interest in this child.

Task concentration: Leah's ability (or willingness) to concentrate on the task was minimal,
though occasionally she was observed to work for
brief periods. On one of these occasions (after
being reminded by the teacher) she set up books
on and around her work so as to separate herself
from others, which could either be interpreted
as a way of blaming others or as an indication
that she was aware of her own high distractability. Leah made a show of getting books,
arranging papers, etc., but rarely concentrated
for more than a few moments. In the reading
group Leah did not attend when others read,
tended not to listen to instructions and, as
a result, had the wrong book or assignment.
This also might get her attention from other
children.

Grade 6, high SDL (Tania, female, black, about
12 years old)

Interaction with teacher: Tania communicated
readily with all her teachers. She was well-
liked by her teachers who seemed to really
respect her academic competence. "She *always*
gets her work done," noted her math teacher
proudly. Tania's teachers seemed to be quite
aware of her at all times. She was carefully
monitored by her teachers who tended to remind
her to "keep working" even when she was momen-
tarily distracted. She tended to finish assignments quickly and she usually went immediately
to the teacher or aide to have her work checked.
She asked questions and was always observed to
participate in group discussions at the teaching
center.

Task concentration: Tania concentrated even
when a room was very noisy. She worked well
whether alone, in a group, or with the teacher.

On only one of twelve observations was she observed to be really "fooling around" and that
was a class that was unusually noisy. It was
also quite close to lunchtime. During all other
observations she received ratings at the "high"
end of the continuum. Tania's ability to concentrate was especially noteworthy given her
popularity. Tania's ability to concentrate
for long stretches of time carried over into
all her academic subjects.

Grade 6, low SDL (Ilsa, female, black, 12 years
old)

Interaction with teacher: Because Ilsa was
such a quiet child, she tended to attract
little teacher attention and she rarely initiated communication of any type with her teachers.
The few interactions observed were teacher-in-
itiated. On only two occasions did Ilsa display
willingness to initiate communication with her
teacher. Both were learning center activities,
one in science and one in reading. On these
two occasions Ilsa was genuinely interested in
the lesson, was listening carefully and voluntarily participating in group discussions. In
general, however, she remained as inconspicuous
as possible in the classroom.

Task concentration: Ilsa generally displayed a
low level of involvement in her classroom activities. She engaged in all kinds of activities
which might reasonably be called self-distracting
(e.g., fixing her belt, tying hair ribbons, playing with erasers or paper clips). She spent a
lot of time moving around at a slow pace. It
typically took her a long time to find the appropriate ditto, discussion card, pencil, or
whatever. On two occasions she left the classroom ostensibly to find some needed materials
and did not return until the class was nearly
over. Her somewhat lethargic approach to things
carried over into actual work habits. During the
observations when she was actually working on
something, I observed that she would take a long
time to head her paper or to write only one
sentence. After a few strokes of her pencil she

would always stop to examine what she had done or to just
look around the room. During one session at the teaching
center when she was supposed to be listening to a teacher
presentation, she spent the whole time copying the class
schedule which was clearly and permanently posted in all
classrooms.

As is often the case, the excerpts from the narrative summaries add impressions that are not necessarily evident in summaries of quantitative data. The two high SDL's appear to have
behaved in quite similar fashion in the classroom in spite of
differences in age, sex, and race. Both gave the impression
of being academically able, responsible, well-organized, able
to concentrate well, liked by the teacher, and popular with
peers. They were, in short, the kind of student who would be
"liked" by school teachers anywhere and at any level of schooling.

The two low SDL's, in contrast, were alike in sex and
race, though different in age. They were also alike in their
apparent inability to concentrate when working alone or to attend when the teacher was giving a lesson. They differed in
personal style - one being almost hyperactive and the other
quite passive and withdrawn. As a result, one was constantly
noticed by the teacher and the other frequently ignored. These
differences apart, both got very little work done and seemed to
require constant direction.

Summary
        Both quantitative and qualitative information show that
high and low self-directed learners behaved differently, both
in the home and in the classroom. Observers found the high
SDL's to be more task involved in the classroom and to be much
more able to shift smoothly to engagement in a new, planned
task. Contrary to expectation, low SDL's were rated as more
planful and better at dealing with unplanned changes such as
interruptions. These results are somewhat difficult to interpret, since "planning" was not a regular or commonly observed
activity among students in the Community School, and the lower
task involvement of the low SDL's may have been the reason that
they appear to be less sensitive to unplanned changes in their
environment.

Teachers and parents saw the two groups of students in
very similar ways, the latter providing an independent verification of the initial selection of the high and low SDL's by

the former. However, parents differentiated between the two groups on all four dimensions only for older learners. There was some evidence for maturation on the part of the learners (and for construct validity of the ratings) in that average ratings tended to be higher for older learners.

The high SDL's present an almost stereotyped image of the model student, possibly in part reflecting biases the teachers brought to the nomination. However, it is equally possible that self-directed children at this age-level merely adjust well to the type of environment provided by the Community School and display their self-direction by taking relatively full advantage of the opportunities that are available. With these two possibilities in mind, the findings from a similar study of somewhat older children in a different culture and school/community context will be of particular interest.

FINDINGS: THE ARELLANO HIGH SCHOOL STUDY

In the Philippine study, high and low self-directed learners were compared in a variety of ways. Although the procedure for identifying the two groups of learners was quite similar in the Philippine and U.S. studies, the latter depended primarily on observations and ratings for its comparisons, while the former placed greater reliance on self-report inventories and questionnaires. Additional information was collected from observations and interviews.

Interviews

Moderately structured interviews of fifteen high and twelve low SDL's yielded a variety of types of information. The interviewers explored the topics of *family, motivation for schoolwork,* and *career ambitions.* Given the small number of participants, the responses did not always lead to clear cut differences between the two groups. However, a few rather striking qualitative differences did emerge in the patterns of responses from high and low SDL's.

When responding to the question, *"What factors make you want to get good grades and obtain more schooling?"* almost all the high SDL's cited some relationship with teachers - the teacher as a model, teachers' expectations, or teachers' confidence and support. Five members of this group also referred to their own competitiveness in the academic situation. Six others traced academic motivation to cooperative relationships with

other students. When asked, *"Who encourages you?"* a similar
pattern emerged, with teachers the primary source of encouragement and other classmates an important secondary source.

In contrast, the low SDL's cited classmates more often as
sources of motivation than teachers. Moreover, the kinds of
relationships with classmates described in the answers were of
a dependent type - assistance, advice, and tutoring, as contrasted with the cooperative, sharing (though sometimes competitive) relationships described by the high SDL's. Encouragement
from others as a source of motivation was mentioned by a minority of the low SDL's. The teacher was named by only one member
of this group.

The other clear difference in the two groups was in response to a question about career aspiration. With one exception ("finish studies and free family from poverty") the high
SDL's chose professional occupations. None of the low SDL's
mentioned a professional occupation, but rather cited jobs such
as automotive or television repair, secretary, sales person,
etc. This contrast in career aspirations reflects, in part,
the generally higher occupational level of parents of the high
SDL's, although even here only three of the parental occupations
were clearly professional. Several were comparable, status-
wise, with occupations of parents of low SDL's.

In spite of being older and from a different culture,
high SDL's in the ISOS program at Arellano High School responded
in ways similar to what one would reasonably be entitled to expect from Community School high SDL's by the time they got to
secondary school. Particularly noteworthy were their close
positive relationships with teachers, their partly competitive,
partly cooperative, relationships with other students, and their
high career aspirations.

Students' Self-Perceptions
An initial pool of about 100 self-rating items that might
differentiate between high and low SDL's were developed for
assessing student characteristics. After a study of item analysis data derived from the entire ISOS student population (n =
566), 72 items were retained for the following scales:

Self-acceptance: The student has a positive view
of himself/herself as a learner.

Planfulness: The student is able to identify
learning needs, set appropriate

goals in the light of those needs,
and devise strategies appropriate
for accomplishing those goals.

Intrinsic
motivation: The student undertakes and persists
in learning in the absence of ex-
ternal awards and sanctions. The
student delays and foregoes gratifi-
cation in order to proceed with
learning.

Internalized
evaluation: Self-directed learners can give accurate estimates of their performance
based on evidence they collect themselves.

Openness
to experience: The student engages in new kinds of
activities which may result in new
learning or goal setting.

Flexibility: The student is willing to change
learning goals or strategies and
use exploratory trial and error
approaches.

Autonomy: The student is able to question
normative standards of a given time
and place as to what kinds of learning are valuable and permissible.

Responsibility: The student assumes responsibility
for "house-keeping" tasks in the
classroom.

Learning climate: Ratings on seven subscales including
teacher expectation, conviviality,
expectations of success, inter-
learning, satisfaction, affinity,
and competitiveness.

Incorporating
learning outside Student sees relevance of learning
school: to life and importance of various
sources of learning outside the school.

Decision-making: The student makes decisions for
himself/herself.

The first seven of the above scales correspond to the
hypothesized learning characteristics on which the study was
based. Statistical comparisons (analysis of variance) between

the high and low SDL's on these scales revealed the former to rate themselves significantly higher on five of the seven scales (in spite of the probability of relatively low power for the statistical test due to the small number of cases involved). The two groups did not differ significantly on *Internalized evaluation* and *Autonomy*, which were very short scales of three items each. The Philippine report notes that these scales (especially *Autonomy*) may not be valid in a national context in which adolescents tend to be more highly dependent on their parents than are children of the same age in many other cultures.

Of the other three scales on the self-perception instrument, high SDL's rated themselves significantly higher on *Responsibility* (in relation to school) and the general category of *Learning climate*. The latter was composed of several subscales whose independent contributions were not reported separately. One or more of the sets of items measuring constructs such as "learning outside of the school", "satisfaction with classwork", and "liking of classmates", may have accounted for the considerably higher average score obtained by the high SDL's. However, the significant overall score on *Learning climate* was probably indicative of a more positive attitude toward school and a constructive approach to the learning experience on the part of the high SDL's.

Generally, the high SDL's described themselves in ways that were consistent with the basis on which they were presumably nominated by their teachers. Superiority of high over low SDL's was not born out statistically in the case of *Internalized evaluation* and *Autonomy*, but it was firmly established in the other five dimensions that have been hypothesized to characterize self-directed learners.

Student Attitudes

Attitudes of high and low SDL's were assessed on five scales, two of which were adapted from the literature and three constructed for the case study. The items used in the final analysis were selected on the basis of evidence of discrimination between high and low groups on total scale scores for the ISOS population as a whole (n = 566). Scale titles and illustrative items follow.

Problem-solving attitude:	"I like games that make me think."
Attitude toward teachers:	"The ISOS teachers give individual help willingly."

Attitude toward SDL:	"I like to help plan learning activities for myself and my classmates."
Attitude toward learning and knowledge:	"School is one source of information, but there are others."
Attitude toward pupil activities:	"I like teaching younger schoolmates, brothers or sisters."

High SDL's rated themselves higher than did low SDL's on all five of the scales, and the differences were both statistically significant and subjectively large on all but the *Problem-solving attitude* scale. There was a particularly large apparent difference on the *Attitude toward self-directed learning* scale. The twenty-two items included on this scale cover a variety of attitudes that appeared to be consistent with the concept of self-direction, e.g., positively scored items included, "I like it when answers are not given immediately and I have a chance to find out for myself", while negatively scored items included, "I learn only from a teacher".

The Philippine case study report discounted the single negative finding on *Problem-solving attitude* on the grounds that its items were not relevant to the kinds of school related activity in which the students had been observed to engage. Rather, the items referred to abstract problem-solving activities instead of the kinds of practical problem that were assigned in the learning kits and in other aspects of the curriculum.

Overall, the high SDL's showed a pattern of attitudes that was consistent with the conception of self-direction on which the research was based, especially in their apparent liking for activities that were directly representative of self-directed learning itself.

Student Values
High and low SDL's were also compared on the *Survey of Interpersonal Values*, a theoretically-based personality inventory developed by Gordon. The scales of this inventory reflect the degree to which respondents value six different types of relationship with other people:

Support:	Being treated with understanding, receiving encouragement from other people, being treated with kindness and respect.

Conformity: Doing what is socially correct,
                       following regulations, doing what
                       is accepted and proper.

Recognition: Being looked up to and admired,
                       being considered important, attract-
                       ing favorable notice and recognition.

Independence: Having the right to do as one pleases,
                       being free to make one's own decisions
                       and do things in one's own way.

Benevolence: Doing things for other people,
                       sharing with others, helping the
                       unfortunate.

Leadership: Being in charge of others, having
                       authority, holding a position, leader-
                       ship or power.

Statistical comparison between the high and low SDL's on
the six scales revealed significant differences on only two,
Conformity and *Independence*. These were the two scales on
which one would logically expect the two groups to be different.
However, the direction of the difference turned out to be the
reverse of what one would predict, in that the high SDL's described themselves as higher in *Conformity* and lower in *Independence*!

This finding at first appears to run counter to other
findings of the Philippine study as well as to the conception
of self-directed learning itself. In this regard, it has already been observed that interviews revealed the high SDL's to
be quite ambitious both academically and in terms of their
choice of careers. Their apparently close and positive relationship with teachers has also been noted. The Philippine
report suggests, by way of explanation, that conformity - as
implied by doing the "right" thing and avoidance of the kind of
independent behavior that is implied by "doing as one pleases" -
is a socially valuable mode of adaptation from the perspective
of a culture that places great value on dependent relationships
of children with adults. In other words, the high SDL's may be
individuals who are especially willing and able to behave in
ways that make the school and the wider society work for,
rather than against, them.

This finding and its interpretation in the Philippine
report is particularly interesting because it independently

OSTE-G*

raises a question already discussed in relation to the U.S. study of the Community School. Are self-directed learners identified by teachers primarily model students who also manifest some characteristics of self-direction, or do genuinely self-directed learners respond to the environment of the school by behaving in a way that allows them to make maximum use of its offerings, thus appearing to be conforming? If the latter is the case, a fresh look needs to be taken at the concept of independence in relation to self-direction. The two studies taken together raise the issue rather than resolving it. But as is often the case, findings contrary to prior expectations may help advance conceptualization.

Observations and Daily Activities

Observations of the high and low SDL's were conducted, using a coded observation form containing twenty-six items covering the following categories:

1. *Cognition* ("applies knowledge from other disciplines");

2. *Motivation* ("seeks new learning on his own");

3. *Participation in planning, execution, and evaluation of learning* ("participates in planning both in-school and out-of-school activities");

4. *Development of self-learning* ("uses opportunities for individual learning"); and

5. *Development of inter-learning* ("shares knowledge with younger or slower students").

High and low SDL's were observed during five minute-periods in the regular classroom.

The striking finding from the observational data was the way in which the high SDL's were found to engage in a variety of activities across the four grade levels, while the range of activities for the low SDL's was very narrow. The only activity observed in the latter group at more than one grade level was the simple "use of processes" such as taking notes or observing. In contrast, the high SDL's were found at all four grade levels to engage actively in the instructional process in a variety of ways. The pattern of differences observed in fact suggests the distinction "active *versus* passive" as a way of summing up the differences in the classroom behavior of the two groups.

These results are paralleled by self-reports of daily

activities. High and low SDL's were asked to list their daily
activities for a one-week period. The two groups differed in
their responsiveness to this request, with all of the high SDL's
returning the requested records as compared to only about half
of the low SDL's. Moreover, about three-quarters of the former
provided specific time schedules as compared to none of the
latter. The range and number of activities reported by the low
SDL's was significantly more limited, although to some extent
this may be an artifact of the lower response rate of this group.

The observational and self-report data in general portray
the high SDL's as more active in and out of school and also more
responsive to the request to contribute systematic information
about their own activities. School activities were not only
more varied for high SDL's, but also were not confined simply
to passive types of student behavior such as listening or
taking notes.

Intelligence
All students in the ISOS program were administered the
IPAT (scale 2), a non-verbal, culture-free test of intelligence
developed by Cattel and his associates. In addition, the school
population took the *Test of Abstract Thinking*, modified by
Acuna and da Silva from Shipley's original version. This latter
test measures the ability to abstract and use a rule from a set
of examples, and can be taken as a measure of abstract intelligence.

The high SDL's were significantly superior on both of
these measures. No theoretical relationship has yet been postulated between self-direction in learning and performance on
measures of intelligence. To the extent that the usual teacher-
biases might have influenced the nominations, it is not supris-
ing that the high SDL's would score higher on intelligence.
But it is also possible that learners with superior cognitive
abilities would more readily develop patterns of self-direction
because of repeated experiences of success in independent learning and problem-solving. The nature of this possible relationship remains to be explored. High I.Q. is presumably neither a
necessary nor sufficient precondition for self-direction in
learning.

Cognitive Style
High and low SDL's were compared on the *Group Embedded
Figures Test* developed by Witkin and his associates. This is a
paper and pencil measure of field independence or the ability

to ignore distractions in the perceptual field by focusing on the relevant aspects of a complex stimulus. Performance on this test is correlated with other aspects of the personality construct of independence, and it might be expected that individuals high in self-direction in any aspect of their lives would score more highly on this test.

The above prediction turned out to be confirmed. The high SDL's scored significantly higher on the Group EFT than did the low SDL's, not only in the narrow sense of statistical significance, but in a practical sense as well (the high SDL score averaging over twice as high as that of the low SDL's). Cognitively, the high SDL's were, as predicted, much more field independent, in contradistinction to their apparently conforming behavior in the regular classroom situation.

Correlation Analyses
    Three types of correlational analyses were conducted on the data to learn more about the pattern of relationships between the various predictors and the high versus low SDL dichotomy. These data should be interpreted cautiously because of the small number of cases included in the intensive study of high and low SDL's.

    Bivariate correlations: Biserial correlations between high versus low status on SDL and nine of the ten student characteristics scales, the five student attitude scales, the learning climate scale, the six value scales, and the three cognitive measures were calculated. Sixteen of the thirty-four relationships were statistically significant and these are reported in Table 8.1 (see next page).

    While chance significance is potentially a factor in multiple significance tests such as those reported in Table 8.1, there can be no doubt that the correlations are virtually all consistent with the relationships hypothesized earlier between self-direction and personal characteristics of the learners. Especially high relationships are listed in the table for *Attitude towards Pupil Activities* (r = .82), which assesses attitudes about teaching others or leadership in inter-learning, *Attitude towards SDL* (r = .79), which deals with activities typically associated with self-directed learning, and *Intrinsic Motivation* (r = .77), which reflects liking to engage in learning for its own sake.

Table 8.1

Correlations of Learner Personal Characteristics, Attitudes,
Values and Cognitive Characteristics with High *versus* Low
Status on Self-Directed Learning

Scale or Test	r_{bis}
Test of Abstract Thinking	.88
Attitude towards Pupil Activities	.82
Attitude towards SDL	.79
Intrinsic Motivation	.77
Self-acceptance	.76
Conformity	.75
Openness to New Experience	.75
Learning Climate Scale	.70
Attitude towards Teachers	.70
Planfulness	.68
Attitude towards Learning	.67
Group Embedded Figures Test	.65
Problem-solving Attitude	.65
Flexibility	.60
Responsibility	.57
Independence	.49

The highest relationship of all, however, was for the
Test of Abstract Thinking (r = .88). This thirty item test
measures the ability to abstract and apply a rule. The respon-
dent is required to generate the rule by examining a set of
examples and then to demonstrate the rule with an additional
example. The TAT has been reported to correlate highly with
Piagetian measures of conservation reflecting attainment of the
stage of concrete operations. The IPAT measure of non-verbal
intelligence was *not* among the variables correlating highest
with high versus low status on SDL, while the *Group Embedded
Figures Test* (GFT) as a measure of field independence was correlated at a moderately high level.

The correlational findings thus suggest that among the cognitive variables, general intelligence is not the most potent factor differentiating between the high and low SDL's. Rather, there is reason to believe that the high SDL's functioned more effectively at a higher level of cognitive development, specifically in their ability to reason abstractly and to ignore a distracting perceptual field. Whether these findings on cognitive variables are merely an artifact of the method of selection of high *versus* low SDL's, or instead suggest a new distinction that should be added to those already made, remains to be investigated.

Factor analysis. In an attempt to summarize relationships in the data, the entire set of measures was subjected to a principle components factor analysis, varimax solution. Extraction was terminated after three factors had emerged due to a sharp drop of the variance accounted for after that point. The scales are related in highly complex ways, and only the most general statements can be made from this analysis.

The first factor was clearly a general factor highly correlated with status on SDL (r = .70). Scales with the highest loadings on this factor were *Intrinsic Motivation* and *Learning Climate*, *Attitude towards Learning*, *Planfulness*, *Flexibility*, and other measures of personal characteristics already found to correlate highly with status on SDL.

The second factor accounted for considerably less variance, but still correlated relatively highly with SDL (r = .60). This factor was clearly bipolar, with the value scale of *Conformity* loading highest positively, and the *Independence* value scale highest negatively. Highly positive loadings were also recorded for *Attitude towards Teachers*, and *Attitude towards Pupil Activities*. This factor appears to reflect at the positive pole the tendency to behave in accepted ways in the school situation, especially with regard to using human and material resources in a constructive way. At the other end of the continuum is the sort of independence that is associated with the right to do whatever one wants and to make one's own decisions irrespective of the consequences. Here again there is the image of the high SDL as a student who makes full use of resources by behaving in a way that is socially appropriate in the classroom context. The high SDL, at any rate when nominated by teachers, is definitely not a rebel in the classroom.

The third factor accounted for a very small proportion of

the variance and had only a low correlation with the high versus low SDL dichotomy. It will not be discussed.

Discriminant analysis. A discriminant function analysis was run in order to identify that particular subset of scales and tests which contributed most to differentiating between high and low SDL's. Fourteen variables that differentiated significantly between high and low SDL's were selected for this analysis (although even this is a relatively large number of variables given the small number of subjects involved).

Table 8.2

Variables Identified in Discriminant Function Analysis of
High *versus* Low Self-directed Learners

Variables	Standardized Discriminant Function Coefficients
Test of Abstract Thinking	.66
Openness to Experience	.43
Attitude towards SDL	.23
Non-Verbal Intelligence (IPAT)	.16
Embedded Figures Test (EFT)	.10

Table 8.2 presents the five variables that in combination were found to classify 100 per cent of the cases correctly as either high or low SDL's. The standardized discriminant function coefficients indicate the relative contribution of each variable to the classification. Once again, both cognitive and personality or attitudinal components contributed to the prediction. The test of abstract thinking ability (TAT) made the largest contribution to the differentiation between high and low SDL's. In spite of its relatively low correlation with the high versus low SDL dichotomy, the measure of non-verbal intelligence (IPAT) also made an independent, though much smaller, contribution. There can be no doubt that the high SDL's identified by teachers in the ISOS program at Arellano High School were more cognitively able than were their counterparts among the low SDL's.

Among measures of personality and attitudes, *Openness to Experience* and *Attitude towards SDL* appear as the second and third most powerful factor differentiating high and low SDL's. The former is a relatively short scale of only five items, all of which are listed here in order to better define this apparently highly relevant personal characteristic:

"I go beyond the tasks in class and try new experiences."

"New activities are opportunities to provide me with new experiences, and I like them."

"I try things even if I don't understand them completely."

"I do not go beyond the tasks in class." (scored negatively)

"New kinds of activities are opportunities to provide me with new experiences, but I don't like them." (scored negatively)

Attitude towards SDL is a longer scale of twenty-five items. While all cannot be reproduced here, the following five items provide a flavor of the scale as a whole:

"I like to help plan learning activities for myself and my classmates."

"Students should learn to recognize what type of material is best for them."

"I like working in groups and learning from other students."

"I learn only from a teacher." (scored negatively)

"I like it when answers are not given immediately and I have a chance to find them for myself."

Examination of these items (as well as the twenty not listed above) suggests that more than a single characteristic of self-directed learning is represented in the *Attitude towards SDL* scale. For example, in the items listed above there is the suggestion of *Intrinsic Motivation*, or *Curiosity*, *Planfulness*, and *Self-evaluation*. While also better at abstract thinking than the lower SDL's, the learners identified by teachers as high in SDL appear to perceive themselves to be high on nearly all of the characteristics of self-directed learning hypothesized in this research.

Summary
The case study of Arellano High School used a variety of measures in assessing the differences between high and low SDL's. It was clear from several types of measures that the high SDL's were consciously and behaviorally oriented toward using the resources provided by the school, including teachers and other students, as effectively as possible. They tended to have close relationships with teachers as a part of a general pattern of position identification with the school. This high degree of goal orientation in school was consistent with significantly higher career aspirations and an overall conformity or "good student" image.

The high SDL's rated themselves as higher on five of the seven hypothesized characteristics of self-directed learning. Likewise, their attitudes about learning, the role of teachers, and engagement in activities that are characteristic of self-direction, were found to be remarkably consistent with what would be expected from self-directed learners.

Contrary to expectation, the high SDL's rated themselves as higher on values relating to conformity and lower on those relating to independence. This important finding is consistent with the behavior of the former in the classroom. As in the U.S. study of younger children, the high SDL's make full use of the school's resources, and in doing so they displayed willingness to conform to the expectations of the system. It is also important to recognize that "independence" as measured by the scale in question referred to "having one's own way", a type of independence that may be more a sign of immaturity than of self-direction.

Finally, the high SDL's were definitely superior in their ability to think abstractly and in non-verbal intelligence. These types of intellectual differences were not hypothesized as dimensions relevant to the high versus low SDL distinction and may in part be an artifact of the method of selection of the groups. However, the particularly wide difference between the two groups on a measure of abstract reasoning suggests that the high SDL's may have been more mature cognitively, and this may turn out to be an inevitable concomitant of self-direction in learning, whatever the method of selection. The high SDL's also scored as more independent on a cognitive measure of field independence. This particular cognitive difference is quite relevant to the conception of self-direction on which the research was based.

IMPLICATIONS OF THE TWO STUDIES

In spite of differences in cultural context, the age level of the learners, and in the types of measure used, the Philippine and U.S. studies of high and low SDL's yielded remarkably consistent findings that, taken together, raise at least one basic question about the concept of self-direction presented in this book.

Both studies show that high versus low SDL's as identified by teachers behave differently in the classroom and elsewhere. With the probable exception of characteristics which could not be adequately addressed in either study, (especially autonomy) there is ample evidence that high SDL's work harder, show more intrinsic interest in learning, are more flexible in adapting to change and in the use of resources, including other people, and in general behave consistently with most aspects of self-direction hypothesized in Skager (1978). These findings provide considerable support for the conception of the self-directed learner on which the research was based.

As is often the case, the findings which are consistent with prior thinking are in a sense less interesting than findings which are inconsistent or at least unanticipated. In this category there are two significant items:

1. in both studies the high SDL's appeared to be conforming rather than independent with respect to the classroom and its rules and expectations; and

2. in the Philippine study the high SDL's were clearly superior in abstract thinking and, to a lesser extent, in general (non-verbal) intelligence.

While measures of cognitive ability were not used in the U.S. study, one suspects, given the other remarkable similarities among the findings of the two studies, that the same finding would also have emerged.

It remains for future work to either incorporate these two findings into a revised conception of the self-directed learners, or to demonstrate clearly that they are merely an unintended artifact of the method by which the groups were identified. By way of anticipation, some speculation seems in order.

It is natural to assume that a self-directed learner would be independent rather than conforming. But one must be more specific about what is meant by these terms. There is a kind of independence that is non-productive as far as learning is concerned. There is also a kind of apparent conformity that is quite useful. The high SDL's in this study manifested that type of conformity by making full use of the resources available to them, including teachers and other students. They worked harder, had higher aspirations, were more open to new experience, moved from one task to another more smoothly, were seen by themselves and others as liking to engage in behaviors that were consistent with self-direction, and generally fit into the school environment successfully and productively. They also openly identified with teachers.

The above could be interpreted as conformity. But it also is the kind of behavior that might be expected from learners who are intrinsically motivated, flexible in their approach to learning, and good at self-evaluation. In other words, as long as the classroom offers legitimate opportunities for learning, the self-directed learner will behave in ways that take advantage of these opportunities, and such behavior understandably will have the appearance of behavior that is merely conforming.

There still remains the fact that the high and low SDL groups were nominated by teachers, and the biases that teachers bring to the task might favor the student whose behavior is conforming without being self-directing. Future research could investigate this question by selecting and comparing high and low self-directed learners by more than one method. In other words, it would be important to determine whether different groups, such as peers or trained outside observers, would nominate the same individuals high or low in self-direction as those nominated by teachers. If there were differences, then the nature of those differences would help to reveal whether or not there were other groups of learners less "conforming" in the classroom but equally self-directing in their learning behavior.

The findings on cognitive aptitude are less easy to explain. It may be that self-directed learners of school age, identified by any method, would turn out to be higher in general intelligence and more mature in abstract reasoning skills. It may well be that learner self-acceptance is more readily developed in learners of higher cognitive capacity who experience success more frequently and with less effort. Perhaps other aspects of self-direction are likewise facilitated in such learners through reinforcement for successful performance. Confirmation of these speculations would require significant modification of the concept presented earlier. It is not an especially appealing modification, because self-direction was not conceived as closely related to intelligence.

On the other hand, the relationships between aptitudes and self-direction may also be an artifact of the selection process. Future research should attempt to identify individuals who possess only moderate abilities cognitively, yet who are highly self-directed. It might also attempt to distinguish between high and low SDL's who are equally able with respect to abstract reasoning ability and general intelligence. If these distinctions cannot be made, then modifications in the conception of self-direction will be in order.

Chapter 9

Principles, Theories, Findings, and the Facilitation Versus Training Assumptions

The four institutions studied in this research differ in many respects. They are located in different countries which contrast significantly in culture and in political organization. They enroll students of different age levels. Their programs incorporate different approaches to the allocation of authority, somewhat different emphases in their curricula and great variation in approach to the teaching and learning process. The institutions even fulfill, in a number of respects, different functions within their respective educational systems. This level of diversity would presumably frustrate any attempt at syntheses.

At the beginning of this book it was suggested that there may nevertheless be an advantage in such diversity. The latter might lead to the emergence of larger issues which would perhaps not have surfaced if a sample of homogeneous schools in a single society had been studied. The plausibility of this seemingly optimistic expectation was first evident in the parallel studies of high and low self-directed learners described in the last chapter.

Comparisons between the students in the high and low groups revealed in both studies that hypothesized characteristics of self-directed learners were, in the main, confirmed by observations of behavior and other means of assessment. However, it was also apparent that the characteristic of autonomy required careful reinterpretation in the light of the fact that the high self-directed learners in both the Philippine and U.S. classrooms were strikingly conforming in their behavior as students and in a number of other respects as well. These students also made full and constructive use of the learning opportunities they found in their environment. They were certainly not non-conforming "loners", and they did not mind obeying rules and regulations. They simply behaved in ways which took full advantage of whatever was relevant to their own development.

With apparent conformity, one of the hallmarks of the self-directed learner in the classroom, autonomy, takes on a more distinctive connotation. Self-directed learners can still show autonomy in avoiding the social and other environmental distractions to which their less motivated peers may be prone. They may also orient their behavior in and out of school to longer term, and more adult goals. However, autonomous learners may still work constructively as members of cooperative groups and fully comply with the norms of such groups. These observations remain as potentially fruitful hypotheses for future work.

ASSUMPTIONS ABOUT ORIGINS

Virtually all the practices observed in each of the schools appeared to reflect one or other of two apparently incompatible assumptions about self-direction in relation to schooling. This contrast emerged during the discussion at the final project meeting. It was quickly perceived to relate to the theoretical approaches that educators might be likely to adopt in designing school environments which encourage self-direction.

On the one hand there is the assumption that some or most individuals, as young children, are fully capable of growing into self-directed learners if the environment is appropriately arranged so as to permit this characteristic to manifest itself. This assumption leads to a conception of the school as a learning environment which should facilitate a natural growth process. The key concept here is *facilitation*. A facilitating environment is designed to permit and encourage a "natural" kind of growth, rather than deliberately to bring about such growth through prescriptive education and training.

There are liberal and conservative branches of this first orientation. Liberals hold that self-direction is inherent in the repertory of virtually every normal child. It merely remains for the environment to be arranged so as to provide sufficient freedom for self-direction to be fully expressed. The more conservative view is in the tradition of the psychology of individual differences. It assumes that only some people possess whatever is necessary for developing fully into independent

and self-directed learners. The task of the educator is to
identify such individuals as early as possible so that they may
be placed in environments which facilitate rather than suppress
their stronger-than-normal self-directive tendencies.

When it comes to the practice of pedagogy, both of these
views are fully compatible with *humanistic* theory, as the latter
was described in Chapter 3. However, the less global theories
about the intrinsic nature of *curiosity* and *exploratory behavior*
are equally relevant. The motivation for self-actualization on
which humanistic theory is based can find expression in environments which are non-threatening and open enough to maximize the
development of positive self-regard. Only learners who think
positively about themselves will be independent enough to become
their own evaluation agents and, e.g., develop internal rather
than external loci of evaluation.

The contrasting assumption is environmentalist, regarding
self-direction as a characteristic which can be developed deliberately in most individuals through proper kinds of training
and experience. It leads to a strong emphasis on appropriate
pedagogy, with freedom for the expression of self-direction
coming at the end of a successful process rather than at the
beginning. The operative concept here is *training*. The assumption is that people can be trained to be self-directing.

This second position is more or less compatible with any
of the other theories discussed in Chapter 3, although the concept of competency motivation, and especially attribution theory, and the related concept of personal causation are particularly relevant. Indeed, attribution theory and its application
in personal causation training almost seems to have been developed specifically for the design of educational environments
which are activist in their approach to the development of self-
direction.

It should be apparent from previous chapters that none of
the four schools can be categorized fully into either the "facilitation" or "training" camp. Rather, the practices that each
school has built into its curriculum probably reflect both of
these orientations, although to different degrees. This in no
way detracts from the fact that the basic distinction about
assumptions is a useful structure for summarizing both what
has been learned about the schools as well as what remains to
be studied in the future in other schools.

198   Organizing Schools to Encourage Self-direction

Illustrations from the Classroom
     The distinction between assumptions about the origins of
self-direction arose from certain observations in the study of
the Community School. The report on this school concluded that
environment seemed to have a strong influence on the manifestation of self-directed behavior. For example, self-directed
learning would, for understandable reasons, be very difficult
to detect in classrooms where there were no choices and where
teachers fully structured the content, sequence, and mode of
instruction. But less obvious might be the fact that self-
directed behaviors are almost equally rare in the classroom
where there is lack of structure to the degree that students do
not understand how they are supposed to behave. The case study
report suggested, in the examples which follow, that some degree of structure might be needed in order to adequately support self-directed learning.

     One upper grade classroom seemed to have the sup-
     porting structure. The students appeared to
     understand what they were expected to do. The
     teacher's expectations of the students included
     self-directed learning behaviors. For example,
     she reminded them that they could choose what
     they wanted to do, but that they must choose and
     not waste time. She praised them for asking
     questions, for being interested in their work,
     for concentrating. She attended to the entire
     class while she was instructing small groups,
     continuously observing and commenting on student
     activity. Many of the children seemed to be
     motivated, planful, self-evaluative, and flexible.

     The report went on to make clear that the teacher worked
constantly to make children aware, at first at a very basic
level, that they could make choices which would facilitate their
own learning, e.g., "When you get your book what are you going
to do? ... No, that wouldn't be a good place to sit, because
you need a *quiet* place to read." In other words, the teacher
gradually shaped the behavior of her students in the direction
of making choices which would promote and sustain effective
learning. This teacher was consciously or unconsciously acting
out the second of the assumptions - that self-direction can be
taught.

     The case study report also described a classroom in which
a radically different situation obtained.

By contrast, in another upper grade classroom,
students were noisy and off-task. The teacher
kept up a stream of ineffectual reminders about
assignments and tasks. Very few children paid
her any attention. In this room most students
did not appear motivated, planful, self-directed
or flexible.

These observations led to the proposal at the final project meeting that one could conceive of two types of environments, depending on the "readiness" of the students. For
children who are already capable of self-directed learning, the
environment would be highly open and flexible, with the guiding
principle of organization that of providing a maximum number of
choices. Here the principle of *flexibility* from Chapter 3 would
be fully articulated with a full array of options about what to
do, and how, when, how often, and with whom to work. The principles of *teaching as a facilitating activity* and *democratic
relationships* could be fully applied, since authority would not
be needed as a motivating, controlling device. Likewise, the
remaining six principles would be fully operative since the
students would be prepared to take advantage of the opportunities available.

The second type of environment would be much like that
described with the first classroom above. Here children who are
not yet self-directing would be initially helped and guided in
making choices. Planfulness would be deliberately taught by
exploring the consequences of various choices. Teachers would
exercise authority as necessary, depending on the level of development of the student. The gradual tactic of "shaping" would
be used methodically to guide behavior in the direction of event-
ual self-direction.

These two practical approaches to organizing the learning
environment may thus be equally valid, depending on the level
of development of the learners. In other words, some learners
may already be capable of a significant degree of self-direction.
For these learners an environment organized according to the
principles of humanistic theory seems to be appropriate. But
perhaps other learners can be taught how to be self-directing.
Here a more or less eclectic approach could better be used, one
which draws on more than one theory about learning.

Strong arguments for theoretical liberalism emerged in
the research reported in this book. For example, at the Katalin

Varga School, students who selected the advanced examination option stood out as individuals for whom learning was a hobby, who had high aspirations, and who received a great deal of approval and encouragement from peers and adults. The high self-directed learners in the ISOS Program had similar characteristics plus excellent relationships with teachers. Both of these groups along with the much younger self-directed learners at the Community School appeared to be naturally occurring subgroups of highly self-directed learners within a larger school population. The fact that a similar group was not detected at the Oberstufen-Kolleg may merely reflect the fact that in this case data on individuals were not collected in ways that would permit the identification of high and low self-directed students.

By contrast, there were, in both the Community School and ISOS Program, groups of students who were mainly unable to take advantage of the opportunities at hand. These students stood out especially in the ISOS Program because their inability or unwillingness to choose to work and persevere was highlighted by the off-school experience. Some of these students were studied extensively in both the Philippines and U.S. projects, but there is some evidence that similar students could be found in the Katalin Varga School. Some of the students at that school who had chosen not to take advantage of the advanced examination option, described themselves as lacking in perseverance and in need of the kind of systematic preparation that effective teaching can provide.

The ISOS and Community School studies revealed how easily low versus high self-directed learners can be identified. In the school setting, the distractability of the former makes it difficult for them to persevere in situations lacking structure and tangible incentives for performance. From a theoretical perspective, reinforcement and attribution theory appear to offer alternative approaches for bringing about positive changes in this type of student. Freedom and lack of structure were obviously not helpful. These findings underline the potential dangers in the universal application of purely theoretical assumptions about the development of self-direction (or any other pattern of behavior) without regard to pre-existing characteristics of individual learners.

APPLYING THE FACILITATION *VERSUS* TRAINING DISTINCTION

The distinction between approaches which are primarily facilitative and those which undertake the deliberate training and shaping of behavior is a useful device for organizing the findings of this research. The distinction readily separates the theoretical orientations which are likely to be implicitly or explicitly selected and applied, but it also makes possible the classification of particular practices in terms of the underlying assumption about the origins of self-directive learning behavior.

In the three tables which follow, the schools will be compared with respect to

1. organization as it relates to opportunity for choice on the part of students;

2. curriculum; and

3. teaching and learning processes.

Each feature identified will be classified in relation to the facilitative *versus* training distinction. It will be readily apparent that both types of assumption were simultaneously in operation in each institution.

Organization and Student Choice
Application of the principles of flexibility and freedom to make choices is directly dependent on the way in which schools are organized at the level of instruction. While all of the eight principles for encouraging self-direction are deemed to be important, the availability of options and the opportunity to make choices among those options seems especially central to the enhancement of self-direction from the perspective of school organization. Table 9.1 (see next page) summarizes findings in this area for the four schools.

Community School. The Community School has gone through a period of development following an initially open-structured emphasis on extensive choice for students. The active role of parents in decision making, especially through the mechanism of the evaluation questionnaire, brought about a perceptible shift away from a predominantly facilitative approach to the adoption of training and shaping strategies. Choice is now to be guided by teachers in most areas, although students are still mainly free to choose to work alone or with others they select, to work at various places in the classroom, and to do some work at home or in school. The development of the individual student profile of competencies reflects the training orientation. It formalizes the evaluation of individual performance by providing explicit feedback on accomplishment and may provide a concrete

Table 9.1

School Organizational Features in Relation to the
Facilitation *versus* Training Distinction

School	Theoretical Orientation	
	Facilitation	Training/Shaping
Community School	Open-structured freedom of choice (initial) Choice of study partners, location, and extra work	Development of behavioral code, teacher-guided choice (later) Development of individual student profile for recording mastery of specific competencies
ISOS Program	Schedule and arrange visits to Learning Centers Pacing decisions on SLK work	Questions at Learning Centers initially framed by teachers, later by students
Katalin Varga School	Use of outside facilities (library, museums, etc.) Use of school facilities (work-study groups, cabinet room, library	Choice of optional subjects for study in facultative groups Selection of advanced examination option with individual study under teacher as supervisor
Oberstufen-Kolleg	Full membership of school governing bodies (Assembly, Conference Curriculum Committee) Full membership in RDP groups Choice of content, mode, place, time of optional and complementary course work Choice of achievement indices and evaluation criteria Choice of work/ community exposure	Choice of program of study after orientation semester and counseling by tutors

model for later internalized evaluation. The Community School thus incorporates both a facilitative and a training orientation with respect to choices made by students, although the latter are now more predominant than formerly.

ISOS Program. Table 9.1 reveals that students in the ISOS Program make relatively few choices relating to organizational and structural arrangements. They are responsible for scheduling and arranging visits to the learning centers and are fully on their own in making decisions about pacing on the self-learning kits during the out-of-school portion of their programs. These two types of activities are classified as representative of the facilitative approach because there is little or no adult involvement. On the other hand, questions asked of adults at the learning centers are originally specified by teachers and later mainly left to the students. This latter type of choice reflects the training or shaping approach.

Katalin Varga. At the Katalin Varga School only the use of the wide variety of learning resources outside the school reflects choices left primarily to the student. The selection of the advanced examination option with individual study under the supervision of a teacher is more consistent with the training/shaping approach. The choice of optional subjects to be pursued in one of the facilitative groups depends on the student, although the group operates under the close supervision of a teacher. This option is thus also consistent with the training approach. In general, the Katalin Varga School, given its role of preparing students for the University and strong academic traditions, will turn out to operate under this second assumption more often than not.

Oberstufen-Kolleg. In the case of the Oberstufen-Kolleg, the balance shifts considerably to the facilitation approach. Students make choices as full participants in various school governing bodies and working groups. Only the choice of the program of study appears to be deliberately integrated with a period of training and preparation. This occurs during the first or orientation semester. During this period students are encouraged to gain direct experience with various fields of study before making their ultimate decision. This process is also facilitated by contact with the students' tutor/counselor.

In other important activities, students function as full participants. They are members of the three school governing bodies. They also serve as full members on the Research,

Development, and Planning (RDP) groups, the organizational
structures through which the dual role of the college as a research and teaching institution is carried out. In the instructional situation, students choose content, mode, place and time
of work in optional and complementary courses. These choices
may or may not be made cooperatively with other students selected as working partners. Finally, students make choices relating
to how, and by what criteria, their work is to be evaluated.
All of these decision areas confront students with a great deal
of freedom and corresponding responsibility, and they clearly
reflect the hypothesis that self-direction develops when learners
are allocated major responsibilities.

Curriculum
        From the perspective of the formal curriculum, the schools
tend to locate themselves relatively consistently under either
the facilitative or training/shaping approach. Thus, Katalin
Varga School and the ISOS Program reflect the latter, and this
is predominantly the case for the Community School as well.
In contrast, the Oberstufen-Kolleg, through its basic course
structure and plan, creates situations in which students confront the possibility of functioning very much on their own
(see Table 9.2 next page).

        Community School. In the curriculum at the Community
School, the individualization theme found tangible expression
in the use of tactics such as multi-age grouping and emphasis
on small group and individual study. These strategies were
under the supervision of teachers who generally exercised control as it appeared to be required according to the maturational
level of the student. While the classroom resource centers remained as a reflection of the original open-structure approach
characteristic of the facilitative assumption, the curriculum
had shifted significantly to the training/shaping side of the
spectrum at the time of the case study. Other aspects of the
curriculum were standard for schools of the state, except for
the multi-ethnic emphasis which was not related to the individualization theme.

        ISOS Program. Without question, the two main components of
the out-of-school curriculum of the ISOS Program both fit under
the training/shaping assumption. In fact, the learning kits are
an excellent illustration in concrete form of this assumption.
Behavioral objectives are stated for the student, activities
suggested, learning is guided through cues and instructions,
and self-assessment exercises are incorporated. As noted in

Table 9.2
Major Curriculum Components in Relation to the
Facilitation *versus* Training Distinction

School	Theoretical Orientation	
	Facilitation	Training/Shaping
Community School	Resource centers in classroom	Individualization through multi-age grouping, group and individual study, etc.
ISOS Program		Self-learning-kits emphasizing guided learning, self-assessment, etc. Community learning centers for research skills, knowledge of industry and government
Katalin Varga	Resource centers in classroom	*Studium Generale* program for "learning to learn" Facultative groups for research and presentation skills Other school organizations and classes
Oberstufen-Kolleg	Optional and complementary course combinations for integrated study Project courses for integrating outside work *Praktikum* course for integrating outside work	

the previous section, only the self-pacing decision is left
fully to the student. The SLK's themselves guide and shape
learning behavior.

Visits to learning centers were also found to incorporate
a significant degree of structure, with questions provided by
teachers (except for older students), student leaders asking
these questions, and reports presented by the student leader or
by the whole group. Thus, the development of information-seek-
ing skills and knowledge about the community and the world of
work is quite tightly structured, especially at the beginning.
Students are definitely not free simply to find out for themselves.

Katalin Varga School. The *studium generale* course and
the facultative groups both articulate the training approach.
The former concentrates on the development of a significant variety of learning skills, but within a formal classroom setting.
These skills, in turn, are applied in the facultative groups
(and to some extent in regular classes) which encourage students
to engage in research and to present their findings in short
lectures or by other formal means. Taken together, these two
innovative elements of the Katalin Varga curriculum encourage
the student to follow a carefully guided path of personal development which has already been characterized as "learning to
learn".

There is also extensive involvement by students in learning activities held at the school outside of regular classes.
Other activities are available in the community. The previous
section made it clear that students were free to choose among
these activities, reflecting the facilitative orientation.
However, the activities themselves were mainly structured as
classes, formal discussion groups, and the like, implying the
operation of the alternative assumption.

Oberstufen-Kolleg. At the Oberstufen-Kolleg students are
responsible for implementing the basic integration theme in
their own coursework. The flexibility built into optional and
complementary course combinations provides one means by which
integration can be achieved. Students are responsible for
putting together the curricular choices they have made into an
integrated knowledge base. Likewise, they have to find and
carry out ways of applying what they have learned in project
courses.

This kind of responsibility implies the facilitative principle, not only in the original choice of optional, complementary, and project courses, but also in the manner in which those choices are carried out. Resources in the environment, including other people, are there to be used and even depended upon if the student so chooses. But it is also possible to lead others, to work quite independently or even entirely alone. This is likewise true of the short *Praktikum* courses in which students integrate work experiences that they have themselves selected.

Teaching and Learning Processes

A number of aspects of teaching and learning processes have already been anticipated - for example, that the learning kits of the ISOS Program provide for guided learning and self-evaluation. One general observation is that, in contradistinction to the section on curriculum, practices turn out much more mixed in the Community School and in the ISOS Program. By contrast, teaching and learning processes at Katalin Varga and the Oberstufen-Kolleg are much more consistent with the picture derived from the study of their respective curricula. (See Table 9.3 next page.)

Community School. Observations of Community School classrooms revealed two characteristics consistent with the facilitative assumption. First, interactions between teachers and students were highly informal. Observations revealed a good deal of warmth and accessibility. Secondly, interactions among students in the classroom were freely permitted. There was considerable tolerance for off-task interactions, unless the latter became distracting for others. These two characteristics reflect the persistence of the initially open-structured approach adopted at the time the school was founded.

By contrast, the training assumption was apparent in the basic learning cycle, which typically began with a part of the class receiving instruction from the teacher and then adjourning to do exercises and other learning activities in small groups or individually. This assumption was again apparent in the use of written response materials as the dominant mode of learning, significantly exceeding learning through didactic teaching. Students were found to be less teacher dependent in learning activities than in the typical classroom, but they did encounter a good deal of structure from the learning materials used.

The Community School demonstrates that it is possible to

Table 9.3

Teaching and Learning Processes in Relation to the
Facilitation *versus* Training Distinction

School	Theoretical Orientation	
	Facilitation	Training/Shaping
Community School	Informal relationships between students and teachers Relaxed classroom atmosphere, student interaction encouraged	Learning cycle begins with teacher, moves to small group or individual work without teacher Written response materials the dominant mode of learning
ISOS Program	Students must maintain own work schedule out of school Students learn communication skills by interviewing, etc. Learn to work in groups out of school	Students in teaching role in school, informally out of school Other adults function as teachers in learning center program
Katalin Varga Grammar School	Students develop own strategies for individual study	Emphasis on development of responsibility and perseverance (self as origin) Participatory learning modes develop in facultative groups (debate, discussion, group planning) Teachers are advisors, counselors, and encourage choice, self-evaluation
Oberstufen-Kolleg	Students plan and contribute independently to courses through planning and adjunct groups Most frequent working mode small groups without teacher Students also choose individual, autonomous study Students responsible for own evaluation in courses, also assess value of course Teacher/student relationships informal Teacher role facilitative, advisory	Teachers evaluate some types of student work Teachers attempt to be active agents in developing SDL through questions, structuring situations, etc.

mix practices implicitly derived from each of the two assumptions about self-direction, as long as conflicting messages are not given to students. Thus, the highly democratic relationships between teachers and students and relative permissiveness with respect to interactions among students did not conflict with the greater structure provided by the commonly-used written response materials.

ISOS Program. The two assumptions were also both evident in the teaching and learning process of the ISOS Program. Work in the classroom was relatively structured, although observers recorded a generally accepting, encouraging attitude on the part of teachers. Within this context, practices consistent with the training assumption included the informal way in which adults in the learning centers acted as teachers (this was fully recognized and accepted by regular teachers) as well as the extensive degree to which students themselves functioned as teachers and tutors, both in school and out of school. The ISOS Program clearly does not abandon formal teaching functions, instead they are extended to students themselves and to adults who have no real connection with the school.

On the other hand, students had to learn and perform in other ways very much on their own. Most critical was the need already mentioned to maintain an appropriate level of work activity outside of school. Likewise, communication skills such as interviewing were learned in the field, as was working with others cooperatively on learning center related projects. Comments of both teachers and students suggested that not all students assigned to the ISOS Program were ready for this kind of responsibility, especially working without the supervision of others.

The ISOS Program thus used practices characteristic of both assumptions. By virtue of its unique out-of-school program it was inevitable that significant reliance would have to be placed on the intrinsic motivation of students under conditions of unsupervised study. The learning kits reflect the training assumption, but their use outside of school depends on student motivation. The program of students who were not mature enough to work on their own, remained to be dealt with through more careful selection on the ISOS student body or by somehow providing more structure for such students during the out-of-school phase of the program.

Katalin Varga. Without question, the case study showed
the Katalin Varga Grammar School to be consistent in opting for
approaches to the development of self-direction which reflect
the training assumption. Probably most important is the way in
which the atmosphere of the school has led students to attribute
personal success or failure to their own self-discipline and
perseverance. The close relationship between this attitude and
attribution theory and the concept of personal causation is
readily apparent.

Students are responsible for a good deal of autonomous
study of a traditional type at the school, e.g., studying to
pass examinations. Information from both students and parents
suggested that most students managed to develop personal strategies for study through a gradual process. Students also learn
participatory modes of learning and teaching (the "learning to
learn" emphasis) such as lecturing, discussion, debate, and
group planning. This is a controlled, supervised process with
considerable structure initially.

Teachers at the Katalin Varga School encourage original
research and problem solving. They are seen by students as approachable and are consulted as counselors and advisers. On
the other hand, the teachers maintain authority in their separate roles. Many teachers place high value on didactic teaching,
especially in the regular classrooms.

The Katalin Varga Grammar School thus operates mainly
under the training assumption for encouraging self-direction.
This is consistent with its role as an academically oriented
institution, preparing students for competitive university entrance examinations.

Oberstufen-Kolleg. With the Oberstufen-Kolleg, equally
a university preparatory institution, the balance shifts dra-
matically to processes that reflect the facilitation assumption.
Students function on the planning and adjunct groups, with or
without instructors, to plan courses and bring special topics
into the learning process. They can - and frequently do -
choose to work autonomously rather than in groups, although the
most common mode of work is in small groups without the teacher.
Students have a significant degree of input into how their work
will be assessed in a course, they participate in evaluating
the work of other students and they provide both assessments
of their own work as well as evaluations of the course itself.

Relationships between students and teachers are quite informal at the Oberstufen-Kolleg, with the typical role of the
teacher that of advisor and resource person. However, students
did not see all teachers as having fully given up the authority
role. Teachers evaluate some aspects of the work of students,
especially individual work which does not lend itself to group
evaluation. Teachers also generally believe that they should
be activists in helping their students become more self-directed
by asking questions and structuring situations.

While the Oberstufen-Kolleg has been found to operate predominantly under the facilitative assumption, this does not
mean that it is merely a place where students are "free". The
school incorporates an atmosphere that stresses participation
in every type of activity, from administration to teaching.
Students have to respond to this atmosphere by making choices
about the nature and quality of their own participation. Nevertheless, the Oberstufen-Kolleg operates in a manner which is
predominantly consistent with the postulates of humanistic theory as cited in Chapter 3. As such, it probably reflects the
most consistent theoretical orientation of any of the four institutions studied in this research.

FINAL THOUGHTS

This book has looked at four schools through a particular
set of lenses - the eight characteristics of environments which
encourage self-direction. The principles of flexibility in
learning, maximizing opportunity for choice, emphasis on facilitative aspects of teaching, encouraging self-evaluation on the
part of learners, democratic relationships, capitalizing on intrinsic motivation, emphasis on expressive objectives, and
learning outside of the school have, by their adoption, determined the categories of findings in this research. If other
principles had been applied, it is certainly possible that somewhat different pictures of the four institutions might have
emerged.

The theories outlined in Chapter 3 would have provided an
alternative way of structuring the empirical investigations of
their research. This perspective was not selected because
schools are rarely if ever designed and operated on purely theoretical grounds, let alone from the perspective of a single
theory. Schools tend, in operation, to be pragmatic and eclectic in their selection of teaching and learning strategies.

OSTE-I

The eight principles just reiterated were expected to shape the case studies in ways which would be most sensitive to important characteristics of the teaching and learning process. By and large, this expectation appears to have been justified.

In spite of the above, the argument also emerges from this research that the study of self-direction and schooling would be greatly advanced if schools, or diversified programs within schools, were established on the basis of consistent philosophies such as could be derived from one of the three most comprehensive theories reviewed in Chapter 3: reinforcement theory, attribution theory, and humanistic theory. Admittedly, one of the institutions in this research did reflect a more than ordinarily consistent theoretical orientation, but this is a very unusual event.

Failing to reflect a single, consistent theoretical orientation is by no means a criticism of the schools studied in this research. It merely seems to be a desirable condition for learning more about the relationship between self-direction and schooling. A consistent theoretical orientation could presumably maximize the impact of the school (or program within a school), since all of its elements would work in an integrated way to achieve the same ends. Likewise, knowledge of the theory around which the school was designed, would help even more to focus empirical research on what is presumably important.

At the same time, individual differences in students emerged in this research as a very important consideration in both practice and research. Authors are entitled to their own preoccupations as long as they are identified as such. Individual differences have always been one of mine. But perhaps no preoccupation about the significance of individual differences was needed, since it appears to be abundantly evident in the findings reported that at least three of the schools enrolled learners who differed radically in their ability to learn in a self-directed manner in the environment provided. The successful encouragement of self-direction in learning appears to require that schools take a differentiated view of the learners in their care, especially with respect to whether or not particular individuals would develop best in a learning environment which is primarily open and facilitating as compared to one which is more structured in the direction of specific training for self-direction.

Appendix A

Participants

The following are individuals who had major responsibilities in the case studies or for the project as a whole.

PEOPLE'S REPUBLIC OF HUNGARY

Dr. Jozsef Bernàth   Professor, Teacher's College, Pécs (Leader, Research Team)

Dr. Màrton Horvàth   Director, Institute for Educational Research, Hungarian Academy of Sciences, Budapest

Dr. Ottó Mihàly   Head of the Department of Educational Theory, Institute for Educational Research, Hungarian Academy of Sciences, Budapest

Jànos Pàldi   Headmaster, Varga Katalin Gimnàzium, Szolnok

FEDERAL REPUBLIC OF GERMANY

Dr. Karl-Heinz Flechsig   Professor and Director, Pedagogical Seminar, University of Göttingen

Elke Geil-Werneburg   Oberstufen-Kolleg, University of Bielefeld

Volker Liewald   Pedagogical Seminar, University of Göttingen

Dr. Savvas Semertzidis   Oberstufen-Kolleg, University of Bielefeld

PHILIPPINES

Dr. Jasmine Acuña-Gavino   Assistant Director, Science Educa-
                              tion Center, Education Development
                              Center, University of the
                              Philippines, Quezon City

Dr. Dolores F. Hernandez   Director, Science Education Center,
                              Education Development Center,
                              University of the Philippines,
                              Quezon City

UNITED STATES OF AMERICA

Dr. Adrianne Bank   Associate Director, Center for the
                              Study of Evaluation, Graduate School
                              of Education, University of
                              California, Los Angeles

Sandra Graham   Research Associate, Center for the
                              Study of Evaluation, Graduate School
                              of Education, University of
                              California, Los Angeles

Robert Murar   Research Associate, Center for the
                              Study of Evaluation, Graduate School
                              of Education, University of
                              California, Los Angeles

PROJECT COORDINATOR

Dr. Rodney Skager   Professor,
                              Graduate School of Education,
                              University of California,
                              Los Angeles

Appendix B

Organizing and Planning
the Project

NATIONAL RESEARCH TEAMS

The identification of members of the four research teams was in many respects as important to the success of the research as was the identification of participating institutions. The primary criteria for recruiting potential leaders of research projects were knowledge of educational research methods and interest in the topic of self-direction in learning. Participating researchers were contacted either directly by the Unesco Institute or indirectly through some other organization, such as the Unesco Regional Office in Bangkok in the case of the Philippines and the Institute for Educational Research of the Hungarian Academy of Sciences in the case of the Hungarian study. As it turned out, all of the principal researchers were on the staff of colleges or universities.

The research teams operated with differing levels of resources, depending on the funding available locally. All of the teams were able to enlist the voluntary assistance of school personnel in the collection of data and, in some cases, in the preparation of the case study report as well.

PROJECT PLANNING

The initial conceptualization of the project preceded contacts with researchers and participating schools. Once the cooperation of the former had been secured, however, the next task involved developing project materials to inform participants, especially members of the research teams, about the specific goals of the project, the nature of the case studies envisioned, the aspects of the schools and learners to be investigated in the case studies, the forms that data collection

might take, and the specific questions to be answered in the
case study reports. These materials took the form of several
reference documents distributed to the head of each research
team at the first project meeting. These documents have been
referred to at relevant points in the text.

The intention guiding development of the reference documents was to provide a common framework for the case studies in
terms of the objectives, research methods, and questions to be
addressed. However, only the latter were expected to be standardized for all four of the studies. The particular form the
studies took, under the broad concept of the case study as defined in this research, was subject to locally available resources and considerations of appropriateness.

Considerably in advance of the first project meeting, the
case study directors were provided with the project document
describing and illustrating the basic qualitative and quantitative research strategies that might be used in their research.
No preference was indicated for any particular approach, quantitative or qualitative. It was to be understood from the beginning that the basic questions to be dealt with in the case
studies could be explored by a variety of methods, and that
choice among methods was to be entirely the responsibility of
the case study directors and their associates. The determining
considerations in selecting methods of data collection were

1. the resources the method would require in order
   to be used successfully, and

2. the acceptability of the method itself in the
   environment in which it was to be used.

These organizational aspects of the research were of
great importance to the final result. The reference documents
were the primary means by which the national studies, widely
separated in both distance and context, were encouraged to develop along parallel lines. The notion of parallelism was dominant, the idea of replication never considered. But there had
to be sufficient comparability of focus in the four studies to
facilitate their synthesis in this book. This was generated
first by agreeing on the basic questions to be dealt with in
all four of the case studies, and only secondarily by the making
available reference documents describing alternative approaches
to the collection of data.

PROJECT MEETINGS

Project meetings were held at the Unesco Institute, the first during late February 1978, and the second in early July 1979. The meetings were attended by the directors of the case studies, UIE staff, and other interested parties, including two members of the teaching staff of the Bielefelder Oberstufen-Kolleg, located in northern Germany.

The meetings were working conferences, and the results of their deliberations are reflected in this book. The first meeting dealt with orientation and planning. Clarification of administrative considerations, such as roles and responsibilities of the various participating agencies and persons and setting the target dates for critical phases of the work, were obviously one objective for the first meeting. On a substantive level, the concept of lifelong education and its relationship to self-direction in learning were clarified and discussed. The purpose of the project within this broader framework was addressed first. Next, the case study directors provided descriptions of the schools they would be studying and summarized the reasons why each had been selected. Turning to the research itself, the basic qualitative and quantitative methods for collecting information in participant and non-participant observational research, and other approaches to collecting data potentially useful in case studies, were reviewed. The first session ended with the preparation and presentation of preliminary research plans for each case study, including the types of measures and indices to be selected or developed.

On returning to their own countries, the study directors prepared final case study designs incorporating suggestions offered at the first project meeting as well as considerations that may have arisen later. These designs were sent to the Institute along with later interim reports after the case studies were underway.

Final case study reports were made available to all participants prior to, or at the time of, the closing project meeting. The purpose of this second meeting was to prepare for the final phase of the project - the drafting of this report. Each case study report was summarized by its study director and discussed by the group as a whole in order to clarify specific findings and to identify commonalities. The primary goal was to find ways to synthesize the findings of the separate studies, rather than to present each as an isolated piece of research.

Appendix C

Case Study Research Strategies

This appendix describes the overall research strategy selected by each of the case study teams. The types of measure
used for collecting empirical data will be described in general
terms. Further information about specific measures is given in
the summary of specific findings of the case studies in Chapters
5-8.

THE COMMUNITY SCHOOL STUDY (U.S.A.)

This study relied primarily on observation and interview
techniques, although one questionnaire was developed for selected groups of learners, parents, and teachers. The study incorporated both informal and formal approaches to the collection
of information. It was divided into two phases, the first being
exploratory and qualitative in its information base, and the
second more specific and based on systematic quantitative data.
The methods for collecting information chosen in this study reflect in part the preferences of the study team and in part a
general climate of resistance to the use of instruments which
assess "personal" information such as attitude questionnaires,
personality tests, and the like. In contrast, direct methods
such as interviews and observations were quite acceptable. So
were questionnaires that dealt directly with the school and the
reactions of the children to the school and its programs.

Goals of Phase 1
The goals of the first phase of this case study, mainly
accomplished during the spring and summer of 1978, were

1. to observe classroom settings, the role of the
   teachers, and the activities of the students;

2. to interview parents and students about their
   views of the school;

3. to synthesize the data from these sources
   into a composite picture of the school along
   the dimensions selected for study; and

4. to use all of what had been learned up to that
   point to conceptualize the second, more specific
   phase of the study.

Procedures for Phase 1

Six observations of classrooms by the Project Director
and a rotating team of observers were conducted. The primary
purpose of the observations was to record in the form of field
notes the extent to which the classroom environment and the
teaching style of the staff provided opportunities, role models,
and reinforcements for self-directed learning on the part of
the children. Notes were taken independently by the observers
and compared afterwards.

A seventh observation period in which one observer was
assigned to each of the six classrooms for a day was held after
the initial observation period. Observers were instructed to
record the physical setting, the social and emotional climate
insofar as it could be inferred, and the activities of teachers
and students. Conversations were recorded verbatim where appropriate. Observers later met to summarize their impressions of

1. the amount of choice available to students;

2. the nature and kind of feedback to students;

3. the classroom ambience;

4. the physical environment of the classroom; and

5. the role of aides and volunteers.

In addition, an attempt was made at this meeting to determine
whether teachers were consistent in their approach to children
across grade levels and whether they appeared to regulate their
own behavior and expectation to the developmental level of the
children.

Interviews with students. Two children from each classroom (along with an alternate) were randomly selected for student interviews. These interviews lasted about half an hour
each and were designed to provide the investigators with a picture of the child's day in school. There were questions about
the ways in which home and school activities were related as
well as about specific learning-related skills such as the use
of the telephone, the library, the dictionary, maps, etc. The

The interview format was of the moderately structured variety, with standard initial questions followed by optional probing questions or requests for explanation of the initial answer.

Interviews with parents. These were conducted primarily in the homes of the selected children. The interviews with parents lasted for about an hour and a half and covered aspects of the school such as its history, governance, parental involvement, communication, funding, evaluation, and satisfactions from the parental viewpoint. Parental interviews were somewhat more structured than the interviews of children, with answers to standard questions recorded verbatim. A general discussion in which the parents raised questions or added other information was encouraged at the end of the interviews.

Goals of Phase 2

The second phase of the Community School case study was focused on a sub-study of high and low self-directed learners that paralleled a similar sub-study conducted by the Philippine research team. The purpose of these two sub-studies was to test the conception of self-direction adopted for this research. More specifically, the research team studying the Community School sought to determine

1. whether or not children nominated by teachers as either high or low in self-direction differed in predicted ways on several of the characteristics of self-directed learners listed in Chapter 2; and

2. the extent to which the child's own view of the self with respect to self-direction in learning was consistent with that of teachers, parents, and observers.

Procedures for Phase 2

Four of the hypothesized characteristics of the self-directed learner were selected: *planfulness, intrinsic motivation, internalized evaluation,* and *flexibility.* What had been learned about the school in phase 1 suggested that these four characteristics would be observed in at least some students. In the Community School, students are allowed to work without direct adult supervision, are not systematically rewarded or punished for task-oriented or non-task-oriented behavior, are provided with a variety of ways for evaluating their own work, and are frequently permitted to change activities. In other words, if these four characteristics did distinguish between high and low self-directed learners nominated by teachers, they would be freely expressed in the atmosphere the school provided.

The behavior of high and low self-directed learners was recorded by means of an observation schedule developed for the study. This instrument combined a running record of the child activities during each of the observation periods with a check-list that included items such as the dominant class activity during the observation, the role of the teacher, the content of the learner's activity, the degree of involvement of the child, and the types of communications made by the learner.

One observer was assigned to each classroom. Each observation period for a single child lasted from five to ten minutes, after which the observer moved immediately to the next of the four children, recycling after all four had been observed. A total of twelve observations on at least three different days was made of each child. This totaled roughly sixty minutes of observation time for children in grades one to three and about twice as long on average for children in grades four to six. Observers were not informed as to whether individual children had been nominated as high or low in self-direction. Observers were given prior practice in the use of the observation schedule and remained as unobtrusive in the classroom as possible.

THE ARELLANO HIGH SCHOOL STUDY (PHILIPPINES)

The study of the ISOS Program made use of the full range of instrumentation potentially useful in research of schools. A total of twenty-two different locally developed measurement procedures, including a coded observation scale, attitude scales, rating scales for students and observers, interview schedules, nomination forms, self-reports on daily activities, a standardized test of personality and several cognitive tests, were used in the research.

In general, data from a variety of measurement methods were applied to each of the basic questions to be addressed in the case studies. Many of the instruments or procedures applied to more than one question. The best way to organize an overview of the research strategy of the Philippine team is in terms of the focus of a given set of instruments or procedures on particular aspects of the ISOS Program or its participants. Material relating to the special study of high *versus* low self-directed learners will be separately identified, as was the case for the U.S. study.

Classroom Observation.

Both qualitative, non-participant and coding observational procedures were used in the study. The latter were applied both to comparisons between high and low self-directed learners and for recording teacher verbalizations according to the system for assessing classroom climate developed by Withal (1967). Henry's cross-cultural outline served as the basis for the non-participant observation of ISOS classrooms conducted to provide a general picture of the in-school instructional process. Teams of two trained observers observed all day for four consecutive days at each level. Results were pooled after the observations were completed.

Other observation instruments included:

1. a form for observing high and low self-directed learners along six dimensions at five minute intervals;

2. a seven-point observation scale focusing on aspects of the curriculum that were not necessarily related to particular academic disciplines;

3. an eighteen-item rating scale dealing with the learning climate established by the teacher as well as the social closeness of teacher to students;

4. a checklist on classroom teaching methods (used on a sample of teachers only); and

5. an eighty-item rating scale dealing with the eight hypothesized characteristics of environments facilitating self-direction in learning plus general classroom climate.

Interviews

All interviews were of a moderately structured type, with lead and follow-up questions prepared in advance, but leaving use of the latter to the discretion of the interviewers. Four types of interview were included in the research:

1. a brief student interview on opinions about the ISOS Program;

2. a teacher interview focused partly on the Henry category of "Who teaches?" and partly on teaching objectives, including those relating to self-direction;

3. another teacher interview on attitudes to the
   ISOS Program; and

4. interviews with the superintendent, principal,
   assistant principal, supervisor, teachers, and
   head of learning centers on the organization
   and governance of Arellano High School and the
   ISOS Program.

Self-Rating Scales
   While rating scales were also used by observers, both
teachers and students contributed self-ratings. Students responded to

1. a 107-item, four choice rating scale with items
   representing the hypothesized personal characteristics of the self-directed learner described in
   Chapter 2, as well as items bearing on responsibility, expectations of success, decision-making,
   learning outside of school, etc.;

2. a self-descriptive attitude scale dealing with
   attitudes toward learning (problem solving,
   teacher's role, etc.); and

3. a fifty-nine-item rating scale on various aspects
   of the ISOS Program, which partially matched the
   basic research questions described in the first
   section of this Appendix. This latter instrument
   was also responded to by teachers and parents.

Teachers rated themselves on

1. a seven-point scale of agreement on specific
   behavioral aspects of self-direction in learning,
   e.g., "I attend subject-matter lectures (not
   directly related to my teaching) in my area of
   specialization"; and

2. an instrument with the same format dealing with
   attitudes to various aspects of teaching.

Self-Reports
   Learners in the high and low self-directed learning groups
were asked to fill in a daily time schedule of activities.
These students also wrote brief essays on the ISOS Program.

Content Analysis
   The self-learning kits (SLK's) used by ISOS students in
the out of school portion of the program were analyzed using a

form developed for the purpose. The analysis emphasized factors relating to self-direction in learning. Notebooks of high and low self-directed learners were also reviewed for the same purpose.

Nomination Form
A form for nominating high and low self-directed learners was used by teachers. This form and the way in which it was used has been described in Chapter 8.

Tests
Standardized tests administered to all ISOS students included

1. the *Survey of Interpersonal Values* measuring six personality scales including "conformity" and "independence";

2. the *Test of Abstract Thinking* adapted from Shipley's test of abstract reasoning by Acuna and da Silva, which measures the ability to abstract principles and use rules;

3. the *Culture Fair Nonverbal Intelligence Test* (IPAT Scale 2);   and

4. the *Group Embedded Figures Test* which measures field dependence/independence.

THE KATALIN VARGA GRAMMAR SCHOOL STUDY (HUNGARY)

Each instrument and procedure for the collection of data in the Hungarian case study was directed at only one of the basic questions to be investigated in the research. This makes it possible to summarize the research strategies of the Hungarian study by the question addressed. In other respects the Hungarian study was similar to the Philippine study, in that local conditions permitted the use of a wide variety of approaches to data collection. However, the Hungarian research did not include a sub-study of high *versus* low self-directed learners, though it did identify a group of fifty-one high, average, and poor "target learners", proportionally represented by form level, for intensive study.

Organization and Governance
This aspect of the school was studied by three methods:

1. an informal study of pertinent school documents,
   including school rules, curriculum plan for the
   year 1978, and materials for supervisors;

2. moderately structured interviews of knowledgeable
   administrators (ranging from the deputy head of
   the local Education Department to the head of the
   students' hostel and including the headmaster)
   on how the organization and governance of the
   school might contribute to the development of
   self-direction in learning; and

3. teacher ratings of the degree to which the
   school governance process contributed to each
   of the eight characteristics hypothesized to
   encourage self-direction.

Characteristics of Learners

The group of target learners were administered a series
of multiple choice or self-rating questionnaires dealing with
personal characteristics such as self-acceptance, planfulness,
internalized evaluation, openness to experience, flexibility,
and autonomy. In addition, fourth form pupils were asked to
write brief essay answers to three questions on the way the
school may have fostered motivation for lifelong learning.
These answers were considered to reflect primarily the learners'
attitudes about themselves. Finally, members of the research
group observed each of the target learners in three different
school situations and produced an anecdotal record of their
behavior.

Characteristics of Teachers

Teacher characteristics were identified in three ways:

1. students were given statements from a published
   test describing a list of personality traits and
   were asked to indicate which ones applied to their
   teachers;

2. teachers were asked to describe their students
   positively or negatively with respect to competence in self-direction (on the assumption
   that the descriptions reflected the teacher's
   own standards and system of self-evaluation);
   and

3. teachers answered, in writing, open-ended
   questions about how the role they had developed

as a teacher helped them to facilitate the development of self-direction in their students
and what factors helped or hindered the realization of this role.

Decision-Making in the Teaching/Learning Process

Three specific approaches to decision-making in the teach-
ing/learning process were developed, although information was
also drawn from student questionnaires described in relation to
other questions:

1. a questionnaire was sent to parents of students
   in all four forms asking for their perspectives
   on this aspect of the school's functioning as
   well as their own reasons for enrolling their
   child;

2. interviews with learners taking advanced examinations on their reasons for deciding to do so;
   and

3. observations by library staff of student use of
   the library and its resources.

How Teachers Teach

Teachers' approaches to teaching were examined through
three methods:

1. the fifty-one target learners were asked a series
   of questions in an informal interview, e.g.,
   "Is there a possibility of choice in learning -
   in that teachers let you decide about what, how,
   when, or where to learn?";

2. fifty-one observed lessons were rated on bipolar
   scales covering various attributes of teaching,
   e.g., the extent to which teachers take notice
   of, and respond to, questions from students;
   and

3. a questionnaire, made up of both multiple choice
   questions on teaching as well as open-ended
   questions in a suggestion format, was sent to
   285 former students of the school (all individuals
   who took the final examination from 1975-1978).

How Learners Learn

The ways in which students learned were investigated by
four approaches:

1. members of the research team sat in on twenty-four lessons (three lessons per observer), rating it on a set of seven-point scales for characteristics such as amount of questioning by learners and the extent to which there was debate in a lesson;

2. all learners in the school were asked to answer in writing a set of questions about how they approached studying;

3. a set of cognitive, problem-solving tasks designed to elicit creative thinking was administered to students; and

4. a meeting of parents of students in the third form was held in which the former discussed how their children approached learning, the results being recorded for later analysis.

Characteristics of the Teaching Materials
Teaching materials were examined through two types of content analyses:

1. an analysis of syllabi according to categories such as *source* (teacher, text, periodical, etc.) or *role of teacher* (motivating, demonstrating, etc.); and

2. an analysis of final examinations of five classes in 1978 and 1979 to determine what types of material would most facilitate successful performance.

What Learners Learn
Text books were also investigated by two methods:

1. a content analysis of the first and last chapters of thirty-one texts from a variety of fields was constructed through the use of a predetermined set of categories, e.g., "Is content primarily factual and descriptive, factual plus explanatory, or primarily comparisons between conflicting issues and ideas?"; and

2. through essays contributed by 329 of the students on the main substance of their learning in and out of school.

Opinions about the School

    Four methods were used to obtain the opinions of outsiders about the school and its programs:

1. unstructured interviews were held with community and other figures likely to be knowledgeable about the school, e.g., the head librarian, the directors of the house of culture, officials in the town, the head of the parents' association, etc.;

2. requests were sent to authorities at seven universities and colleges, asking for evaluations of individual graduates of the Katalin Varga School who were currently enrolled in their institutions;

3. moderately structured interviews were made with several graduates of the school who provided accounts of their own preparation for higher education in relation to the expectations of those institutions; and

4. pertinent information from questionnaires sent to graduates of the school (mentioned above) was analyzed for this purpose.

THE BIELEFELDER OBERSTUFEN-KOLLEG STUDY
(FEDERAL REPUBLIC OF GERMANY)

    The approach taken to the collection of information for this case was qualitatively different from the other three. It would be misleading to represent this particular study as primarily empirical research, although some formal data were collected and reported. The study of the OSK mainly used an approach akin to one which would be adopted by a journalist conducting an in-depth report. The approach involved the development of relationships with people within the school who were especially interested in the study, and depending on these contacts to facilitate participation in the various types of activity that are part of the OSK program. The means of collecting information were also primarily journalistic rather than scientific, consisting of informal interviews; conversations; observations in the form of note-taking at various types of school meetings, classes, or study groups; and reading through documents describing the school and its programs.

    This approach was undertaken for two reasons. First, the

resources available to the case study were more limited than
those available to the other studies. Fortunately (and essential to the success of the case study), two members of the
teaching staff of the OSK were willing to contribute significant proportions of their own time. Even with this assistance,
elaborate approaches to the collection of data were not feasible. Second, however, even if there had been more resources,
the use of formal approaches to the collection of data characteristic of social science research would probably have been
counterproductive in the atmosphere of the OSK. Whereas conversation, discussion, and even participation were acceptable,
tests, questionnaires, or formalized recording of behavior by
means of non-participant observation would probably have been
counterproductive. It was judged early in the study that such
methods ran the risk of being "reactive", e.g., likely to generate events as a result of their use that would not have otherwise occurred in the normal life of the school. (Perhaps this
observation is itself a useful insight into the OSK and its
students.)

Mode of Collecting Information
      Information about the OSK was collected by means of
several types of activity:

1. initial guided overview of OSK plant and various
   types of regular activity conducted by a staff
   member participating in the case study;

2. examination and analysis of documents and publications describing the OSK;

3. attendance of meetings of governing bodies of
   the school;

4. observing learning activities in small groups
   or combined meetings;

5. participation by observer in a class field trip;

6. reports in essay form by students from a regular
   secondary school who visited the OSK to interview
   students and observe teaching and learning activities;

7. interviews with students on the subject of self-
   direction in learning as applied to the OSK (in
   a number of cases standard questions were used
   and responses tallied numerically); and

8. interviews with teachers at the OSK on self-
   direction in learning.

For observations of students in group learning situations an "activity card" was developed which included a rough drawing of the seating arrangement of participants, with arrows drawn chronologically between participants representing

1. questions;

2. declarative statements; and

3. whether communication was addressed to an individual or to the group as a whole.

These records were used qualitatively rather than quantitatively to summarize the nature of group learning activities.

It should be added that Harder's (1978) description of the history of organization and operational context of the OSK was an important supplement to the case study in the preparation of this book.

SUMMARY

Perhaps the single most critical factor in the success of the project as a whole was the attempt to focus the case studies on a common set of research questions while at the same time allowing each research team sufficient flexibility in the design of their own study. The respective teams had to be free to select specific indices and data collection procedures consistent with available resources and appropriate to the local context.

The research strategies ultimately adopted by the four research teams did manifest variations attributable to local norms and resources. The U.S. study emphasized interviews and non-participant observation in the form of coding, ratings, and field notes. The Philippine and Hungarian studies used these approaches to measurement, along with self-ratings and objective measures of attitudes, personality, and cognitive characteristics. Content analyses of materials such as tests or other curriculum materials were also conducted. Finally, the F.R.G. study differed qualitatively in taking an approach much like that of in-depth journalism, using mainly informal observation, interviews, and inspection of documents, plus some formal counting of responses to specific questions. All four of the studies, however, dealt with the nine basic questions which provided structure for the project as a whole.

References

Bandura, A. and Walters, R.H. *Social Learning Theory and Personality Development*. New York: Holt, Rinehart & Winston, 1963.

Bandura, A. "Self-reinforcement theory: theoretical and methodological considerations". *Behaviorism*, 4 (1976), pp. 135-155.

Bandura, A. "The self system in reciprocal determinism". *American Psychologist*, 33 (1978), pp. 344-358.

Berlyne, D.E. "Curiosity and education". In Krumboltz, J.D. (ed.). *Learning and the Educational Process*. Chicago: Rand McNally, 1965.

Biggs, J.B. "Content to process". *Australian Journal of Education*, 17 (1973), pp. 225-238.

Blaney, N.T. et al. "Interdependence in the classroom: a field study". *Journal of Educational Psychology*, 69 (1977), pp. 121-128.

Chickering, A.W. "Developmental change as a major outcome". In Keeton, M.T. and Associates (eds.). *Experiential Learning*. San Francisco: Jossey-Bass, 1976.

Coleman, J.E. "Differences between experiential and classroom learning". In Keeton, M.T. and Associates (eds.). *Experiential Learning*. San Francisco: Jossey-Bass, 1976.

Cronbach, L.J. "The logic of experiments on discovery". In Schulman, L.S. and Keislar, E.R. (eds.). *Learning by Discovery: A Critical Appraisal*. Chicago: Rand McNally, 1966.

Cropley, A.J. "Some psychological reflections on lifelong education". In Dave, R.H. (ed.). *Foundations of Lifelong Education*. Oxford: Pergamon Press, 1976. (Advances in Lifelong Education, Vol.1).

Cropley, A.J. and Dave, R.H. *Lifelong Education and the Training of Teachers*. Oxford: Pergamon Press, 1978. (Advances in Lifelong Education, Vol.5).

Dave, R.H. *Lifelong Education and School Curriculum*. Hamburg: Unesco Institute for Education, 1973. (UIE Monographs 1).

Dave, R.H. (ed.). *Reflections on Lifelong Education and the School*. Hamburg: Unesco Institute for Education, 1975. (UIE Monographs 3).

De Charms, R. "Personal causation training in the schools". *Journal of Applied Social Psychology*. 2 (1972), pp.95-113.

De Charms, R. *Enhancing Motivation*. New York: Irvington Publishers, 1976.

Eisner, E.W. "Instructional and expressive educational objectives: their formulation and use in curriculum". In Popham, W.J. et al. (eds.). *Instructional Objectives*. Chicago: Rand McNally, 1968, pp. 1-18. (AERA Series on Curriculum Evaluation, No. 3).

Faure, Edgar et al. *Learning to Be. The World of Education Today and Tomorrow*. Paris: Unesco, 1972.

Fredriksson, L. and Gestrelius, K. *Lifelong Learning in Swedish Curricula*. Malmö: University, School of Education, 1975. (Didakometry, No. 48).

Glynn, E.L.; Thomas, J.D., and Shee, S.M. "Behavioral self-control of on-task behavior in an elementary classroom". *Journal of Applied Behavioral Analysis*, 6 (1973), pp. 103-105.

Goodlad, J.I.; Klein, M.F., and Associates. *Behind the Classroom Door*. Worthington, Ohio: Charles A. Jones Publishing Co., 1970.

Goodman, Paul. *Compulsory Mis-Education*. New York: Horizon Press, 1964.

Greenfield, P.M. and Bruner, J.S. "Culture and cognitive growth". In Goslin, D.A. (ed.). *Handbook of Socialization Theory and Research*. Chicago: Rand McNally, 1969.

Harder, W. "The Oberstufen-Kolleg in Bielefeld". In Nissen, G. and Teschner, W.P. (eds.). *Curriculum Research and Development*. Kiel: Institut für die Pädagogik der Naturwissenschaften, 1978. (IPN Report-in-Brief).

Hargreaves, D.H. "Deschoolers and new romantics". In Flude, M. and Aheir, J. (eds.). *Educability, Schools, and Ideology*. London: Croom Helm, 1974, pp. 186-210.

Heider, F. *The Psychology of Interpersonal Relations*. New York: Wiley, 1958.

Henry, J. "A cross-cultural outline of education". *Current Anthropology*. 1 (1960), pp. 269-305.

Joyce, B. and Weil, M. *Models of Teaching*. Englewood Cliffs, New Jersey: Prentice-Hall, 1972.

Kagan, J. "Learning, attention and the issue of discovery". In Shulman, L.S. and Keisler, E.R. (eds.). *Learning by Discovery: A Critical Appraisal*. Chicago: Rand McNally, 1966.

Keeton, M.T. and Associates (eds.). *Experiential Learning*. San Francisco: Jossey-Bass, 1976.

Keifer, E. *The Effects of School Achievement on the Affective Traits of the Learner*. Paper presented at the annual meeting of the Educational Research Association, New Orleans, February, 1973.

Kreitler, S.; Kreitler, H. and Zigler, E. "Cognitive orientation and curiosity". *British Journal of Psychology*, 65 (1974), pp. 43-52.

La Belle, T.J. and Verhine, R.E. "Nonformal education and occupational stratification: implications for Latin America". *Harvard Educational Review*, 45 (1975), No.2, pp. 160-190.

Lebouteux, F. "The school in an age of continuous education". *Education and Culture*, 21 (1973), pp. 8-14.

Lee, D. "A socio-anthropological view of independent learning". In Gleason, G.T. (ed.). *The Theory and Nature of Independent Learning*. Scranton, Pa.: International Textbook Company, 1967.

Lengrand, P.. *An Introduction to Lifelong Education*. Paris: Unesco, 1970.

Lepper, M.R.; Green, D., and Nisbett, R.E. "Undermining intrinsic interest with extrinsic reward: a test of the 'overjustification' hypothesis". *Journal of Personality and Social Psychology*, 28 (1973), pp. 129-137.

Lepper, M.R. *Generalized Effects of Modeled Self-reinforcement Training*. Final Report. Washington: National Institute of Education, 1976. (NIE Project No. NIE-G-74-0027).

234   Organizing Schools to Encourage Self-direction

Marbeau, V. "Autonomous study by pupils". *Education and Culture*, 31 (1976), pp. 14-21.

March, J.A. "Model bias in social action". *Review of Educational Research*. 42 (1972), No. 4, pp. 413-429.

Maslow, A. *Motivation and Personality*. New York: Harper, 1954.

Maw, W.H. and Maw, E.W. *An Exploratory Study into the Measurement of Curiosity in School Children*. Washington: U.S. Office of Education, 1964. (Cooperative Research Project No. 801).

Peters, R.S. *Psychology and Ethical Development*. Oxford: George Allen and Unwin, 1974.

Peters, R.S. "The development of reason". In Benn, S.I. and Mortimore, G.W. (eds.). *Rationality and the Social Sciences: Contributions to the Philosophy and Methodology of the Social Sciences*. London: Routledge and Kegan Paul, 1976.

Rogers, C.R. "A theory of therapy, personality, and interpersonal relationships, as developed in the client-centered framework". In Koch, S. (ed.). *Psychology: A Study of a Science*. New York: McGraw-Hill, 1959. (Vol.3).

Rogers, C.R. *Freedom to Learn*. Columbus, Ohio: Charles E. Merrill, 1969.

Sawin, E.I. *Evaluation and the Work of the Teacher*. Belmont, Ca.: Wadsworth, 1969.

Sears, P. "Implications of motivation theory for independent learning". In Gleason, G.T. (ed.). *The Theory and Nature of Independent Learning*. Scranton, Pa.: International Textbook Company, 1967.

Skager, R.W. and Dave, R.H. *Curriculum Evaluation for Lifelong Education*. Oxford: Pergamon Press, 1977. (Advances in Lifelong Education, Vol.2).

Skager, R.W. *Lifelong Education and Evaluation Practice*. Oxford: Pergamon Press, 1978. (Advances in Lifelong Education, Vol.4).

Skager, R.W. "Self-directed learning and schooling: identifying pertinent theories and illustrative research". *International Review of Education*, 25 (1979), pp. 517-543.

Spaulding, S. "Life-long education: a modest model for planning and research". *Comparative Education*, 10 (1974), pp. 101-113.

Thoresen, C.E. and Mahoney, M.J. *Behavioral Self-Control*. New York: Holt, Rinehart and Winston, 1974.

Tough, A. *The Adult's Learning Projects*. Ontario: The Ontario Institute for Studies in Education, 1971. (Research in Education Series, No. 1).

Vidler, D.C. "Curiosity". In Ball, S. (ed.). *Motivation in Education*. New York: Academic Press, 1977.

Weiner, B. *Theories of Motivation*. Chicago: Markham, 1972.

Werdelin, I.; Bondesson, E. and Larsson, G.B. "The effectiveness and transfer value of two methods of concept learning". *Scandinavian Journal of Psychology*, 12 (1971), pp. 198-204.

White, R.W. "Motivation reconsidered: the concept of competence". *Psychological Review*, 66 (1959), pp. 297-333.

Whyte, W. *Street Corner Society*. Chicago: University of Chicago Press, 1955.

Wilhelmi, H.-H. "The school system in the Federal Republic of Germany". *Bildung und Wissenschaft*, (1979), No. 12 (e).

Withal, J. "Evaluation of classroom climate". *Childhood Education*, 43 (1967), pp. 403-408.

Wroczynski, R. "Learning styles and lifelong education". *International Review of Education*, 20 (1974), No. 4, pp. 464-473.

Index